S0-BPI-922

The Good Old Rule

...the good old rule
Sufficeth them, the simple plan,
That they should take, who have the power,
  And they should keep who can.

William Wordsworth

The Good Old Rule

GENDER AND OTHER POWER RELATIONSHIPS IN A RURAL COMMUNITY

Gretchen Poiner

•A15043 219134

HN
850
.N4
P65x

WEST

**SYDNEY
UNIVERSITY PRESS**

SYDNEY UNIVERSITY PRESS
in association with
OXFORD UNIVERSITY PRESS AUSTRALIA

© Gretchen Poiner 1990
First published 1990

This book is copyright. Apart from any fair
dealing for the purposes of private study,
research, criticism or review as permitted under
the Copyright Act, no part may be reproduced,
stored in a retrieval system, or transmitted, in
any form or by any means, electronic, mechanical,
photocopying, recording, or otherwise without
prior written permission. Inquiries to be made to
Oxford University Press.

Copying for educational purposes
Where copies of part or the whole of the book are
made under section 53B or section 53D of the Act,
the law requires that records of such copying be
kept. In such cases the copyright owner is
entitled to claim payment.

National Library of Australia
Cataloguing-in-Publication data:

Poiner, Gretchen.
    The good old rule : gender and other power relationships
    in a rural community

    Bibliography.
    Includes index.
    ISBN 0 424 00160 8.

    1. Sociology, Rural—Australia.   2. Social psychology—
    Australia.   3. Social role—Australia.   4. Sex role—
    Australia.   5. Australia—Social conditions.   I. Title.
307.720994

Edited by Heather Kelly
Cover design by Peter Shaw
Cover illustration by Jane Poiner
Typeset by Best-set Typesetters Ltd, Hong Kong
Printed in Hong Kong by Condor Production Ltd
Published by Sydney University Press in association
with Oxford University Press,
253 Normanby Road, South Melbourne, Australia

CONTENTS

List of Tables viii
Acknowledgements ix
Marulan and district map x

Chapter One
INTRODUCTION 1
The study: background, interests and method 1
The district 5
Commuter farmers 10
District history 14

Chapter Two
GUIDELINES TO UNDERSTANDING: SOME
BASIC CONCEPTS 20
Power 20
Consciousness and conflict 22
Mobilization of bias 24
Interests 25
Hegemony 28
Ideology 30

Chapter Three
HISTORICAL PERSPECTIVES AND RURAL
VIEWS 33
From idyll to ideology 39
Attractions of rural self-portraits 45
Conservatism in the country 49
Rural ideology 50

Chapter Four
CLASS RELATIONSHIPS: DIVISIONS CONFUSED OR CONTAINED   53
Social closure   57
Class relationships in Marulan   59
Conclusion   77

Chapter Five
IMAGERY IN ACTION   79
Symbols and groups   79
Upper-status farmers   82
Farming families   84
Townspeople   87
'Rough' townspeople   89
Marulan and beyond   90
Social views and social action   92
Differences denied   95
Awareness in context   98
The clarity of hindsight   102
Two-faced status   103
Conclusion   105

Chapter Six
WOMEN IN MARULAN: INDEPENDENT AND TIED   107
Faceless women and women as an underclass   109
Marulan women   113
Landholding   121
Women in the workforce   124
Conclusion   128

Chapter Seven
MALE AND FEMALE RELATIONSHIPS: POWERFUL BELIEFS   131
Radical feminism in the country   131
Male dominance—an ideology   136
Happy families   144
Spheres of action   149
Sex role behaviour—the real and the ideal   154
Conclusion   156

Chapter Eight
TRIAL BY FIRE   158
Events of 1965   161
Fire: 1979   165
Fire fighters: formal structures and informal participation   166
Women's role in crisis   171
Threat of disaster, reality of crisis: human responses   174
Aftermath assistance   176
Convergence   177
Communion   178
Conclusion   180

Chapter Nine
CONCLUSION   183

Bibliography   191

Index   201

TABLES

3.1 Percentage contribution of agricultural exports to total exports 42

3.2 Percentage contribution of farm product to gross domestic product 42

4.1 Employment in the rural sector 67

4.2 Strikes at quarry—Marulan South 1977–78 71

4.3 Strikes at Blue Circle Southern Cement Plant—Portland 1977–78 72

4.4 Voting patterns in Marulan 74

6.1 Land transfers—Marulan and district 1.1.38–30.6.77 125

6.2 Land sales—Marulan and district 1970–76 126

6.3 Sex of single agents in land sales—Marulan and district 127

6.4 Years of residence in Marulan district 128

7.1 Scores for people cited as influentials 140

7.2 Age at marriage 147

7.3 Age at marriage—people thirty years and younger 147

7.4 Age at marriage—Anglican Church Register 1970–77 148

7.5 Marital status 149

7.6 Proportion of Australian population never married—1977 150

7.7 Attitudes to women's working 151

7.8 Attitudes to sex-specific domestic tasks 152

ACKNOWLEDGEMENTS

I am indebted primarily and principally to the people of Marulan. It scarcely needs saying that without their help and co-operation this study would have been impossible. Well beyond a level of courtesy and interest, I was warmly accepted into district social life and into people's homes. During bushfires I was gratefully aware of their concern. More than that, they extended friendship to me. I offer them my special thanks.

The research was in the first place undertaken for a PhD, for which I was fortunate to have the advice and support of two supervisors, Ron Wild and Marie de Lepervanche, successively. Their stimulation and comment were invaluable.

Numerous colleagues and friends have helped in discussion and offered criticism and encouragement. I do not venture to name them individually—it would be a very long list—but I am grateful to them all.

I certainly owe a considerable debt to Valerie Perrin for her excellent typing of the manuscript and keen editorial eye, and for her tolerance.

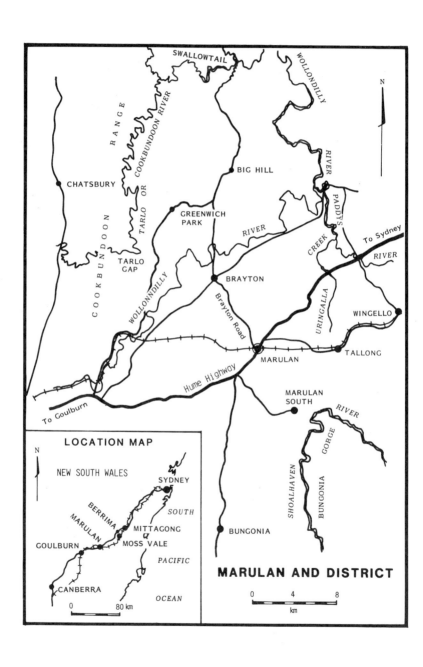

SWALLOWTAIL

WOLLONDILLY

RANGE

COOKBUNDOON RIVER

TARLO OR

CHATSBURY

BIG HILL

RIVER

PADDYS

GREENWICH
PARK

COOKBUNDOON

RIVER

To Sydney

RIVER

TARLO
GAP

CREEK

BRAYTON

WOLLONNDILLY

URINGALLA

WINGELLO

Brayton Road

Hume Highway

MARULAN

TALLONG

To Goulburn

MARULAN
SOUTH

RIVER

SHOALHAVEN

GORGE

BUNGONIA

N

LOCATION MAP

N

NEW SOUTH WALES

SYDNEY

BERRIMA

SOUTH

MARULAN

MITTAGONG

MOSS VALE

GOULBURN

PACIFIC

BUNGONIA

CANBERRA

OCEAN

0   80 km

MARULAN AND DISTRICT

0   4   8
km

CHAPTER ONE

INTRODUCTION

THE STUDY: BACKGROUND, INTERESTS AND METHOD

This study is of social relationships in a country district in the Southern Highlands of New South Wales. The district includes the small highway township of Marulan and the surrounding countryside. A central consideration of the study is gender.

For three years before the formal beginning of this project, my family and I had been associated with the district on a part-time basis. Like many others, we spent weekends and holidays there and were fortunate in meeting and making friends with a number of residents. Apart from individual connections and informal social associations, which opened up a wider network of friends and contacts, one event especially created the conditions for our acceptance. Soon after our move into the district one of the fires which break out nearly every summer in that region blazed in the country behind our small farm. Wind direction and local topography meant that for the safety of the district to the north and west the fire should be stopped at our place; it had at that stage moved to one of our boundaries. For a couple of days and nights shifts of men came and went, indeed many just stayed, and an assortment of heavy equipment rumbled around. During this time, while the men of the family were out fighting the fire, the women made 'tucker'—tea and sandwiches—for the fire fighters. The communal bonds which were established in the shared experience of that fire furnished the basis for the development of district associations and friendships. I felt that, through it, our presence in the district was in some measure both recognized and accepted.

Over the period of intermittent residence preceding fieldwork I was particularly intrigued by the high social visibility and influence of women (despite their secondary role during bushfire). At that time women had received relatively little attention in studies of local social systems, but in Marulan it was obvious that specific forms of female-male relationships articulated with many other dimensions of social organization. Thus during my time in the district certain questions relating to the attitudes of local inhabitants and to social relations were firming in my mind. The following chapters address these questions.

At the beginning of 1977 I took up full-time residence in the district for that year, with many working visits made subsequently. I believe that living in the rural—as opposed to the town—sector of the district brought positive benefits, despite the isolation. I was accepted by country dwellers, and then as if by some flow-on process, by the townspeople. As is the custom in many farming districts, the voice of the farming population carries considerable weight. I suspect that residence in the town would not have provided the same opportunities for contact and work with farming families, or acceptance by them. Although the time came when I had to finish fieldwork as such, I retain my association with the district.

Continuing residence, albeit part-time and with reduced participation in district affairs, has made me, as a researcher, particularly conscious of my responsibilities to the people with whom I worked. It is more than a matter of conscience and being answerable from a distance: I continue to be directly and personally accountable to them. This is underlined by the general local understanding of the network of interdependence which ties people in the district together, a network of which my family is now part. I have been direct in recording my observations and interpretations but I do not believe that this has been destructive in any way. Most of my fieldwork reports and much of the discussion present nothing new or surprising to the people of the district—they are aware of most of it in its general form. Certainly residents who read it in the form of a doctoral thesis endorsed the material and accepted the interpretation. I have called places by their real names, which I believe makes more interesting reading for locals, but in case any individual might be embarrassed I have not used residents' names. It is true that the details of individual style are usually consistent with the social position an individual occupies, but in the context of this research I maintain that it is possible to convey social processes without disclosing personal identity, although I note that local residents, however correctly or incorrectly, are keen to make such identification.

Living in the district as a participant observer allowed me to gain insights which more formal methods of acquiring information cannot elucidate. In everyday life the chance meetings along a country road, or on the street in town, participation in informal social events from dinner parties to handwork sessions, and in formal affairs such as meetings of local organizations, provided opportunities to observe a broad spectrum of social relations and to become aware of people's behaviour and their evaluations and attitudes on a range of subjects.

As appropriate, I joined voluntary associations and attended as many meetings as I could, as well as participating in the back-up events and business connected with a number of such organizations. The knowledge that I was engaged in a social study of the district did not seem to impinge unproductively on people's interactions with me or on observable behaviour. Nor did it apparently affect their acceptance of my participation in day-to-day life.

In addition to participant observation I conducted formal interviews with members of a third of the district's 170 permanent households. The interviews included both women and men.

Historical information concentrating on the district is meagre, but I examined what sources were available, including books and historical writings, articles in Sydney newspapers and relevant items in the *Goulburn Evening Post*, a daily newspaper covering the Marulan district. As well, I consulted residents' personal scrapbooks and papers, church records and the shire council's records of land transfers.

After I completed full-time fieldwork I carried out a second survey, this time based on a random sample covering 50 per cent (n = 85) of district households. My aim in this case was to interview all adult members of each household in the sample. I interviewed each adult separately to reduce the influence of any dominant personalities on the information presented by others in the household.

As it turned out, I did not interview every person in the sample. Members of five of the households were not questioned.

In one case the woman declined on her own and her husband's behalf. In each of the other four cases the women agreed to the interviews but were subsequently overruled by their husbands. In seven other instances the women of the household all responded to the questionnaire but their husbands would not. I one case a man co-operated but his wife refused. Clearly it was the men who were less inclined to co-operate. In eleven out of the thirteen rejections it was townsmen who refused or directed the refusal.

While participant observation undoubtedly provided a rich source of information, there are biases inherent in that approach (see Oxley 1974, p. xv), and certainly the fact that I am a woman opened up some avenues for enquiry and reduced others. Although this study includes both women and men of the district, the emphasis is on women and the female side of social relationships. Most Australian studies of this nature at the time I was conducting mine had been carried out by men, and that generated a male orientation. My intention was to provide some balance and draw attention to the centrality of women in district relationships and, in doing so, establish a ground for a critique of masculinist constructions of society. The point is that while female and male researchers may not present exclusively different pictures, in any society in which gender differentiation is both deeply entrenched historically and currently pervasive, the sex of the researcher must be considered an important factor in many of the directions and findings of the enquiry. Gender, for instance, is significant in opening up various opportunities for participation and association which must then inevitably be reflected in analysis, a highly relevant consideration when we take account of the fact that most researchers in this field have been men.

My overriding theoretical concern in this project is with the exercise of power in several of its forms. I am particularly interested in cultural domination and the way in which ideology operates in power relations. As a system of beliefs and ideas ideology can represent reality and what is 'right' and 'natural' to people who accept these beliefs and order their lives by them. Insofar as the interrelated set of beliefs and ideas of any particular ideology support certain social positions rather than others, such an ideology is also an effective instrument for the exercise of power by people in those social positions (see Williams, R. 1977, pp. 55–71). That is, as the subordinate persons in any power relationship accede to their position, and support the dominant ideology, they contribute to the process of hegemony. Some of the forms of relationships which I investigate are generally accepted by the participants as being 'right' and quite unexceptional. They are assumed as base lines for social interaction, but insofar as people consent, for whatever reason, to these forms, even when it means those who consent are placed in a subordinate social position, such forms are hegemonic. While these relations of power and influence I examine are not in any way specific to any one district, but characterize Australian society as a whole, they are here thrown into clear focus by the acknowledgement and acceptance by district residents of certain ties of dependence which constitute the basis of community.

THE DISTRICT

The study is set in the ethnographic present and although some changes have occurred since 1977 their social consequences have been slight; the tenor and focus of district life has not changed. The township of Marulan lies 170 kilometres south-west of Sydney. At the time of the study it straddled the Hume Highway, the principal road link between Sydney and Melbourne, although a freeway now bypasses the town by a few hundred metres. It is a typical highway small town insofar as the shops and commercial ventures are on the main road and the back streets are residential. There are no pretentious buildings in the township. It is, generally speaking, a tidy place, although some of the buildings have been allowed to deteriorate and this leaves a few scars. The nineteenth- and most early twentieth-century buildings are dotted along the roadside in a modest riband development, although later work has extended the township quite considerably on one side of the highway. There are several service stations, supported principally by passing traffic, which cater particularly for truck drivers; they have cafés which serve a variety of snacks and meals, and they also provide shower facilities. They are well placed to offer these services as there is a lorry checking station at one end of Marulan and the drivers are able, in comfort, to adjust their arrivals to meet timetable requirements.

About half of the buildings along the main road are of heritage value (as are a scattering in the back streets), although not all have been well maintained. Despite their individual attraction they do not determine the character of the town, which draws heavily from the service stations, the trucks and a few vacant allotments. There are three churches—Presbyterian (originally Scots and now Uniting), Roman Catholic and Anglican; a rectory adjoins the latter. The post office, police station and hotel are also on the main road, as are the butcher, a baker and the three general stores, one of which contains a newsagency. The Marulan Hall operates as a focus for the social life of the district. School events, large-scale church functions, club activities and private functions such as wedding receptions are all held in the hall. There is a primary school attended by about a hundred district children who come from thirty to forty family groups. Most secondary school students travel to Goulburn to attend one of the two state high schools there. Some go to independent schools, mostly for religious reasons, although in the case of children from grazing families it is for reasons of status. These schools are usually in Sydney or in the Mittagong–Moss Vale area between Marulan and Sydney. Most children, regardless of religion or status, start their education at Marulan primary school. One medical practitioner has his home and surgery in Marulan. There is also a car smash repair business.

Principally a service town, Marulan has only one industry, and this produces hydrated lime. The limestone crushing works are located towards the edge of the built-up area, although sufficiently within it to create a dust and noise nuisance for residents nearby. The limestone is brought from the quarry at Marulan South.

There is a small company town at Marulan South. Blue Circle Southern Cement (now taken over by Boral Ltd), which works the quarry, owns over twenty of the town houses (only six are independently owned), and provides and maintains services and facilities which range from sewerage to the sports oval. Nearly two hundred people are employed at South, and around twenty-five to thirty come from Marulan itself. Yet the two settlements very firmly retain their separateness, despite a number of factors which might have drawn them together in a shared feeling of district belonging. The quarry is a source of employment for men from Marulan and is only 11 kilometres away. A number of other forms of connection and dependence with less general impact link Marulan and South; these include kin relations, and the Marulan shops, which offer a little more than the single store at South. People in Marulan do not consider South as part of the Marulan district. Not only is there clear differentiation between the two settlements but this is often attended by a sense of rivalry. A well-known character from South spoke depreciatingly of Marulan. Defiantly, perhaps wishfully, he alleged that it was really reliant on South, but apart from that it was definitely going downhill. He cited as evidence the proposed downgrading of the post office to 'unofficial' status, the indications that the railway station would soon be unmanned, and the bypass diverting traffic on to the expressway around the town. He predicted that in a few years Marulan would be a forgotten town. Its decay, he said, was already apparent in its physical appearance. At least to this time—1989—and in spite of the bypass, his forecasts have been very wide of the mark.

Marulan may give the appearance of an industrial service town, but historically one of its reasons for existence was as support centre for the surrounding rural district. These days Goulburn, a city of 24 000 people, 29 kilometres to the west of Marulan and now within an easy drive for most of the Marulan district farmers, has taken on most of this supporting role. Certainly it provides goods and services that Marulan cannot. Even so, people continue to turn to Marulan for basic commodities and services. It offers food supplies, newspapers, post office and medical attention, which together or even separately have some centripetal pull on the farming population. Until the 1980s, when it no longer had a resident rector, the Anglican church also acted as a centralizing force. For people with young children the primary school is the focus of attention and the reason for their visits to Marulan. While their children attend the school this orientation becomes habitual, although it may weaken somewhat with passing years. The rural setting and connections provide the basis for people projecting an image of country life, and for the self-identification of the inhabitants as country people. This is not simply a matter for those living in the surrounding country, because district residents from in town as well as out of town strongly support rural values and believe in the superiority of rural life in aesthetic, emotional and social terms. That is, they are pleased to register Marulan as a country town and themselves as country people.

The district surrounding the town is taken up by small and large farming enterprises. The largest properties belong to upper-status graziers, the smaller ones to twentieth-century battlers. Quite a few holdings are large in area but fall within the category of small farming because of poor land and/or lack of capital which makes improvements impossible. The largest grazing properties are over 1000 hectares which, although not comparable in size with the vast properties further inland, is quite large for this part of the southern tablelands and is economically viable. The smallest concerns operating as farms require a hundred or so hectares. Sheep and cattle are depastured by small- and large-scale farmers. Until the last several decades the emphasis had been on sheep, and the size of the dams on old properties attests that, but in the 1960s when the market for wool slumped badly and cattle prices rose, most people endeavoured to diversify. Today more people are breeding horses. These include high-quality bloodstock, quarter horses, unpretentious stock horses, hacks and ponies. Newcomers are venturing into goats and even deer. Apart from paddocks put down to oats or lucerne for hay, very few crops are grown. A few hectares are often given over to growing potatoes and some special stock feed for grazing, such as millet or oats, might be sown, but the concentration is on pastures.

The land is very variable in productive potential. There are a few seams of rich red basalt country, but generally the soil is poorer and includes rough conglomerate outcrops and very light-weight sandy soils. Apart from the river flats and some grassy open plains it was heavily scrubbed and wooded at the time of the first settlement; the hilly country, particularly in those areas where there are huge rock outcrops, still is. Coming to Marulan from Sydney, the productivity of the land clearly falls off south of Berrima (42 kilometres north of Marulan). In good and bad seasons the difference in pastures is noticeable. This is not only related to soils but more directly to rainfall. Marulan is further on the western side of the slopes of the Divide than Berrima and therefore receives a lower rainfall, averaging 691 millimetres per annum. There are a number of minor creeks and ephemeral water sources in the district and although many are dry for most of the time, in a wet season they give the country the illusion of being extremely well-watered. The largest and most reliable source of water in the district is the Wollondilly River, which supplies the town's not very palatable water. In parts the river's water-holes are wide and deep; in other places, in drought years, there is no surface flow at all and even the puddles, which is all that can be seen of the river then, dry up.

The district's boundaries are clearly defined and recognized by nearly all residents. Newcomers have the greatest difficulty and perceive them hazily, but members of old families in the district have no trouble in citing them almost without hesitation. They appear as a compound of historical and geographical factors. The northern extent of the district is defined by Uringalla Creek which the highway crosses about 10 kilometres on the Sydney side of Marulan. The southern frontage lies about 6 kilometres beyond the town on the Goulburn side, but there is some disputation about the location of this boundary; a number of people would have it drawn at the turn-off to Marulan South. Relatively little land is included on the coastal side of the highway although the boundary does extend to encompass several properties, including the early grant made to George Barber. The country becomes more rugged and starts to drop to gorges a few kilometres on this eastern side. The other side, however, embraces thousands of hectares, including rough and heavily-timbered country and arable land. A road from Marulan goes out through what used to be the hamlet of Brayton to Big Hill and beyond to the Cookbundoon River. This waterway definitely marks the extent of the district at this point. Although the road could be said to cross through it, these days only four-wheel-drive vehicles venture to do so, and not when the river is carrying much water. In the past horses and buggies could negotiate it, but the crossing lies in a deep gorge and the topography would have made it extremely laborious and even hazardous.

The fact that Marulan is on the railway line and indeed for a year was the railhead, has exerted a centripetal attraction on people in the surrounding country. This was emphasized by the presence of a post office. It is evident that in the region generally the existence of a railway and a post office, avenues of communication, created a cell-like pattern of settlement and social orientation. This applied also to the Marulan district, though here geographical features may demarcate the boundaries more sharply.

During the period of my fieldwork abut 520 people, including children, resided full-time in the district. There were 44 households in the country sector and 126 in the town. There have been minor fluctuations, and an increase in the last few years, but for the previous three decades no marked changes occurred in the size of the population of full-time residents. In the century from 1868 there was an increase of 300 persons. In absolute terms this represents a significant increase, but it has not had much impact on development and pales in comparison with the population growth of what are now the large towns in the southern highlands, even though the initial populations were comparable in size (see for example Wild 1974a, p. 23). Over recent years, with an upsurge of commuter farming, the number of part-time residents and associates of the district has increased.

COMMUTER FARMERS

Whereas full-time residents of the district generally feel a strong attachment to it, and are seen to belong to it, there is more to being an accepted resident of Marulan than simply owning land or living in the area. There are some families, generally newcomers, who have neither fitted in nor been accepted. They do not see themselves, nor are they seen, as Marulanites. The we–they division may operate for several years, but time inevitably softens it, and although some continue to remain aloof and outside district affairs, their presence in the district over many years means that they become recognized as district residents. Indeed this sort of minimal acceptance of their presence is inevitable, as they have no other residential connections.

There is another kind of person who is not only not of the district but only infrequently in it. This category is made up of commuter farmers and comprises two different sorts of people with different interests. On the one hand there are 'Pitt Street farmers' (other places have their own form of this colloquial expression). These are people from Sydney who seek to direct city-made money into rural enterprises. The general aim is to lower the taxation burden while investing money in capital forms which will at least hold in value, or more likely appreciate. For these people the business of primary production may not be run at a profit, but as long as the loss simultaneously enhances the value of the investment it is acceptable, even desirable, as that loss can be written off against taxation. It is, in short, a way of converting income into capital. Clearly it is an avenue only open to some.

On the other hand, commuter farmers include hobby farmers—one of the locals refers to them as 'smoggies'. These people are not primarily interested in the land for its financial return, although no doubt they would like to see their money outlay as a secure investment. What they are seeking is some form of rural retreat. They see the land as somewhere to go for weekends and holidays and possibly as a place for retirement. In the land boom of the 1970s the subdivision of properties made many small 16-hectare-or-so blocks available, and these were swiftly snapped up by city people at what turned out to be exorbitant prices. Either for reasons of finance, or because the local council did not approve home building on the smaller blocks, there have been few houses built on these lots. Some people camp, others have caravans, and there are a couple of Nissen huts, erected as temporary shelters. Quite a number of buyers have wanted to resell their land, which has sometimes presented problems because of the owners' need to recoup their original inflated outlay (often made in the belief that they could build).

Hobby farmers do not aim to farm the land but simply wish to be in the country. This does not preclude growing, say, fruit trees and some vegetables, or even keeping stock, but this is really not done on a commercial basis and certainly not on any scale. These people may not even seek good farming land. One country resident related with askant humour a story demonstrating the quirks of hobby farmers:

I was driving along the river road when I saw a girl standing with a tiny little spade. I asked her what they were going to do with the land. 'Nothing', she said, 'just nothing. We don't want to move a stone—we just want it left as it is.'

The spade, my informant explained wryly and with derision, was for digging thistles. While she was highly amused at people owning land and not cultivating it, or using it for any form of farming, this woman was sympathetic towards hobby farmers because, she said, she could understand people wanting to escape the city. There is a general compassionate understanding in the district of city people's need for a country retreat (a view held among both town and farming populations), but this does not necessarily mean that they are welcome. The general feeling in town towards their presence is indifference. Residents there had nothing to do with hobby farmers and most are unaffected by their incursion. Some, however, stipulate that city farmers are really only acceptable if they do not bring their provisions with them but buy them locally, thereby contributing something to the town. Others are more critical. One woman said, 'They put up unsightly bits of sheds and they do nothing with the land. One can do without them. They're no benefit to a small community'.

Farmers are even less tolerant of their presence. One couple explained to me that there was only limited good tableland country for farming and that in a few years the bulk of the country might be taken out of production by carving up the land for the development of hobby havens. Subdivision of this sort, they said, brings about violent fluctuations in land values and consequently in the rates that farmers have to pay. As a result of the growth of hobby farms crops are not being planted, which means that machinery is not required. Machinery hire firms therefore move away, and the farmers who are left have to go further afield for implements and pay increased costs. Moreover, they argued, subdivision is self-generating and there is a general push of tableland farmers westward onto land of lower productivity.

Farmers know smoggies are unproductive, which in itself is unforgivable, but in addition they are known to present a fire hazard. They often let the vegetation on their blocks grow out of hand, and they are also thought to light fires mindlessly in unsafe conditions and even during fire bans; yet they are seldom there to fight fires. Nor are the farmers' fears without substance. In 1975 a fire started in a smoggy's caravan on a block with a river frontage. Opinions differ as to whether it was fat in a pan which ignited or portable gas equipment. Whatever the case, the flaming article was thrown out of the caravan door into the long dry summer grass on the block, and from there the blaze spread rapidly. The fire was put out in a few days but in that time it burned through more than 100 hectares and threatened one house.

Two local stories, based on incidents which occurred in 1977, are told in a vein of ridicule and derision. They highlight the ineptitude and stupidity of the city people and the residents' contempt for them, and thus succinctly sum up attitudes. The threat of fire weighs heavily on the minds of country people and one of the events is again concerned with fire. On this occasion a group of hobby farmers and friends had been barbecuing on a block by the river. The cooking fire spread in the surrounding grass. Some of those assembled endeavoured to extinguish it with towels, but failed. One young man ran to his car to move it away, unfortunately clutching his now-burning towel, which became caught half out of the car door as he drove off, thereby leaving a well-set fire trail.

The second tale was told by a farmer who saw some cattle on a small block. Knowing that the land had no water, he asked the man he saw tending the animals what he did for water. He was assured there was no problem, it was simply a matter of putting a hose in a neighbour's dam and siphoning water out. The irony was that the dam belonged to the interrogating farmer.

Far from seeking to enjoy the pleasures of rural life, Pitt Street farmers may visit their properties infrequently. Some holdings have managers living on them, working them on a full-time basis. Others are looked after by locals who work on them part-time. There is general resentment directed to Pitt Street farmers, and unlike the attitude to hobby farmers, it is not softened by sympathy. Only one or two residents, from either town or country, condone their presence, and the basis for such acceptance is that city farmers could afford to open up the country and undertake expensive development beyond the reach of other farmers: 'they turned what was a jungle into cattle-producing country'. It is also sometimes said in their favour that Pitt Street farmers create employment, but these capacities do not redeem them in the eyes of the population as a whole. Again, it is particularly the farming population which is antipathetic. One ex-farmer from the town held that there were far too many city people undertaking farming with too little experience. He said they were raising animals—cattle and horses in particular—which are of poor quality and thereby lowering the standard of the national herd. Further, he said that poor beasts on the market depress market prices generally. Many others share his attitudes. Usually the criticisms are directed at Pitt Street farmers for 'farming on paper'; they are not totally committed to it as a lifestyle and really only do it as a tax dodge. But people take the argument against the presence of city farmers further, and claim that by sinking money into improvements they cause a re-evaluation of land. As one farmer said, 'the rates are now inflated beyond the earning capacity of the land'.

Another farmer, who undertakes a good deal of contract work and begrudgingly acknowledges that Pitt Street farmers provide locals with employment, was none the less very definite in his condemnation of them. He made a number of points:

1 They devalue farm products because they have other sources of income and can afford to run at a loss.
2 They displace full-time farmers.
3 Because they are absent for most of the time their ownership and their absence erodes the sense of community; social life falls right away.
4 Their absence means reduced labour in times of crisis, for

instance during a bushfire when a small fire-fighting force of residents has to cover a large area, much of which is un-attended by owners.

Local attitudes exhibit distortions and exaggerations, but many of the criticisms have substance, and the farmers who have hung on to their land have been left with a backwash of problems caused by the departure of neighbours. Above all, what these comments indicate is a resentment, not necessarily to any known individuals, but to changes to the face of the district and to local lifestyles, which have been brought about without any input from the farmers who remain, but by people who are remote and anonymous. It is interesting that no censure attends the farmers who sell out—they are rather to be pitied. The resentment against city newcomers is compounded by the knowledge that access to finance enables the new, but absent and probably ignorant, farmers to achieve what others have been struggling for over many years. What is important in this study is that commuter farmers are for the most part socially invisible. They are known to be there but as individuals very few take part in any district affairs or are even personally known to locals. As a category, if they are thought of at all, they are separated out by and from district residents. Despite a landed presence they are not seen as part of the district. For this reason they are not included in any of the following discussions.

I draw attention to what will already be apparent, that is, a division in the population between town and country residents. Basically this relates to occupation and physical location, but there are flow-over effects in the allocation of social honour and in the relative social standing of the two sections. The country group is also further subdivided by the recognized separation of the large-grazing from the small-farming population. This demarca-tion is significant in social-class terms. It is a basic division in this study.

DISTRICT HISTORY

The Aboriginal population of this area dispersed, died from disease and were killed in the early decades of European settle-ment. Very early reports attested to numbers of Aborigines being seen around the district, but accounts soon dwindled to isolated and passing comment on the presence of very small groups. If the present bird and animal population is any indication, there was a variety of food resources available which would also have included indigenous edible plant forms, but the carrying capacity of the land for Aborigines would have been profoundly changed and reduced by the pastoral expansion. In 1826 it was reported that Aborigines killed, and are said to have eaten, a shepherd employed at Greenwich Park—just on the outskirts of the Marulan district (Wyatt 1972 [1941], p. 107). I was told of a later episode by one of the locals who related that years ago (unspecified), a member of his family took a couple of Aborigines 'down the back'. The white man returned alone and the implication was that the Aborigines had been shot. They had apparently been annoying the man's wife. Whatever the alleged offence, the punishment was dire. For one reason and another, all bearing on the advent of white settlement, the local Aboriginal population and culture were soon shattered. It is the same shocking and dolorous tale here as can be told for so much of Australia.

The earliest whites to have visited the area were in a party led by Henry Hacking, the quartermaster of the *Sirius*. This expedition, which took place in 1798, had no effect on plans for settlement. Exploration in 1818, however, influenced plans for the rural development of the country and from that time people moved into the area. On 4 September 1819 Hannibal Hawkins Macarthur was granted 1000 acres (400 hectares) in the newly discovered country to the south, although at that time he was not given permission to depasture stock there. The grant formed the kernel of his very extensive outstation. Then in the 1820s permits were issued to persons to take their cattle south of these parts. Subsequently several were issued with 'tickets of occupation'. Some of those who were originally permitted this untenured occupancy did, however, later receive grants and lived and died in the district. Grants could be quite generous. In 1834, 800 acres (324 hectares), to become the estate of Glenrock, were given to George Barber. Major Edmund Lockyer, Surveyor of Roads, was initially given 600 acres (243 hectares). Later grants and purchases increased the latter estate—named Lockyersleigh—many times. When offered for sale in 1853 it incorporated 11 810 acres (4780 hectares).

The original site of Marulan was on the line of road to Goulburn at the turn-off to Bungonia. The design for the village was formulated in 1834. Jervis (1946, p. 123) quotes from the *Sydney Morning Herald* of 14 September 1845, which described it as 'a small village with two inns, one store and a few bark huts'. Then again, from an edition published on 11 January 1847: 'the village of Marulan which differs little in its features from the other villages of the interior, being a small cluster of houses with two inns, a post office and three or four stores, procuring custom, nobody knows how'.

There was development but it was checkered and somewhat precariously based. Then in 1868 The Great Southern Railway was extended to Marulan and caused a change in the fortunes of the settlement. In fact the location changed too, as the line terminated some distance from the original site of settlement. Lots of land were offered for sale in the vicinity of the station and the old village declined as the population moved to the new centre. The new township was named Moorowoolen but was later renamed Marulan. In 1877 it had a population of 112 persons (*Illustrated Sydney News*, 31 March 1877). For the period of just over a year, when the township was the terminus for the railway line, it was busy serving coaches to Goulburn and Braidwood.

By the time the Robertson Land Acts were framed in 1861 most of the useful land in the Settled Districts had already been taken up, either by the large properties of the socially ascendant grazing élite or by struggling smallholders. Thus if the selectors who were encouraged onto the land by the new legislation chose to remain within the limits of location they had to pick out the best of what was left, which on the whole was rugged, inaccessible and generally poorer farming land (see Jeans 1972, p. 214). Many, however, preferred to do that than push forward into the empty interior.

Despite the difficulties of this sort of settlement, it occurred. The churchyard at Big Hill was built in 1878 and contains graves of members of early settling families dating from 1882. Parish maps from the 1880s onwards show a steady increase in the numbers of smallholdings taken up, and it seems that at that time the district took on the character which has persisted. True to the general model, large estates covered most of the good cleared rural land, while the small blocks worked by settlers were in hilly, uncleared and often 'light' country. The large estates were run by gentlemen farmers—a classificaton sought and conferred. Their properties were able to support them in a satisfactory manner. Smaller settlers, however, were not always able to eke out a living on their holdings. They grazed sheep and cattle and some dairy cows and were involved in cropping hay, wheat, maize and potatoes—the usual agricultural constellation for these parts. Even so, they often had to seek work elsewhere. Rabbiting of course was an activity available to farmers (as well as towns-people), but they were also engaged in more arduous work. Many took on part-time work, ring-barking and scrubbing—labour greatly in demand to clear timbered and scrub-covered areas for grazing. Shearing has always provided work at certain times of the year, and in difficult periods the men went away to shear, even as far as the big sheds in the west. Closer to home they were often taken on casually as general station hands on the large properties in the district. It is relevant to observe that however critical the role of women in the labour history of the district, the actors are recalled and registered as men.

With the extension of the railway to Goulburn in 1869, Maru-lan's role as a highway town was somewhat reduced until the advent of the motor car. By the last decades of the century the township had a dual role, serving the surrounding farms and supporting a variety of small industries. Earlier this century industry in the district was diverse. Rabbit trapping, which employed about fifty men, was more profitable over winter months, although freezing works operated in the summer as part of this industry. Rabbiting on this scale stopped around 1920. There was a tanning factory on the Goulburn side of the settle-ment, the process carried out in pits in the ground, using wattle bark. Inevitably this required further labour for stripping, stack-ing and bagging the bark for tanning. For a long time there was a sawmill out of town which employed a number of men. One elderly man stressed the great call from the railways for wood for sleepers and for burning in the engine. The railway also required numbers of men to maintain track, rolling stock and other equipment, and many present townspeople give their fathers' occupation as fettler. Nowadays this form of transport does not compete with road haulage for a large range of goods. For this reason, and because of increased mechanization, the numbers of people employed have declined.

Mining and quarrying have provided the most persistent and stable employment opportunities. Quarrying for stone has a long history in the area, and indeed continues. Not all strikes or workings fulfilled their early promise, however, and many enter-prises were short-lived. For instance gold was found but fossicking provided small returns, and although ochre, kaolin and coal were all mined for a period, the supplies were soon exhausted. In the past the district yielded fine marble, sandstone and granite and more recently blue metal. It has been the massive deposits of limestone, however, which have supported the largest-scale industry, and for many years, although they lie at Marulan South, just outside the district as defined. In 1830 Charles Sturt is said to have remarked on the outcrop. It has now been quarried for over a century. In 1875 limestone was sent to Sydney, although it was only a few years before it was burnt locally, producing an output of about 350 tons (357 tonnes) of lime per week (Carne & Jones 1919, p. 142). Until 1928 the deposits were held under adjoining leases by two separate concerns. Over the years there have been several changes and now the quarry is managed by Blue Circle Southern Cement Limited, itself recently wholly acquired by Boral Limited. It is thus part of a huge and diverse enterprise with operations in various parts of Australia. In 1928, 82 000 tons (83 640 tonnes) of limestone were produced: technological development and expansion of the operation have increased this and in 1979, 2.4 million tonnes were taken out for the manufacture of hydrated and quick lime, with a production capacity of 100 000 tonnes per annum. The quarry at South is a large concern and has deposits which give it a future of many decades, but although it provides employment for so many Marulan men, the town itself is little affected by it (either physically or socially).

Despite some changes, Marulan does not appear to have developed significantly from the turn of the century until today. A number of individuals and companies have established various small-scale industries at different times, and with considerable fluctuations in fortune. Their effect has been principally on the town population or itinerant workers.

Farming and grazing, which have the oldest history of any enterprise in these parts, have remained virtually untouched by local industrial ups and downs, but members of the farming population are fearful that the rural face of the district will change. Many small farmers are experiencing hard times; apart from their marginal position in the rural economy, the drought of the early 1980s amplified the difficulties and some may be forced to move. There should be no lack of buyers. As less land is available near Sydney for hobby and Pitt Street farmers, there is an expansion in the frontier of commuter farming. Marulan, just a little further away, is attractive for these ventures. At the same time some of the larger estates, which are viable enterprises, seek to expand their holdings when they can. The nett result of this conjunction of factors is that it seems that the presence of small farmers in the district will be reduced.

CHAPTER TWO

GUIDELINES TO UNDERSTANDING: SOME BASIC CONCEPTS

POWER

The exercise of power is crucial in the form and process of social relationships. It is clearly evident on a grand scale in the operations of national and international capital and is evident in the working of government, with consequences, however indirect and attenuated, for the structure and form of district life. Power may not be evident, but it remains significant in the formal and informal interactions of people as social collectives, and as individuals. Given my concerns of gender and social class relationships, the concept of power is the theoretical anchor of this study. In this case its exercise is more often covert than directly apprehended. It shelters in community identification, rural imagery and traditional values. Low key and assiduously unrecognized as it is by the actors, it is none the less basic in the pattern of social relationships.

While power in both its conceptualization and theoretical application has been beset by problems, I do not intend to review either the particular arguments or the general debate which must be seen as both a consequence of, and a contribution to, the concept's theoretical development and in turn its practical usefulness. Instead the starting point for discussion will be Lukes' view of power (1974). His analysis incorporates clear critiques and reviews of approaches which emerged from the 1950s onwards. In effect, initially born of the rejection of crude élitist positions, from the ashes of each argument a new one arose.

Power as a relationship concerns the effective control that people (as individuals, or collectivities—formally or informally constituted) have or seek to have over their own affairs and those of others. As Lukes points out, we are all constantly affecting each other in our interactions, although left at this the notion does not have strong explanatory value. The concept of power, however, homes in on ranges of affecting, which can be identified as *significant* in specific contexts (Lukes 1977, p. 4). And it turns on the notion of interests. It is significant insofar as it is important for whoever achieves it and/or for whoever is affected (White 1972, pp. 488–90).

A focus on distinctive features in the areas of decision-making, issues, conflicts and interests (Lukes 1974, p. 5) draws attention to power relations as an integral part of structure, although manifest through the behaviour of specific human subjects. Giddens (1973) distinguishes these two aspects of power as the 'institutional' mediation of power and the mediation of power in terms of 'control'. That is, on the one hand the institutionalization of bias in the social system which favours certain groups and, on the other, the effective power held, and wielded, by members of dominant groups.

In this connection it is necessary to note that while at any one moment the institutional form (of say the state, gender, or class relations) can express power relations without reference to agency, agency is inevitably structurally framed. Over time specific forms of power relations may be engulfed by structural change and structures themselves recreated or remodelled by, and in, new power relationships. The process is dialectical and historical.

This is not to say that structures actually exercise power or benefit from it, which would be manifestly absurd, but that structures favour people in certain and often institutionalized sectors of the society; and those in power take care to maintain the system of differential privilege. The returns to these dominant individuals and groups are frequently unquestioned by subordinate people because of their broad acceptance of the structural conditions (see Urry 1981). Such acceptance may directly reflect the dominated people's lack of choice in the matter or, less directly, their involvement in ideological processes (which may also limit choice). There is the added complication that in some cases institutionally framed objectives may obscure the identity of those who stand to benefit most. The dependent spouse rebate, for example, is likely to have special significance for middle-class families where women are not in the paid labour force. An obvious example in the context of a rural study is how the principal beneficiaries of rural subsidies tend to be large-scale farming/grazing enterprises.

CONSCIOUSNESS AND CONFLICT

In both formally and informally constituted power relationships the element of consciousness requires attention and helps in explicating the nature of such relationships.

How individuals perceive and understand social forms and relationships provides an analytical key to the conscious and deliberate exercise of power by agents operating within or extending their structural brief, or flouting it. For instance, if subordinate and dominant members of society see power as traditionally vested in certain structural arrangements, more specifically as the right and responsibility of people in a dominant sector, then its exercise by these individuals may be accepted as legitimate. It is by invoking tradition—what is and always has been right and proper—that the powerful frequently exercise control. Their interests lie in maintaining the established order and its supportive ideology. Thus any view of power must take into account the awareness or non-awareness of the actors involved. That is, a primary feature for consideration must be the awareness, not only of the existence of a power structure and variations in the exercise of power, but also of the fact that control of the means of production gives power and in turn power controls access to scarce material and social resources.

While it is safe to assume that those participating in a social system conferring unequal rewards recognize its hierarchical nature, it is not necessary that they perceive any inequity in it. Consciousness takes two forms: the first as simple knowledge, a passive recognition best described as awareness, and the second, which is a further development, where consciousness carries with it a predisposition to action. Consciousness on the part of a subordinate group can really only be identified in its developed form when, through experience, the members perceive their relative deprivation, have some hopes of improving their position and seek to take action. From being passive or active contributors to the conditions of their existence, they take an active stand against them. In the process, the various features of power come into sharper focus. In this respect one can emphasize 'consciousness as inseparable from conscious existence, and then...conscious existence as inseparable from material social processes' (Williams, R. 1977, p. 59). It is not necessary at any particular time for individuals to perceive themselves as operating in, or to identify their social being as linked with, any given set of material social processes; or if they do make such identification that they should be aware of and articulate the essential nature of their relationship with others involved in the same processes. This does not imply that consciousness is merely a secondary phenomenon, an appendage to social process; rather it is an integral part of it and a crucial means of its manifestation (see Williams, R. 1977, pp. 61–2). Yet it only operates and is visible to the observer at certain moments in that process.

Social conflict is often an ingredient of power relationships but the question of actual social conflict only arises in circumstances in which people are conscious of their present or potential inequality, resent their circumstances and try to change them. (This does not preclude cases in which power is wielded mindlessly or perhaps even unconsciously but which then lead to conflict. Rather it emphasizes the significance of the response of the subordinate group.) Even so, the matter must be taken further than this. People may be aware of their unequal position but accept it as part of a natural order which is not only acceptable, but right and proper. That is, they do not interpret their inequality as inequitable. Further, they may contribute to the perpetuation of the assymetrical relationship either passively and unconsciously by simply accepting the status quo, or actively and consciously by rationalizing it and defending it. In both instances such acceptance of the structural relationship operates as a generative mechanism by which the bias of the system is reproduced. At such moments in power relationships notions of actual conflict have no place.

Once people identify domination there is the possibility of latent conflict. On the question of power controlling access to scarce resources, the potential for the exercise of power is in itself usually systematically created as a scarce resource. Yet depending on the strength of the ideology supporting the system of domination and legitimizing it, there may be only an inkling of the likelihood of the dominated people recognizing fully that their interests may differ from those of the people who dominate them. Conflict here can be seen as a possibility only. In this case latent conflict must inevitably have a particularistic cast and so be discretely issue-related because of the underlying acceptance of the hierarchical structure.

When the dominated recognize clearly that they are dominated and are aware that their interests differ from those of people with power over them, then conflict may become observable. It can move from particularistic, issue-related matters to embrace a challenge to the whole structure of the relationship and the underpinning ideology. Under these circumstances opposition none the less surfaces on a series of separate fronts. Challenges to the embracing ideology erupt around different issues exhibiting the basic inequalities of the system in rejection. Thus, there is a shift in focus from challenges over particular matters, which are seen as autonomous or not necessarily related issues, to challenges to the structure of domination itself, wherein individual issues are acknowledged as particular expressions and instances of the broader, contestable, inequity. In the first case people accept and do not criticize the overarching structure, in the second they reject the structure itself. This sequence is apparent in the (relatively recent and Western) history of social relationships between women and men. Earlier in the twentieth century, for example, individual issues such as women's right to vote or to equal educational opportunities were not generally perceived as firmly embedded in a wide-ranging criticism of and challenge to male domination. For many of the women and men involved they constituted independent issues. Today, however, instances of specific sexual discrimination are more likely to be understood as expressions of a broader and unacceptable female subordination. As particular matters they will each be challenged, but at the same time this is a direct critique of the overall and unequal social cast of female–male relationships.

MOBILIZATION OF BIAS

Consciousness in the form of the identification of interests is itself a generative mechanism in power processes. Schattschneider's argument on the mobilization of bias (1960), although developed particularly in respect of political pressure groups, bears critically on power studies in other social arenas. He holds that 'organization is the mobilization of bias' (1960, p. 71), in that people drawn together on the basis of interest are already predisposed to organize, and in the preparation for action bias is mobilized. The bias of a group is evident in its form or organization and in the very act of organizing. With the institutionalization of action, bias inheres in structure and ensures 'a set of predominant values, beliefs, rituals, and institutional procedures ("rules of the game") that operate systematically and consistently to the benefit of certain persons and groups at the expense of others' (Bachrach & Baratz 1970, p. 43). Some issues are organized into the system and some organized out. It is, however, inappropriate to order thinking in terms of the exercise of power as assimilated in either structural determinism or methodological individualism (see Lukes 1974, p. 54). Inevitably every decision or non-decision is made in a structural context and further, outside the realm of decision-making, there are structural limitations to action, non-action (a conscious and deliberate response from a position of power or perceived potential for power) and inaction (an often unconscious response of the alienated) in power relations. But, just as inevitably, the notion of action refers to human agency. In all its expressions the exercise of power is part of social process. As process it quite clearly involves not only individual subjects acting within the confines of structural positions, but circumstances wherein both the limiting structure and therefore the range and nature of choice in the practices of individuals are constantly changing. These are responses made not simply to exogenous factors, but above all to the internal dynamics of their interlocking.

INTERESTS

The question of interests is embedded in any view of power, whether or not this is explicitly acknowledged or whether there is any endeavour to come to grips with it. Power itself is a dialectical relationship exercised within a framework of limited or even no choice, which rests on the realization of the interest of one particular group or individual over the interests of others, whatever the status of such other interest: subjective and identified, or objective and masked. While subjective interests by definition are acknowledged by those who hold them, and are therefore much more accessible in any investigations of actual power relationships,

the argument that people have interests which existing conditions prevent them recognizing but which they would acknowledge if only conditions were different, i.e., when they may be presumed to be able to make the choice, contains little that need be disputed. (Hindess 1976, p. 330)

In some instances unexpressed objective interests might be swiftly and unambiguously identified. Yet in other instances, and at any given time, the identification of real interests becomes a matter for debate (Martin 1977, pp. 40–1; Lukes 1974, pp. 33–5; 1976, p. 129; Saunders *et al.* 1978, p. 68).

Consider for example the problem of unambiguous identification of the interests of the various sets of people who live out the beliefs surrounding the merits and responsibilities of rural land ownership. Identification of the subjective interest of large landholders in particular, which are embodied in these ideologies, may present no difficulty. In this same context, however, it is not such a clear-cut task to separate the objective interests of landless workers, aspiring landholders, or more particularly small landholders, unless there is an underlying assumption of either 'real' identification with, or 'real' opposition to, already acknowledged subjective interests. It is difficult, that is, if one does not already presume to know what the answer ought to be.

Moreover, it is likely that different orders of identified interests will arise from differences in methodology employed in endeavours to identify these interests. Real interests which have been separated by a negative approach—a certain action is not in the interest of an individual (or collectivity) and therefore her or his interest is an unspecified 'other'—are less accessible and less precisely bounded than real interests which have been positively identified and are therefore specific in form. 'It is not in the interest of landless labourers or small farmers to have most of the land locked up in the hands of a small élite' is a different order of statement from: 'It is in the interest of landless labourers and small farmers (a) to be able to acquire (more) land, (b) to have a measure of economic independence, (c) to have a choice of employment opportunities'.

Equally problematic is the reduction of situations involving multi-stranded benefits to single-stranded interest arguments; a conflation or an excision which must result from considering some interests as having primacy over others. This is of course intricately tied to the question of choice. It is not simply a question of competing interests in respect of the same person(s), and this can be a dilemma confronting both actor and observer (see Connelly 1972, pp. 474–7). Some sort of delineation and narrow evaluating focus appears to be necessary in order to get analysis off the ground, but this does violence to the complex and contingent nature of social factors operating at any time. Let us take a case where, in a time of high unemployment, agricultural labourers and their families live and work in a country district where it is common practice to use chemical crop sprays which contain an identified, unacceptably (albeit contested) high level of toxic substances, potentially dangerous when breathed or in contact with skin. There is continuing risk to the whole family, particularly the agricultural worker. Nobody would doubt that it would be in the interests of the people not to be poisoned, but the threat of unemployment, apart from cutting loose from supporting kinship and friendship networks, and maybe with other complicating factors such as forcing other family members to leave employment or breaking up the family, complicates, for the actors at least, interest identification.

I revert to the theme of consciousness in power relationships, which draws investigation away from objective towards subjective interests. This is not because I consider the former line of enquiry to be a worthless pursuit. On the contrary, and following Lukes, I believe that it is worth while, despite the dangers attendant upon it. To enquire into the workings of society exclusively on the basis of direct evidence, without any conception of real interests, is to reproduce the bias of the system in the analysis (Connelly 1972). For present purposes, however, the concept of consciousness is more immediately useful to an understanding of aspects of local social relations. By investigation of the conditions under which people's consciousness is triggered (or not), we may come to see in a clearer light the relations between levels of interests. While the concern in this study is principally with smothering any consciousness of domination by powerful ideology, in other contexts concentration on class or gender consciousness and their formation may reveal the possibilities that exist for mobilization around particular concrete objectives.

It is the notion of consciousness which acknowledges and identifies subjective interests and which alerts people to differences in interests within any hierarchical arrangement (Thompson 1963). This assumes the further but previously established requirement that there is not only an awareness but a resentment of inequality. It is in the light of this discordant dialectic that objective interests can be identified. The development of feminism is a good example of this process. There is clearly a time factor involved; indeed, it is with the passage of time and the aid of hindsight that the confusion clears somewhat, and an understanding of real interests may be developed. Not all identification of real interest is on a retrojective basis, but it is usually less beleaguered.

Frequently there is an elision of real interests and emergent subjective interests, but that is not the point; what is critical is that in structurally similar situations of inequality, those who have developed or are developing a consciousness of divergent interests behave differently from those who have not. In doing so the former, in their behaviour, reflect and contribute to modifications in social reproduction. While consciousness does not always carry with it an imperative for action, it does provide a charter for it, and the basis for mobilization. On the other hand, simple awareness, knowledge with no critical edge, provides no directives for change. At the least it encourages acceptance, at the most a stamp of approval.

HEGEMONY

It is significant that an understanding of social arrangements in terms of domination and subordination does not inevitably invoke the question of conflict, although with the development of a consciousness of inequality, increasing account must be taken of it. Moreover, when conflict erupts, the exercise of power then appears to many people to be attributable more to individuals or identifiable collectivities than to the nature of the social structure itself. Not that the exercise of power is ever consigned solely to either the realm of individual behaviour or to structure, as neither exists as an independent entity, either on the ground or in any productive theoretical analysis which has not lost touch with reality. Prior to the emergence of consciousness on the part of the dominated, or when it is inchoate, one of the forms that power takes is in hegemonic relations. Such cultural domination circumscribes and impedes attempts at resistance, although in the longer term it is likely to defuse the form a mobilizing social consciousness will take and the nature of its development—say towards an alternative or counter hegemony.

The concept of hegemony is not without problems. The recognition of interaction and process in hegemonic relations avoids any suggestion of static categories of power, but the concept has what R. Williams (1977, p. 112) describes as a 'totalizing tendency' in which there is a move from specific experience to more-encompassing perception. This tendency, which in itself is a crucial feature, may, however, easily be lost in a conversion into an 'abstract totalization', that is generalization no longer anchored in a known and identifiable reality, which at the same time presents as more static and uniform (see for example Chamberlain 1983). Such transformation robs the concept of its effectiveness in practical application, for the growth of an umbrella-like abstract concept makes the connections difficult to trace and understand.

Williams' formulation of the concept of hegemony is clear and helpful:

Hegemony is. . .not only the articulate upper level of 'ideology', nor are its forms of control only those ordinarily seen as 'manipulation' or 'indoctrination'. It is a whole body of practices and expectations, over the whole of living: our senses and assignments of energy, our shaping perceptions of ourselves and our world. It is a lived system of meanings and values, constitutive and constituting—which as they are experienced as practices appear as reciprocally confirming. It thus constitutes a sense of reality for most people in the society, a sense of absolute because experienced reality beyond which it is very difficult for most members of the society to move, in most areas of their lives. It is, that is to say, in the strongest sense a 'culture', but a culture which has also to be seen as the lived dominance and subordination of particular classes. (1977, p. 110)

As a result of intrinsic and extrinsic pressure, hegemonic relations are constantly being not merely defended, but recreated; such adjustments are made in order that the essential nature of the structural arrangements should not be impaired.

Hegemonic relationships are not without dissension and threats—the triumphs of which guide major directional changes in history—but the essence of the survival of any given hegemonic form is that it should be responsive to such challenges and able to incorporate them. Overall, and possibly because adaptive responses help to legitimate it and thereby contribute to its re-creation, hegemony rests on a basis of consent. Indeed the 'spontaneous' loyalty (see Gramsci 1971, pp. 196–200) extended to the dominant group by virtue of their social and intellectual prestige (Cammett 1967, p. 204) constitutes a hallmark of hegemony. As Urry (1981, p. 64) points out, however, while hegemony as practice may conceal social contradictions and conflicts, this does not necessarily imply that it bespeaks cultural homogeneity.

IDEOLOGY

Hegemony is more than 'the articulate upper level of ideology', but the concept of ideology is central to the analysis of any hegemonic process, and any hegemonic relationship is ideologically premised. Moreover it is the palatability and persuasiveness of the sustaining ideology(ies) which in the first instance invest structural arrangements with consent—recreated and reinforced by participation in the course of everyday life. The ideology of the family, as the foundation for society and a haven for individuals, with its attendant notions of ties and dependence, has for instance been beguiling enough to recruit people whose economic and social position would logically place them in opposition to it. If, from the beginning, an ideology has limited currency, or if it later loses its potency, then the hegemony to which it contributes may recreate itself with changes in its ideological content, or in some circumstances the hegemony itself may founder or yield to other forms. Over recent times ideas of what constitutes a family and roles allocated within it have undergone radical changes which have enabled the family, as an idealized social form, to resist more destructive challenges.

The frailty or failure of any particular hegemonic form need not, however, totally blight its articulated ideology(ies). In Australia, as part of the process of class formation, a pastoral hegemony was established early in the development of the colony. But it was never really entrenched (Connell & Irving 1980, pp. 62–3) and soon gave way to the rise of a mercantile bourgeois hegemony. None the less the rural ideology which had been established then in an early form continued to be expressed. There have been significant changes in its expression—modifications and accretions—but it persists. In its perseverance it has proved a useful tool in the exercise of power, both within the rural community and between rural and metropolitan interests.

It is necessary to write interests firmly into ideology. Whereas ideation, as a system of ideas such as coherent mental templates in the manufacture of stone artefacts or principles of crop rotation, may have an existence independent of any power relationship, ideology does not. Urry notes that it is necessary for two conditions to hold for a practice to be seen as ideological:

(i) that embodied with such a practice is a concealment of the causes, nature and consequences of that practice or of some other practice; and (ii) that this concealment is in the interests of one or more of the dominant social forces within that society. (1981, p. 45)

The centrality of interests requires him to clarify other critical characteristics of ideology. First, despite the concealment of particular features of its practices, ideology itself is not unified. It has no necessary or special coherence. He also argues that while ideology can only be viewed through its effects, the explanation of its effects cannot be couched in simple functionalist terms. That is, although ideological effects are observable in the advantages they return to certain social sectors, the origins of the practices cannot be explained by reference to those advantages (see for example Delphy 1984, pp. 199–200). Acknowledging the importance of interests, ideology can be viewed as 'the complicated process within which men [sic] become [are] conscious of their interests and their conflicts' (Williams, R. 1977, p. 68).

This is not simply to claim that ideology has a material existence only. It exists, as Urry says, 'within and through ideas, through the relations of concepts and propositions' (1981, p. 60). It is a system of concepts embodied in practice and Williams' understanding of it as process accommodates transformed and transforming practices. It also leads us straight to the critical issue of the relation between ideology and consciousness. However, without further probing what the 'complicated processes' might be, we are left quite simply in the realm of consciousness.

The relation between consciousness and experience is direct. Consciousness can only be born of experience, and thereby constitutive of it, but ideology, as an articulated form of consciousness (Eipper 1981, p. 24), is, in its theoretical systematization, separated from everyday experience (Bourdieu 1979, p. 80). It is, however, reproduced in the system of values and meanings, not as an independent ideas-system, but as part of the ongoing social process and as a result of certain kinds of power relations. By way of example we may look to the dynamic of patriarchy (Connell 1980), or to the development of a feminist critique.

Ideologies support particular group interests rather than others, but present the dominant group's interests as benefiting society generally. Yet they are not necessarily explicitly formulated by members of that group as an instrument of domination. For instance the rural ideology may well serve the interests of large landholders but it is an over-simplification of its complex genesis to see it as promulgated by this group alone, or that landholders themselves are necessarily conscious of their ideological stance.

Such specific social instances and forms explicate the complex and heterogeneous character of ideology and how both consciousness as awareness—with or without a predisposition to action—and ideology as a system of concepts, are part of the social process. Consciousness cannot be divorced from experience: however, at the point of its systematization the link between ideology and experience may be more tenuous. Further, the link is neither constant insofar as not all people who might be expected to subscribe to an ideology do so at all times, and others even remain untouched by it; nor is it necessarily visibly historically grounded.

There is another way in which ideology can be objectively and subjectively separated from social experience, that is, strangely enough, in its operation. While there is, for instance, no question that there are many happy housewives sealing with approval the practical reality of an ideology of family, there is information on dissatisfaction, frustration and depression among other housewives which suggests that in subjective and objective terms, and for whatever reasons, their experience of family life has little in common with any formulated ideology of the family, except in that it may have provided one motivation to marry.

Yet whereas ideology and experience may appear separated, they may also be closely tied. There are cases where the potential for dissatisfaction and unhappiness, within an arrangement underwritten by ideology, are defused because of the persuasiveness of the very same ideology. To take an example from the same context: some housewives hanker in many ways for another sort of social existence, but even when unrestricted by material conditions they accept their role in the belief that this is really how things ought to be.

What is significant is that ideology is manifest in everyday life, it is voiced and acted out and in its fit with experience and in the disjunctions tearing between it and experience, it provides a means whereby people identify their interests and their conflicts.

CHAPTER THREE

HISTORICAL PERSPECTIVES AND RURAL VIEWS

As part of the backdrop against which this study of social relationships must be understood, I turn now to examine aspects of the operation of a rural ideology in Australia's history, focusing on New South Wales. While there are vast areas of the state which lie outside this analysis, because of the time at which they were settled and therefore the nature of their settlement, there are many which fit the pattern. Even so, the present picture is not always replicated because local environmental variables have wrought different consequences.

If rural-mindedness has a long tradition outside Australia, within Australia it has value from the beginning of white settlement, both in promoting settlement and in some measure as an incentive in attracting labour to country areas. Yet the ideology was not always successful in counteracting the loneliness, the harsh conditions and poor pay attending rural labour, and certainly workers were not attracted to the country in sufficient numbers to meet the demands of pastoral interests. In certain historical circumstances the ideology was underwritten by conditions revolving around issues related to land, labour and capital. These particular circumstances were those in which small-scale rural settlement took place in areas where large estates were already established. Such was the case in the Marulan district. It is necessary, however, to probe further back in time because the pattern for the development of rural settlement, and rural relationships, was established in the very early decades of the colony's existence.

Initially land was the first significant form of property in the settlement and could only be secured by grant. For a few this provided a fillip to their fortunes. Coghlan, however, marvels that: 'With every inducement to become worthy citizens, with better chances of success than had many better men without convict taint who remained in England, it is remarkable how few of the convicts became genuine settlers' (1969 [1918], p. 21).

Certainly the acreages, based on English models and an English climate, were often of low productivity and inadequate, but the crux of the issue lies in the availability of labour and capital. In 1793 the first grants were made to officers. These were of 100 acres (40 hectares) each, but the officers were able to consolidate and develop their interests because of their trade monopoly (see Fitzgerald & Hearn 1988; McMichael 1979, p. 45). Not only could they buy up land given as grants to their subordinates in the New South Wales Corps, but they were also able to buy out emancipist farmers who had run into debt (see also Buckley 1975, p. 14). This form of capital accumulation was enhanced by assignment, and such a privileged position in access to free farm labour was bolstered by the availability of the wage labour of expropriated farmers (see Hughes 1987, pp. 284–322; McMichael 1979, pp. 43–6). The official aim may have been to establish a small-farming population answering the agricultural needs of the colony, but the practical consequences of the policy in its early years were to supply a steady flow of land and labour to an emergent class of privileged landowners. Of course emancipists and free settlers were not excluded from the category of successful landholders, and by 1821 neither civil nor military officers monopolized the leading positions (Fletcher 1976, p. 219). But capital was a prerequisite for acquiring enough land, livestock and labour to make farming or pastoral ventures profitable. The difficulties and costs of extracting even a bare living from the land resulted in high casualty rates for the majority of small farmers (Fletcher 1976, p. 219). New lands were opened up for settlement after the Divide was crossed in 1813, and from the 1820s attempts to settle small-scale farmers gave way to explicit support for large landed capital.

By the end of the first quarter of the nineteenth century the foundations of subsequent rural social and economic relations had been established. The differentiation between large and small landholders was at base an economic one, but the separation of pastoral and other farming interests also symbolized status differ-

ences (see for example Robinson 1976, pp. 7–8), which have
endured over time. From the outset of settlement, for those
economically and socially favoured, land seemed to generate land,
and with an availability of capital, rural development was rapid.
Reliance on labour-intensive methods, however, meant that the
demand for pastoral and agricultural labour was constant. The
system of assignment had provided landholders, specifically landholders of large parcels of land, with a number of biddable
workers at low (often virtually no) cost. When transportation was
finally abolished in New South Wales in 1840, the landholders'
access to and control over the labour force was, at least in
principle, circumscribed (see Clark 1973, p. 446). Free (that is
non-assigned) rural labour, which had always been scarce, continued to be so; it was increasingly expensive and the problems of
attracting rural labour were strongly declaimed by the emergent
landed gentry.

The gold-rushes of the 1850s swelled the numbers of immigrants and when the fever subsided many more people wanted to
take up tillable land. The sales of smallholdings rose, but nevertheless fell far short of meeting the demands. It is important to
note that the squatters' expansion of the pastoral frontier from the
1830s had not improved the lot of small farmers. Land-use
patterns followed those established in the Settled Districts and
the land was effectively locked up and made inaccessible to most
small farmers (McMichael 1979, p. 66).

As well as the numbers clamouring for land, and growing
unemployment, the tide of opinion of those not associated with
squatting interests was rising against the rural domination by
squatterdom and a change of policy was demanded in the land
laws. John Robertson framed, and vigorously supported the
changes which were embodied in, two Bills, both of which were
passed and became law in 1861. The Acts were officially intended
to open up the land to persons of small means and to establish a
class of yeomen farmers—a notion which had long been dear to
the thinking of British and colonial administrators as a way of
increasing the agricultural productivity of the settlement according to what was regarded as the successful British model. That the
conditions of settlement and the history of the colony, albeit
short, were hardly conducive to the establishment of a passive and
productive peasantry did not cloud or otherwise impair the ideal.
Under the Crown Lands Alienation Act land was thrown open to
selection before survey at the fixed price of £1 per acre—lots

ranging from 40 to 320 acres (16 to 128 hectares). Given the terms of acquisition and payment it was hoped that men (it was inevitably men) with little capital would be attracted.

While the aim of the Acts was to encourage small cultivators as pioneers of the land, it soon became apparent that it was impossible to unlock the lands in this way without the principal benefits being derived by the rich. Clark (1978, p. 167) claims that in 'the class contest for land' selectors were caught between what had hitherto been the major economic forces of Capital and Labour. Some were able to rise into the ranks of capitalist, others were pressed again into the wage labour force, the very circumstances the Acts sought to change. There was in fact a third outcome, when selectors, unwilling to relinquish their holdings, were pushed part-time into wage labour in order to earn the money their selections could not return—money needed to discharge debts and simply to live. Again, lack of capital and small and unviable acreages all too often made a charade of successful independent farming.

Coghlan examined the rate at which selectors were dispossessing themselves of their land, and in his 1893 report he said that since 1882 (twenty years after the Acts had been passed) 23 157 453 acres of conditional purchases were transferred initially, against 13 986 848 acres which small settlers had later applied to buy. He reports the difference, of over 9 million acres, to have gone to the increase of large estates. Moreover, he draws attention to his finding that:

there appears to be no great tendency among the country-born youth to follow city rather than country pursuits, but among the immigrants there is only a small proportion who are accustomed to country life, or who possess the means requisite for coping successfully with the difficulties which surround a pioneer, while the townbred population show no disposition to embrace a rural life. (1969 [1918], p. 517)

His statement supports the view that not only was rural labour less easy to recruit but the country–city division was firmly established.

According to Fitzpatrick (1969 [1941], pp. 265–6), throughout the 1890s and into the twentieth century it was evident that 'people did not own the land'. The large estates took up most farming property. Further measures were taken by the government to split up the large estates and redistribute the land to smaller farmers; unimproved land values were taxed but with little effect except an increase in revenue. The Discharged Soldiers' Settlement Act after the First World War, in direct contradiction of its aims, merely put more small blocks on the market for those who could afford them. But twenty years after 1917, 50 per cent of soldier settlers in New South Wales had left their blocks. Fitzpatrick cites the lack of capital and the small, economically unviable blocks, as well as the fall in value of primary products and the unsuitability of many settlers, as the reasons for the failure of the scheme.

This perspective of the history of land settlement, and the consequent economic and class relations, reads as a litany of the disasters of small-scale farming. Certainly the failures and tribulations have been manifold. Yet the features of an idealized rural existence, what McQueen describes as 'our land-myth' (1970, pp. 147–71), have operated as an attractive force, drawing some people into the country from the earliest days of settlement. It is worth noting that in its basic form the ideal pivots on owning or working one's land. Without ownership or the hope of it, country living presents a less pleasing prospect. As Coghlan notes, the virtues of the lifestyle did not bring wage labour flocking. Obviously the conjunction of rurality and capital enterprise, from petty bourgeois to large estate, offers the most potent form of the attraction. Even though the idyll in itself is not a drawcard for labour, I argue that it is today invoked by people already living in the countryside or country towns who do not own farming land. The ideal of private land ownership constituted a crucial, if explicitly unacknowledged, element in the policies of settlement. In the oppositions which frequently surfaced between city and landed concerns (see for example Clark 1973, p. 89; McQueen 1970, p. 150), country people united in the interests of large landed capital—in what was interpreted as a common cause. It is true that divisions between small- and large-scale farmers were often bitter, especially those between squatter and selector, but at times, and certainly over time, these were healed by the panacea of rural orientations.

A farming population was attracted to the country by the compelling images and values of rural life and rural ownership. More than this, however, because of the force of the rural ideology, many cleaved to this lifestyle despite the difficulties and deprivations which made their existence precarious and marginal. Not only did the largest areas of land go to the landholder with means, but what was perceived as the most productive country was allocated in the early grants or bought later by those with money. What was left to selectors were the small and poorer blocks whose productivity all too often did not allow for self-sufficiency. Men in such families often went away shearing or did contract work for part of the year, leaving wife and the rest of the family to manage. Work found locally was obviously preferable. What occurred then as a consequence of the history of the settlement system was the creation of a continuously available labour force, whose members could be called upon at critical points in the year to work on large landholdings (see for example Coghlan 1969 [1918], p. 495).

Casual work suited the selector and it was also attractive to employers. As the relative position of labour improved, the demand for workers increased and their wages rose. Being able to call on casual but reliable workers during the critical periods of the farming year, or for help in work projects of limited duration, such as scrubbing or fencing, no doubt represented a considerable saving to employers who would otherwise have had to take on workers on a full-time basis and/or surrender themselves to the demands of an increasingly independent, mobile and assertive rural proletariat.

The features of land settlement and rural relationships which have been the themes in this historical overview are present in the history of the Marulan district. Hannibal Hawkins Macarthur's extensive grazing property 'Arthursleigh' was an outpost of southern settlement until 1820 (see Roberts 1968 [1924], p. 31; Jeans 1972, p. 103). Like other early large grants made in the district it incorporated (indeed still does) long stretches of river frontage and grassy plains. The small selectors' holdings are located on poorer soil or in rugged hill areas and were claimed much later, mostly during the last few decades of the nineteenth century and later. Members of some of the present families living in the district relate how their forebears walked from gold diggings in other parts of the state to take up selections. Some of 'the old names' have disappeared as landowners, but a few have expanded their properties. Not only are past patterns of land allocation and selection detectable in maps of present holdings, but, tied to this enduring model, certain forms of economic relationships persist, for many of the small-scale farmers work at times throughout the year as wage or contract labourers on other properties. They shear, plough, fence, or otherwise provide their skills and labour. Their participation in the labour market varies, not only seasonally, but individually, but it is essentially the same system operating as nearly a century ago when small selectors in the district worked part-time on large properties nearby.

FROM IDYLL TO IDEOLOGY

Newby (1977, pp. 11–21; 1979, pp. 13–24; in association with Davidoff & L'Esperance 1976, pp. 146–52; and with Saunders, Bell & Rose 1978, pp. 63–4) has persistently presented the rural idyll as a factor which must be counted as significant in social studies of rural life in England. It is, however, not confined to England but flourishes as a necessary and primary consideration in the Australian rural scene.

> The core of this tradition can be stated quite simply, life in the country-side is viewed as one of harmony and virtue. The town is disorganized; the country is settled. The town is bad; the countryside is good. Social relationships in the town are superficial and alienating; relationships in the countryside are deep and fulfilling. The images combine when the countryside is regarded as 'natural', the town as 'unnatural'. (Newby 1977, pp. 12–13)

While the Australian convention may be traced back to an English source, there were continuing modifications in the experience of settlement which gave the local form of the idyll a peculiarly Australian colour. Pioneering and the challenge of frontier living have been enshrined in Australian literature as embodying the quintessential characteristics of Australian people— men particularly. Because of their lower numbers and more especially because, traditionally, this was a man's realm, women became background figures in the landscape (see Schaffer 1988). The stereotypical rugged, hardworking, steadfast characteristics were not only said to have created the conditions for the ideal rural existence, in which was to be found satisfying hard work and simple contentment, they were also easily translated into the characteristics defining a farming image. Rural life was also portrayed as a battle against nature, but just like the English picture, the idealized Australian version of this existence attested the triumph of men over the hostile elements of nature and the idyll was then invested with harmony, innocence and peaceful pleasure—a veritable cloak of bucolic virtue. What is interesting is that long hours of toil in frequently most uncomfortable conditions could be presented as desirable, even when the returns were often so low. Indeed for many they remain inadequate as income. It is a testimony to the potency of the idyll that the unpleasant, demanding, even wretched aspects of rural life are filtered out of the image, despite their oppressive reality for so many people, most particularly small farmers and agricultural labourers (many of whom would dearly like to own farms themselves), who must not only face all weathers and all work, but who are so susceptible to the dictates of the market.

The view of country living as 'the good life' is not held by the farming community alone. City people also subscribe enthusiastically to the notion, and laud country life. Whereas once they were content to have holidays in the country, more and more people over the last few decades have wanted to participate in, rather than simply observe, this lifestyle. Opportunities, especially widespread ownership of motor cars, have made this possible. Hobby farms provide a common weekend and holiday retreat for people with either capital or access to reasonable loans. Sometimes it is sufficient just to have the land to visit and enjoy, at other times vegetables or fruit trees are grown and possibly a couple of animals depastured. Running hobby farms, however, seldom involves much more effort than pottering, or at most, easy labour. In Marulan between 1970 and 1976 land sales boomed (see Table 6.2). Most of the transactions involved an input of city money, either in the form of Pitt Street farming or, more noticeably with the subdivision of some larger farm properties, hobby farming.

The ideal of the return to nature, inherent in hobby farming, is also most clearly in evidence in the rise of communes and alternative farming settlements in rural Australia (see Powys 1981; Powys, Nalson & Hickey 1981; Ward & Smith 1978, p. 5). While alternative lifestyles which are followed in commune life are an expression of the dissatisfaction felt with city lifestyles and values, they also acclaim the worth of most of the basic features of a traditional small-scale farming existence. For city people the sentiment and nostalgia surrounding rural life is somehow, and mysteriously, divorced from resentment and opposition to concessions which governments may make to bolster the agricultural sector, and even from the picture of the whingeing farmer which emerges from time to time. Paradoxically, then, if farmers were ever in doubt about the merits of their lifestyle, the attitudes of city people, anxious to experience and extol the virtues of country life, would surely dispel uncertainties and confirm the known. It is not commonly the vision of 'the good life' which attracts Pitt Street farmers to invest in rural property, but even so it is a way of talking about this form of enterprise which may be seen to soften the brashness of the financial purpose. At the same time land ownership in Australia, particularly in large holdings, has brought and continues to bring status (see Oeser & Emery 1954, p. 31).

As R. Williams (1973, pp. 9–12) and following him Newby (1977, p. 18) indicate, retrospect is a crucial element in appraisals and reappraisals of the undeniable worth of rural life. But in Australia it is not merely its essentially virtuous nature, depicted so clearly in the reconstruction of past and halcyon days, which commends it; history also highlights the economically crucial role of farming in the well-being of the nation. In its early days the colony tried to depend on the success of farming for its existence. As the nineteenth century rolled on and the nature of settlement and development changed and concerns moved beyond bare subsistence, pastoralism became the mainstay of Australia's economy. The nation, it is claimed, rode to prosperity on the sheep's back.

In 1888 Coghlan wrote: 'Pastoral property and stock form the largest factor in the wealth, not only of New South Wales, but also of all other principal colonies of Australasia and the return derived therefrom is the largest source of the income of its inhabitants' (p. 293). Sustained by this generally known fact of history, it is a common rural belief that the relative weight of the farming contribution to the nation's economy has not changed dramatically over the years. At an informal social gathering in Marulan in 1977 a grazier from the district stressed his belief that the worth of the man on the land was not fully recognized and questioned the propriety of the state of affairs in which he said '15 per cent of the population is responsible for 50 per cent of the nation's productivity'. Everybody present seemed to accept not only the gist of the statement but the accuracy of his figures. Yet in 1972 Aitkin noted that since the mid-1940s the contribution of the rural industries to gross national product had fallen by half, and the proportion of export income which these industries generated had dropped from 90 per cent to less than 50 per cent. Certainly farming products remain most important to the nation's economy, and the export trade is heavily reliant on grain, meat and wool, but other industries, specifically mining, have risen steadily and have contributed to the relative decline in the input of farm products. In the last few years agricultural exports have contributed less than 25 per cent to total exports (see Table 3.1) and in 1982–83 the contribution of farm product to gross domestic product was 3.29 per cent (that is at current prices; 3.21 per cent at average 1984–85 prices; see Table 3.2).

As Aitken demonstrates, the belief in the overriding importance of primary industries is central to the political ideology of the National Party of Australia. Its members believe that:

Table 3.1   Percentage contribution of agricultural exports to total exports

Year	Agricultural exports
1983–84	18
1984–85	21
1985–86	20
1986–87	17
1987–88	18

Source: *Exports Australia 1987/88*, Australian Bureau of Statistics.

Table 3.2   Percentage contribution of farm product* to gross domestic product

Year	Current prices	Average 1984–85 prices
1974–75	5.68	4.12
1975–76	4.91	4.38
1976–77	4.76	4.38
1977–78	4.14	4.18
1978–79	5.93	4.95
1979–80	6.08	4.21
1980–81	5.13	3.59
1981–82	4.73	4.14
1982–83	3.29	3.21
1983–84	4.74	4.47
1984–85	4.30	4.30
1985–86	3.77	3.98
1986–87	3.79	4.06
1987–88	4.12	3.81

Source: *Quarterly Estimates of National Income and Expenditure Australia*, March 1989 Quarter, Australian Bureau of Statistics.

* Farm product is that part of the domestic product which derives from production in agriculture and services to agriculture.

Farmers and graziers are thus not only owed respect and consideration from the rest of Australia, but it is in everyone's interest to help them to be as productive as possible. The most effective means of accomplishing this end is to implement economic and social policies which will have it as their aim. Since only farmers and graziers really understand the nature and problem of their industries they should be left to devise these policies themselves. (1972, p. 17)

This political ideology is co-extensive with the commonly held image of farming, and holds fast to the rural idyll. Even if country people are not members of the National Party, and even if they do not vote for its candidates, they none the less adhere to the basic notions of the party's ideology, endorsing the worth of farmers and farming.

These basic beliefs concerning farmers, farming and indeed the rural scene generally, are critical to the study of rural society. I do not suggest that *gemeinschaftlich* (referring to community in which relationships are intimate, primary and traditional) and *gesell-schaftlich* (where relationships are impersonal, secondary and autonomous in large-scale society) differences can be plotted on to a rural–urban continuum (see Pahl 1968; Wild 1974b, and more recently Newby's comprehensive discussion of the rejection of a rural–urban continuum in sociology, 1980, pp. 21–31) but rather that the rural idyll, and by extension rural life as ideal, is a factor which must be incorporated in consideration of country living. In Australia agricultural economy has been deemed to be a legitimate object of sociological study, but rural society *per se* has not really been accorded this right (see Nalson 1977, p. 321, and a more recent exception is James, 1989). It is true that people often appear in texts as country people, but only to the extent that they live and work in the country. Yet their life circumstances, their social relations and their expectations, even when not necessarily flaunting rurality, are likely to be intimately tied up with processes directed by rural orientations and ideals. These views must therefore be included as important and distinctive factors in studies of rural areas.

Commitment to the ideals of rural life draws country people together. Thus shared attitudes can be made to minimize, even on occasion to bridge, social class differences, and give a unity to town and out-of-town populations. This is particularly evident when rural and urban values and interests are set against each other and the lines of opposition become clearly seen in economic and especially in social relationships.

Many of the comments I noted, made by Marulan district residents, both town and farming, indicate how people sharpen their focus and appreciation of country life through country–city oppositions. Time and again the friendliness, freedom and health of country life was stressed against the impersonality, the constraints and unwholesomeness of city existence. City people are represented as dissatisfied, materialistic and misguided—none of which characteristics is said to burden country dwellers.

Interestingly, only one country person—an old-timer with a philosophical bent—elaborated on what might be considered an elemental factor in farming existence, the close and direct dependence on the environment and subjection to its vagaries.

Country people are different from townspeople because of the different environment. Townspeople don't understand the problems of the man on the land and what he has to contend with. They don't realize that being on the land is an uncertain way of making a living. You might have a crop and then a hailstorm comes down and cuts it to pieces. That's terrible music. Then there's droughts, you have to live with them. It's either too wet, or too cold, or too windy—the times in between are what you've got to grasp. Those intervals which are favourable for the production of food.

Farming is often said to be 'in the blood'. In this respect it is akin to 'good breeding', which is not only found in animal herds as a consequence of controlled breeding programmes, but is also alleged to be apparent in humans. Here too it is said to be a matter of genetic properties, closely tied to environmental factors. On several occasions country people extended the idiom to argue that, indeed, heredity played an important part in whether or not an individual would be a good farmer. One man put his views in a Lamarckian mould. He maintained that the country way of thinking was different:

When you live on a farm it becomes part of you. Lots of farmers could get better economic returns doing something else but they stay on the land because they are part of the land. It's a feeling of belonging. A city person would view the land simply as a block of ground, he doesn't know it intimately and in detail.

He went on to suggest that the feeling for farming is inherited genetically. This sort of argument goes beyond a statement of difference between city and country people to justify in biological (that is 'natural'), and therefore absolute and unquestionable, terms, the basis of that difference.

The difference is also expressed in other ways. On one evening social occasion, attracting principally grazing and upper-status people from the Goulburn region, the guitarist played a popular song of which the catch line was 'Thank God I'm a country boy'. The assembled male youth was so moved by the song that it was played twice in succession, and the stamping, singing and clapping took on a cultic frenzy as the music played.

ATTRACTIONS OF RURAL SELF-PORTRAITS

It is common for people from even large country towns to perceive themselves as country people and therefore different from those living in the seaboard conurbations.

It is not surprising, then, that Marulan district residents from out of town preserve, and even cherish, a rural self-image which is in harmony with an idealized vision of country life. The circumstances do after all fulfil all the material requirements of life in the country. There are, however, contradictions between ideal and actual circumstances, and between aspects of this interpretation of a way of life, which invite further consideration. Following the pattern of perceptions indicated above, Marulan townspeople see themselves as country people, despite the fact that some seldom, if ever, go into the surrounding countryside but dwell, work and take their pleasure in Marulan or in Goulburn. Two questions remain: why does this view have not only strong, but widespread support in the country; and why today, given the circumstances of their existence, should townspeople subscribe to a country-mindedness?

The overriding consideration is of course the economic and social significance which most Australians and certainly locals accord to farmers. Inevitably this has an impact on the farmers' position in the local social system. Such is obviously the case in Mallee Town also (see Oeser & Emery 1954, pp. 12, 19), where farmers are seen as constituting 'the key unit in the social structure of the community'. In Marulan the farming sector— even excluding upper-status graziers—certainly enjoys more prestige than do the townspeople, and the farming voice carries considerable weight.

While the general attitude to farmers has specific consequences at the local level, their significance in the early development of the district also brings social honour. The town in part grew, and certainly served, as the centre for outlying farms and properties. The descendants of early settler families who were successful in their farming enterprises, even though they are no longer on the land, carry names which continue to be well regarded in the district. These are known to be the families who made the district what it is.

The idealization of rural life works in a number of ways. Among the Marulan farming population people are aware of certain limitations and problems of country life. For instance, many have felt their educational deprivation keenly. They would like to have furthered their schooling, but distance, the immediate need for their labour on their parents' property and the fact that there was little likelihood of turning such education to obviously direct and practical use, meant that they left school as soon as possible. A few regretted it at the time; more regretted it in later years. One woman in her late fifties told me that for most of her life she held a grudge against her father for not allowing her to go to high school, which she so desperately wanted to do. Others have had to live in quite primitive domestic conditions because of the difficulties in keeping the farm going and the need to return all monies made to it. And again, some are sensitive to the isolation of both their work and home circumstances. As one farmer explained: 'Being alone makes you see you can be contented in isolation but it doesn't make you seek it'. That is, people are certainly aware of these and other disadvantages of their rural past and present, but at least by upholding the belief that this lifestyle is qualitatively superior they are able to reinterpret what might otherwise be construed as negative elements in their existence. The virtuous characteristics of innocence, simplicity and steadfastness therefore subsume the kinds of disadvantages and deprivations mentioned above. Thus the barbs and criticism contained in notions relating to country bumpkins, yokels, backwardness, primitiveness and so on, are all deflected by the perception that this lifestyle is intrinsically good; city existence, by contrast and as a logical consequence, is not (see Rowse 1978, p. 16).

With particular focus on Suffolk farm workers, Newby writes that one of the reasons which makes it important to understand the tradition of rural idyll is 'because it has affected the agricultural worker's interpretation of his own situation, for a general cultural approval of the rural way of life is something that an otherwise low-paid, low-status group of workers is grateful to adhere to with understandable enthusiasm' (1977, p. 13).

This reasoning is not only entirely consistent with the material presented above, it is also germane to an understanding of Marulan town dwellers' perceptions. Whether wage labourers or petty bourgeoisie, townspeople manage an improved translation to their social position generally by setting themselves into part of the rural scene. Country-mindedness operates as an alternate frame from which to view what then becomes socially significant. It becomes the means whereby people can set themselves not only apart from, but even above their urban counterparts, although there may be no differences in the material circumstances of their existence. People are happy, or indeed even grateful, to see themselves as somehow imbued with a measure of rurality as a consequence of simply living in a country town.

Country-mindedness as commendation and identification is moreover reinforced in the town by the presence of a number of residents who, for various reasons, have moved in from the outlying countryside. In some cases, for example, partible inheritance resulted in land divisions which were too small to be worked profitably. Under these conditions it is common for one member of the family to buy out others who, in many instances, have then moved into the town and either established themselves in a business venture or become wage labourers. In one case advancing age prompted parents to move off the family property in favour of a son, and although they live in retirement they continue to take an active interest in the farm. Other families, feeling unequal to, or no longer prepared to grapple with, rural recession, the challenges of drought on land of low productivity, hard work and poor returns, and aware of the preparedness of Pitt Street or hobby farmers to pay handsomely for their land, have sold up and gone to live and work in town. Their move, however, does not detract from the strength of their support for country living.

There are also a few who live in town but who are, or were, farm workers, either full- or part-time. Whatever the reasons— whether people lived on the land as children, were themselves farmers or work(ed) on it as wage or contract labour—well over a third of town households have at least one person who feels a strong farming association. This constitutes a substantial number of people whose country-mindedness is based on rural experience.

The rural outlook of these people has social impact, and this is particularly strong in the case of those who are esteemed social participants in district affairs and whose views carry weight with other district residents.

Aitken proposes that the political operations of the National Party, in emphasizing rural and urban divisions, draw country dwellers from farm and town together. He points out (1972, p. 20) that in New South Wales the party has had a remarkable lack of success in achieving the goals of its supporters and, in the face of this failure, its continued existence can only be attributed to its being an ideological party as well as an economic interest group.

The sustaining philosophy, he argues, feeds on the distrust and suspicion with which country people view their metropolitan cousins. It arose in the nineteenth century when farmers, convinced of the intrinsically worthwhile nature of farming pursuits, and the responsibilities they shouldered in national economic terms, looked with hostility at the rise of economic and social power within the cities. Aitken suggests that country-mindedness today overflows into local towns and is associated with the promotion of regional as opposed to sectional interests. The nub of the argument is of course quite familiar now, but in this case it is turned to political uses which further contribute to welding together the attitudes of the farming population and residents of country towns. The National Party embraces wholeheartedly a view of country unity based on the belief that:

Farming settlements and country towns provide the best and most natural communities in which to live, societies in which people from all walks of life mix easily and freely, where there is genuine care and consideration for one's fellow man and the cleanliness and uplift that comes from living close to nature. Such communities are also stable, thoughtful, and suspicious of sweeping proposals for change; they are not prey to the forces of irrationality and mob rule that can take over big cities. (Aitken 1972, p. 19)

In Marulan an extra charge is given to rural attitudes because, for many years, the electoral representative at the state level was not only a National Party man, but lived on a farm not far out of town. He retained an unpretentious and farming image, and participated willingly and often in local events while simultaneously engaged in the machinery and issues of state government—all of which enhanced his prestige and personal following.

People from the town as well as farmers spoke of him sympathetically and familiarly. Even local members of the Labor Party
appeared to be proud of him as a district notable. The very few
who did not admire him kept their views to themselves. In these
circumstances the presence of a political leader, far from being a
divisive force, drew the district population together, and the fact
that the base of his platform was country interests promoted rural
orientations and country identification even further.

CONSERVATISM IN THE COUNTRY

If rural retrospect is a guiding theme in the development of rural
attitudes, that is, if the real virtues of country living are best seen
by reference to past forms and values, then in the pursuit of the
rural idyll 'The first essential element is one of unchanging continuity' (Newby 1977, p. 13). In certain circumstances conservatism may in effect be the consequence of apathy. For many it is
more comfortable to stay with the known and it certainly involves
less effort; and there is no doubt an element of apathy in the
conservative social outlook of most country populations. But
Aitken also suggests that these people are more 'old-fashioned' in
their attitudes because of limited social contact and a time delay in
being exposed to the new. This may once have been so, but these
days it cannot seriously be advanced as an argument which is
relevant to the country population as a whole, or even to most of
it. Television and other media have long been introduced in most
country districts and there is no time lag in country people's
reception of the news. Money permitting, farmers are quick
enough to avail themselves of the latest technological developments if they hold the promise of improved productivity. The
point is that country conservatism is quite selective: it applies
especially to social and consequentially to political issues (see
Baldock & Lally 1974, p. 107). Aitken, however, also offers what
might be called positive reasons for this selective conservatism,
that is, reasons which enhance and secure the position of the conservative (1972, pp. 101–3). His study finds that farm owners out-
number farm workers by nearly two to one (1972, p. 110) and he
contends that in political terms owners' interests are more likely
to be served by maintaining the existing system (see Oeser &
Emery 1954, p. 31 and Gruen 1970, p. 341). Of course change
is inevitably occurring, but it is reinterpreted and managed in
such a fashion as to pose no perceptible threat to a total view of

rural lifestyle. Given the open-endedness of retrospective attitudes in evaluating rural conditions and experiences—for today's conditions constantly change as the present becomes the past (the 'good old days')—then it is obvious that change is managed so that the past assumes a permanence, and basic tenets appear unsullied.

As the rural idyll and associated farming images confer benefits on country dwellers, in some cases tangible benefits, in others perceived or at least assumed, then it is understandable that every endeavour is made to keep the tradition alive and in its recognizable form. Conservatism thus feeds on itself, and nourishingly.

RURAL IDEOLOGY

According to R. Williams, much of the nostalgia surrounding rural beliefs can be traced back to stories and memories of childhood, although he also notes that the same holds for the sentimental backward glances of the urban working class, conjuring up images of gas lamps, corner shops and the like. Yet, he argues, these views are significant for they direct adult consciousness.

It is not so much the old village or the old back-street that is significant. It is the perception and affirmation of a world in which one is not necessarily a stranger or an agent, but can be a member, a discoverer, in a shared source of life. Taken alone, of course, this is never enough... Yet we can see here, in a central example, the true aetiology of some of the powerful images of country and city, when unalienated experience is the rural past and realistic experience is the urban future. (1973, p. 298)

Experience can be turned to confirm sentimental dispositions. The power of country images is such that pleasant days, good seasons, high prices, mutuality and country connections extinguish, or at least etiolate, memories of harsher realities. More than this, bad experiences such as bushfire, drought, flood or suchlike are also used to glorify country living by the elevation of (country) values such as good neighbourliness or doggedness. The value of country life is then attested in conscious practice in country living.

People can and do uphold and act out a rural ideal and derive pleasure from many aspects of their commitment, but this does not mean that the interests of all sectors of the rural population are served equally in the persistence and sometimes in the promotion of this sort of country-mindedness. Aitkin demonstrates that the roseate images of rural life serve as the ideological foundation of the National Party, and while the party may avow that it is as interested in small farms as large-scale agricultural and pastoral enterprises, it is inevitably the latter which are able to maximize on any rural assistance in the form of tariffs and subsidies which the party is instrumental in achieving. Indeed, the returns from political interest and activity commonly benefit not so much (if at all) small, but rather large, rural concerns, even though the image of small farming constitutes the very core of party ideology. As Nalson cogently argues:

Price supports, tariffs, fertilizer subsidies and the like are based on units of output or input. They thus accrue much more to the few large operators who, through their membership and control of farm lobbying organizations and political parties are able to manipulate for their own self-interest, political concern over, and sometimes urban sympathy for, the plight of disadvantaged farmers. (1977, p. 310)

Clearly there are contradictions between the conditions which underlie the forms of rural class relationships, but these are subsumed in the rural idyll which is then transformed into a rural ideology. It is the downplay or ignoring of some information and the deformation or reformation of other data which is central in understanding the transformation of the idyll to ideology and its associated constitution in social process, including the determination of form and emphasis given to attitudes. Larrain writes:

by concealing contradictions, ideology serves the interests of the ruling class, which can display the present order of things as natural and in the interests of all sections of society. Ideology serves the interests of the dominant class not because it has been produced by the ideologists of the class—which may or may not be the case—but because the concealment of contradictions objectively works in favour of the dominant class's interests. (1979, p. 61)

Hence a rural ideology characterizes attitudes and values of rural dwellers generally, and, as their beliefs are confirmed in the experiences of everyday life, this ideology at one level represents reality for them. Farmers acknowledge and for certain purposes even stress the difficulties in farming, but they also say, and they know, that it is the good life. At the same time, and in no way undermining this system of beliefs, but rather dependent on it and promoting its reproduction as part of the material social process (see Williams, R. 1977, pp. 55–71), ideology objectively channels principal benefits in the direction of dominant class interests.

In discussion of rural ideology what emerges is the importance of property 'not only in defining access to, and benefit from the crucial economic resources, but in being one of the major institutions that secures the reproduction of the rural class structure on an intergenerational basis' (Newby 1980, p. 79). In this way the responsibility—which is how it is seen—of making property work, confers rights. It creates a reservoir of power potential which can be called up in crude economic ways or exercised less directly in other social priorities. A rule of thumb recognized and accepted is: the more property, the greater the power potential.

CHAPTER FOUR

CLASS RELATIONSHIPS, DIVISIONS CONFUSED OR CONTAINED

We have only relatively recently become aware of the significance of gender inequalities for understanding class relationships, and the obverse, which is that class is critical in the way we look at sex-based inequalities.

The ways in which patriarchy and class, as systems of power, intersect, interact and indeed constitute each other have generated vigorous and productive debate over this time. Within the context of social stratification Walby (1986, p. 2) reviews a range of approaches to theories of gender inequality. She typifies these according to whether gender inequality is argued to be:

- non-existent or of no theoretical consequence
- deriving from capitalist relations
- an autonomous system of patriarchy—the primary source of inequality
- intimately intertwined with capitalist relations forming one system of capitalist patriarchy
- a consequence of the interaction of the dual but autonomous systems of patriarchy and capitalism.

Her own position is that gender inequality is a consequence of the interaction of the autonomous systems of patriarchy and capitalism, but in which the patriarchal relations of paid work have primacy (1986, pp. 51–69). Franzway, Court and Connell also offer an overview of the debate but criticize the static qualities of analysis when gender and class systems are represented as dichotomous. They argue for a dialectical approach which allows us to see 'gender relations as constituting class relations, in the sense of settling (historically specific) limits to class relations, and vice versa' (1989, p. 26; see also Cockburn 1983, pp. 7, 195). This certainly removes the difficulties of privileging class over gender or gender over class.

Of course, at any one time particular purposes will inform the perspective taken, although as Cockburn points out, while events can be read from different perspectives, '*The events themselves cannot be understood unless read from both perspectives*' (1983, p. 194). (Nor should we take this comment to exclude the constitutive power of other systems of inequality, for example race, although with dreadful irony and as a consequence of the relations of settlement in the district it is no longer a factor in Marulan.)

Australia is, and ever since white settlement has been, implicated in capitalist relations of production, first as a colony and later as an independent country. It is a society premised on class structure, a persisting order of class relations (Connell & Irving 1980, p. 11), which none the less, in the development of capitalism, have undergone certain changes. The role of the state has been an important feature in that development. It presently mediates many of the relations of capitalism, for example through the processes of arbitration and in the field of welfare (see for example Baldock & Cass 1983). The government also makes considerable contributions to private business through mechanisms of control and subsidy. This is especially evident in government rural policies, hallowed in practice, which bolster both failing and successful rural enterprises. A government would seek to tamper with (that is scale down or wipe out) such policies at some peril.

Class relations are generated in the division of labour between those who own and control productive resources and those who do not. Women's visibility in the system appears, at first glance, low. This is because both class and gender, as systems of power, have a material basis (for all that it may also be ideologically expressed) which advantages men. Patrimonial transmission as well as the possibilities of capital accumulation opened through wage labour favour men, thus it is mainly men who own productive property. This is especially relevant in the farming sector, reinforced by the masculine image of the occupation. Moreover, patriarchal advantage in the workplace is evident in the male workforce and culture of quarrying and related activities, including trucking.

Despite clear differences in the ownership and control of productive property at any given time, and for all those directly concerned, class divisions are not necessarily distinctly perceived. For a number of reasons this is certainly the case in Marulan. Classes are not homogeneous, but there are no hard and fast lines internally differentiating them, and at times the ideology underpinning bourgeois hegemony is so successful that the division between owners of productive property and labour appears irrelevant. In this respect I doubt that Marulan is profoundly different from many other places.

Class relations are, of course, relations of power. They are created, maintained and enlivened in relations involved in production. Fundamentally they are grounded in objective economic factors in the production process, but are not simply reducible to them and come into analytic focus more crisply with the emergence of consciousness. Classes are not static categories, but groupings of people, each class 'manifest as a set of closely related inequalities of economic condition, power and opportunity' (Westergaard & Resler 1976, p. 27), which have a fluency in themselves and therefore in the process of class formation.

Status is a socially symbolic statement about instances of class relations, present or past. I use the term status to refer to 'style of life', which is, in the first instance, a matter of consumption patterns, expressed by means of material symbols and nonmaterial attributes, as well as in values and attitudes. It must be evaluative and hence status groups are subjectively defined. While status honour may be established as standing 'in sharp opposition to the pretensions of sheer property' (Weber in Gerth & Mills 1977 [1948], p. 187) it is commonly the case that social expressions of class and status are difficult to prise apart. The directness of the link is particularly clear at either end of the scale of social inequality, and their interaction in social process is intimate. It is both premised on and mediated by power relationships. This occurs on two different levels.

First, when there is recognition or confirmation of position in one sphere with reference to position in the other: for instance, in Marulan the most economically advantaged (and the most economically powerful) group consists of some large landholders who are differentiated from other large landholders (albeit usually not quite as large) by 'good breeding'. As some locals explained to me on one occasion, it meant not money *per se*, but education, social position and lifestyle, which could be traced back through several generations at least. This may indeed not mean money as such, but after all money makes access to valued social forms possible in the first instance and, at the same time, the conjunction of these features establishes a framework wherein access to money is made easier. And this, with higher expectations of lifestyle and life chances, underwrites a further difference evident in the employment of labour. Whereas high-status landholders can afford to employ labour, others rely on the labour of family and perhaps friends. In this case the recognition of differences in class position within the farming sector—even given a similar relationship to property ownership—is etched out by reference to status. The interaction is, however, more than simply referential; the power of status position not only helps in differentiating class position in conceptual terms, it also has impact in practice. (At the same time it is necessary to note that economic advantage has made access to education, valued social position and a prestigious lifestyle possible.)

At the other social extreme, it is also the case that people's perception of the debased class situation of some of the unskilled labourers is thrown into greater relief by the knowledge that they are 'rough'. Again, it is not simply that status confirms class position, but people see the 'roughness' as blighting expectation of any social, or indeed economic, improvement at all.

Secondly, interaction occurs in the case where people use their present relationships in either a status or class system to improve their position in the other sphere. Just as class relations (past and present) prefigure claims, status networks may be activated to improve economic position, extending the interaction of the first example beyond the level of simple recognition or confirmation. In this respect there are obviously double benefits for those already in privileged status positions; professional advice may be freely sought and given at this level, and investment and attractive job opportunities selectively opened. It becomes social class in action.

What is revealed in examining social relationships in Marulan is how status honour functions as ideology and 'assertion of such an ideology even in the absence of legal supports, affects the very manner in which market relations are conceived and articulated'. Moreover, 'the status group appears justified and is generally successful in the monopoly of various positions, occupations and services through preferential recruitment' (Austin 1981, pp. 34–5).

Intriguingly, while women are shadowy figures in relations of production in public settings in Marulan, they are central in creating public images of social class not simply on their own behalf but also on behalf of other family members.

SOCIAL CLOSURE

The exercise of power as a prerequisite in class or status formation and maintenance is clearly expressed in social closure. Indeed 'the vocabulary of closure is readily translatable into the language of power' (Parkin 1974, pp. 5, 15), and closure as strategy is a means of reproducing existing power relations (see Neuwirth 1969, pp. 149–52. Note, however, that I do not employ the concept of community in this way). It is by the process of social closure that social groups of any kind make, sustain and consolidate monopolistic claims to resources in the form of either opportunities or rewards. Drawing the lines of inclusion and exclusion, that is the conscious recognition of difference, may reinforce perceptions of group identity; or it may create them in the transformation of category to group. Any person or collective with the required qualifying attributes is, by definition, a candidate for inclusion.

Australian primary producers today, a very heterogeneous category of people, none the less for political purposes form a group on the basis of ownership and exploitation of rural property and with respect to claims to certain real and believedly deserved financial benefits and social honour. The overarching group is a composite of specific occupations, social origins, status, gender and many other group-defining attributes, and it is certainly easier to mobilize less inclusive associations within the broader division, such as the Livestock and Grain Producers' Association, or the National Farmers' Federation. That the rural division may function most effectively through its component parts does not, however, affect the justificatory basis for its overarching claims. Instead these circumstances highlight the variety of ways in which calls on power relations are made in order to secure or improve opportunities. Hence the more embracing group is seen in the function of its parts and they in turn, justifying particular claims, may do so based on the understanding of their wider affiliation. In this instance, despite differences in the prosecution of particular interests, the rural classification is cohesive in its operation.

Yet the concept of closure presents certain problems in some class applications, for the capitalist class consists of a number of fractions which may have opposing interests and form opposing groups. Such was the case with pastoralism in the nineteenth century, when squatters' interests were in conflict with those of owners. Although the interests of capital, as against labour, may unite wrangling fractions, it is on a piecemeal basis.

A perspective on the constitutive processes of class and gender is opened through the concept of closure. Cockburn, referring to the struggles of working-class men to retain their status as skilled craft workers, writes:

The struggle to keep women competitors out of work and to wrest from the employers a wage sufficient to keep an entire family may have seemed to the men at the time, as it is often represented today, as necessary class struggle, pure and simple. It was, nonetheless, also a struggle by men to assure patriarchal advantage. (1983, p. 35)

While her focus on type of work, time and place is specific, the theory she draws from the study has wide application. In Marulan the definition as men's work of driving the huge Euclids (enormous tip-up trucks) in the quarry, or big semi-trailers, or farming with equipment or strength, serves to illustrate how men can exercise class control over women. As Cockburn points out, there is the argument that because of certain inadequacies—manual, physical and temperamental (characteristics deemed, however, to fit women for family life)—it is alleged that women cannot undertake certain skilled tasks. And then there is the argument that for economic and social reasons they should not compete with men for skilled work (Cockburn 1983, p. 174).

Closure is determinate action. It must therefore be prefigured by consciousness. Passive awareness is an inappropriate premise in respect of closure because it carries with it no message for action, either to maintain or improve economic and social position. In the process of formation, groups call up their capacity to effect closure (Parkin 1974, pp. 2–15; Giddens 1973, p. 107; Wild 1978, pp. 17–23). Moreover, in the recreation of the system closure is the means whereby a group seeks to assert its control over the rewards and opportunities it has gained. It follows that, while closure may be subjectively motivated, there are likely to be real structural obstacles to movement. The broad aims of closure are always the same—monopolization of advantages—and those in dominant positions seek to retain their favoured position by strategies of exclusion (Parkin 1974, pp. 6–9). Interestingly, solidarism as a form of social closure (see Parkin 1974, pp. 9–12), whether based on class or sex, is unlikely to be manifest in endeavours at status mobility, for people work to improve their status position on an independent or family basis, not *en bloc*. Yet it is a significant means whereby those excluded from rewards in the workplace can assert their claims.

Although 'the language of closure can be translated into the language of power' (Parkin 1974, p. 5), it is obvious that the language of power does not simply provide 'a metaphor for describing the [very] operation of this system' (Parkin 1974, p. 15). Closure is predicated on power; it is by the exercise of power that closure is accomplished and power maintenance/improvement is the goal. And in the reproduction of power relations, closure by means of exclusion is considerably assisted by the existing bias of the system.

CLASS RELATIONSHIPS IN MARULAN

Class relationships do not provide a clear blueprint for social behaviour. According to Connell and Irving, class boundaries:

are *normally* 'blurred', uneven, incoherent; they should be expected to be; and they may become more blurred, uneven and incoherent depending on changes in the organisations of production, the fortunes of politics, the processes of cultural change. They may also become more sharply defined; and when they do become sharply defined, then some kind of crisis is normally at hand. (1980, p. 21)

There is no reason to see the circumstances of existence in Marulan as anything but normal. Marulan people recognize that there are economic and social problems in the broader Australian context. Yet often enough unemployed and socially disadvantaged members of society are themselves blamed for the problems which beset them. It is a common enough attitude in society generally. With few exceptions, Marulan locals are not particularly anxious about, or even interested in, any questions bearing on capital restructuring or social justice. Within what they perceive as acceptable limits, recessions, along with the booms, are accepted as given and, as we shall see, inequalities are both accepted and denied. There is certainly no shadow of impending crisis and, as I have indicated, the class picture is far from hard-edged. While this may be a normal state of affairs, there are other specific and identifiable reasons to account for the fuzzy class outlines.

In Marulan class consciousness is both muted and suppressed; some people are petty bourgeois in objective terms, others are in orientation (see Bottomore 1964, p. 35; Metcalfe 1988, p. 136). The virtues ascribed, not just to rural life, but to owning rural land, further obfuscate delineation of clear, consciously accepted class boundaries. The overall district population is small, and as people in different class positions regularly interact across class boundaries, this tends to dilute consciousness of class as such. The relative isolation of Marulan and of its inhabitants from others sharing similar class positions also contributes to the masking of class differences. That is, the expressed or unexpressed recognition of community ties must also be seen as having some effect, as indeed is apparent in the softening of social distinctions. This accords with the broader theoretical point that in a capitalist society class relations are more sensitive, or sharpened, at a national level, and therefore operate as a national rather than as a local bond (see Bottomore 1975, p. 99). Class consciousness at this embracing level may be splintered but it can also be heightened by sectional interests which may take on a localized expression because of circumstances surrounding specific industries (for example the cement industry in Berrima or Kandos, or abbattoirs in particular country towns). Matters of scale become important in this connection. When the operation of the industry is large and the work population high, or alternatively part of a relatively large local social system, then class bonds transcend local influences and must be seen in a wider perspective. On the other hand, when the enterprise is on a smaller scale and/or the work population relatively low in number, other local influences hold greater sway and can, as they do in Marulan, subdue the impact of an awareness of class ties.

The masculine imagery of class relationships often enough appears to eclipse women. This tendency is certainly evident in Marulan, where it is quite easy for both actors and observers to discount women's contribution. Yet despite the masculine construction of much of the paid work and the force of patrimonial inheritance, women do figure in the secondary labour market as wage labourers and in relatively fewer instances as owners of property. More interesting but more elusive is the role they play in assuring the family position as petty bourgeoisie, a position which is often dependent on their labour and skills (and perhaps their property) in say storekeeping or farming.

Out of town

Although in general class boundaries are blurred, locals recognize the superior class position of the large landholders, and this is reinforced by a general awareness of their high status. Even here, however, other factors intrude. Questions of class struggle, of conflict, crucial in class formation and recreation, are reduced to near irrelevance by the ideological value locals generally place on owning rural land and working it.

The properties of the large landholders—all of whom are graziers—vary in size from less than 1200 hectares to above 4400 hectares, which for today in this part of the state is large. Cattle, principally Hereford, and sheep, principally merino and cross-breeds, are the economic focus, although raising bloodstock is also an important activity on one property, and another runs a pony stud.

Some of these graziers employ a number of labourers. The largest property engages seven or eight farm workers of various descriptions—stockmen, managers, grooms (sometimes women) and those whose particular skills lie with machinery, general station hands and so on—who live in cottages on the estate. Another property has two or three workers who live on it. As well as resident labour, workers from the district may work on a full-time, part-time or contract basis on big landholdings. The largest property engages quite a few men in this way. Other large-scale graziers, with different labour requirements, who do not employ resident labour, may hire men from outside, full- or part-time. They also engage contract workers, according to variables such as season, the work programme and plans of management.

The number of farm workers in the district fluctuates but is usually between twelve and fifteen. Around half of them—all men—also own their own land, ranging from less than 50 hectares to nearly 400 hectares, which they work in their spare time. Others hope, with varying degrees of realism, to own some property one day; assuredly it is the ideal. A certain amount of labour is provided on a more casual basis to large landholders by other farmers. They, of course, already own their land, and in order to keep or improve it they take on contract work or hire out their labour. Rarely do they perceive any conflict of interests in engaging in these two sets of circumstances. Sometimes people may feel overworked by their employer, but this is explained and contained at a personal level; the rural ideology overshadows problems of this order which might carry the germ of conflict. Moreover, in a small community people make positive efforts to avoid rifts.

People generally recognize the power potential of some members of the upper class; one smaller-scale farmer explicitly pointed out that 'people in a position to hire servants and farm hands are in a position to influence a lot of the district'. Yet, if anything, the class position of the large landholders is extolled as a virtue insofar as they provide employment—full- or part-time—for district residents. Locals see this as valuable, not only to the individuals, but to the district, as it maintains a local circulation of money. At the same time the labour expended enhances the district, visually and reputationally, in terms of its productivity and the quality of its produce. This becomes common property, as people believe that district identification entitles them to some sort of proprietorial response to the individual achievements of other district residents. In all, the Marulan case provides an example of a near-perfect fit with the arguments presented by Rose, Saunders, Newby and Bell, on the legitimation of inequality at the local level by an ideology of land ownership (1976, pp. 711–12).

Although they may be relieved of many of the more arduous, monotonous or unpleasant duties, upper-status graziers also physically farm. Their participation has a democratizing effect on work in general and while status distance may be recognized in work and non-work contexts, sharing manual labour reduces it, and generally reduces the significance of opposing class interests. Moreover, the circumstances of the workplace mean that aspects of an ideology of land ownership are transmitted across class boundaries (Rose *et al.*, p. 715; see also Pearson's discussion of management–worker rapprochement in small-scale work contexts: 1980, p. 168).

It is only large land-owning families who employ domestic labour. In one case the housekeeper 'lives in'. Otherwise women from town or nearby small farms work on one or two days a week for these upper-status households.

As a whole farming families, as distinct from graziers, occupy positions of a classic petty bourgeoisie, 'fluctuating between proletariat and bourgeoisie and ever renewing itself as a supplementary part of bourgeois society' (Marx & Engels 1952, p. 80). The economic and social commitment of this group is towards land ownership, and despite some ambiguity in their actual class relations, there is no question of identification with proletarian interests. Yet, because of the marginality of their own farming concerns, twenty-one out of thirty-one smallholders take on contract work or are engaged as wage labour casually or on a permanent and full-time basis. The marginality may be a consequence of farm size—they range from 100 hectares or so to over 1500 hectares—and/or poor farming land.

Not all small farmers, however, are drawn intermittently, or at all, into wage labour. The points of differentiation between graziers and ordinary farmers revolve around the scale of the enterprise, the form of profit deployment and the employment of labour. For both types of landholder the aim is primary production for profit, which is largely reinvested in the enterprise. For many of the smaller farmers the profit margin, if and when it exists, is slight; and they may differ from the grazing élite in how they redirect it. The graziers, with larger-scale economic concerns, have a less conservative farming view of how best to make capital work for them. They are more likely and indeed better able to explore new possibilities, and have access to and seek advice on business matters. If a woman from a farming family joins the labour force it is most unlikely to be in any form of farming. It is significant that women from grazier families may also seek paid employment. Thus, if class relationships are defined by occupation then their class position changes. This at least is the theory, although observation of day-to-day relationships indicates no apparent difference.

Interestingly, the information I gathered on income levels is not useful in this connection. For many people, on the land and in town, it is a sensitive topic. Apart from any individual misunderstanding, misgivings or statements of misinformation (indicated by husbands and wives disagreeing in disclosures of family income, or by people declining to answer), certain tendencies become apparent. Large and small landholders, for example, usually stated their income as low—absurdly so in some cases. It is obviously in their interests to have as low an income on the books as possible, and because they are self-employed, and because of the nature of their business, they have some flexibility in determining what parts of their gross income can be classified as deductible costs. By way of contrast, wage labourers from town appear anxious to state their income as high as possible, as though to endorse their social worth.

The productive capacity of the grazing élite is evident in the profit they are able to siphon off into private consumption—behaviour which is not only expected but possible because there is more to redirect. Nevertheless, retention of lands and if possible the acquisition of more, the improvement of existing holdings, upgrading stock and plant, in short, the concerns of rural capitalism, are common to both groups. Essentially, the differences are methodological and ones of scale. Such is not the case in the employment of labour. All members of the grazing élite rely, at least from time to time, on the labour of rural workers. Smaller farmers never employ full-time labour, and only very few—and rarely at that—employ contractors. Family labour, always including and at times extending beyond the immediate household, is very important (see Nalson 1977) and if things get out of hand, then the help of neighbours may be solicited. This is unlikely to be on a paid basis but rather on an understanding of reciprocity.

Predictably, given a rural ideology and a celebration of land ownership associated with peculiar conditions of the workplace, even landless farm workers have a petty bourgeois orientation. This does not imply that people are not aware of differences in class positions, differences which profoundly affect life expectations. Rather, their attitudes suggest that the values underpinning the operation of rural capital are beguiling and sufficiently satisfying in themselves to be commonly held; then, given the worth of rural life, workers consent to their position in it.

The inheritance of land is a crucial factor in the ongoing pattern of class relationships. Landed inheritance, particularly in large quantities, sustains class position and privilege. It is even more significant if it is well-developed property. The pattern of inheritance for both farmers and graziers is usually from father to son(s) and contributes to the reproduction of class and, within a class frame, gender relations. The question of women's part in land transactions is discussed in chapter 6.

As I previously indicated, property size alone is not a clue to class divisions, but in association with the productive quality of the land and the financial capacity to improve it, it is a good guide. Nevertheless class divisions in the rural sector are somewhat indistinct, even in objective terms, and their impact is further softened by people's subjective views of land ownership. The primary division acknowledged in the community, however, is between those who own and farm land and those who do not. This is of course a straightforward class difference, although it has a gender component as well as implications for status evaluations, and in respect of primary production, ordinary farming families and the grazing élite are placed together. This is how those involved are happy to see the arrangement, for such social placement appears to align the interests of all farmers, whether they are large or small landholders. While it is socially pleasing to the small farmers, from the point of view of large landholders it also has tangible class advantages, for in affirming the commonality of interests there is a reduction in the potential for conflict over the disadvantages associated with unequal opportunities and privilege in the class system. For example, there is no doubt that because of their resources, possibly including other productive capital, large landholders are able to negotiate for, and obtain, more favourable credit facilities and terms, and their access to capital makes them better able to rationalize their economic enterprises; in short, whereas small farmers are not in a position to, large landholders can make the system work for them. Affirmation of a common identity as landholders and farmers means that relations are made easier between the levels of capital, and moreover it assures the goodwill of the casual labour force. There is no question that in the rural ideology ownership of land underscores the social worth of men as well as affording them economic and hence political advantage.

For many small farmers the goal of independence is something of a chimera, and Oeser and Emery's comments are appropriate in this context: 'The picture of a self-employing, self-determining farmer was, in the past, true only in a very limited sense. There is every reason to believe that it will be even less true in the future' (1954, p. 23). The limited circumstances and the often dependent nature of smaller-scale farming does not, however, alter the response by locals in which the distinction between larger rural economic enterprises and the farming petty bourgeoisie is only made in follow-up discussion. For those directly implicated there is obviously a basic understanding of difference, but although it is clear enough in dimensions of consumption, nobody is anxious to stress it in terms of the process of production. As I have argued, it is not in the economic interests of the dominant to drive in any such wedge, and there is some overflow of prestige for smaller farmers.

The role and significance of small farming in the structure of rural capitalism is eclipsed by the way of life and the economic impact of large landholders (see for example Encel's discussion, 'Broad Acres', 1970, pp. 293–317). This is understandable because class relations are defined by private ownership of productive resources (see Connell 1977, p. 39), and accepting the proposition that this is the principal determinant in the form of these relationships, it follows logically that a bigger, and a potentially richer, resource base confers greater power on the owners of productive property. Hence large landholders appear as more significant in the reality of class relations, and usually in analysis of them, than those with a lesser potential to exercise power. The relatively higher numbers in the less powerful ownership category may offset this imbalance to some degree, yet petty capitalists generally appear to offer a less attractive subject in sociological literature. While such a focus acknowledges the generative capacity of property (Connell & Irving 1980) and the power potential which inheres in it, it obscures the role of the petty bourgeoisie in the operation of capital and its economic and political consequence.

It is, however, the numbers of small farmers whose economic position is precarious that provide the basis for many rural economic policies. Indeed, it seems that a number of small farming industries have survived only through government assistance. A good example is dairying. While such politics constitute the very core of the political platform of the National Party, they are also seen as key issues by both Liberal and Labor parties. Apart from the non-party-political issue of shoring up what are deemed important industries but which are not self-sustaining, it is obviously in the interests of the National Party especially to formulate policies whose aim is to assist the small farming population, as this is not only likely to win the farmers' votes, but also those of the people in the non-agricultural rural sector who are, in various ways, dependent on the economic well-being of small farmers.

For whatever reasons, government assistance to the rural sector is high. This was acknowledged in a report, *Rural Policy in Australia*, submitted to the prime minister in 1974: 'In Australia,

Table 4.1 Employment in the rural sector

Item	Census years		
	1933 ('000)	1954 ('000)	1971 ('000)
Employers	103	62	50
Self-employed	155	200	135
Total farm operators	258	262	285
Employees and unpaid helpers	234	168	113
Total employed farm workforce	492	430	298
Unemployed, etc.	36	6	n.a.
	%	%	%
Male farm workforce as percentage of total employed male workforce	28	15	8

Source: *Rural Policy in Australia.* (Report to the prime minister by a working group, May 1974, paragraph 2.9.)

as in many other advanced economies, government has, since 1945, assumed an unprecedented degree of responsibility for the functioning and welfare of the economy in general and of agriculture in particular' (par. 2.48).

Other industries, as this report is careful to observe, also receive high levels of government assistance, but it appears especially notable in rural industry. This is no doubt associated with, but at the same time highlighted by, the relatively small and declining contribution of the farming sector to the gross domestic product (see Table 3.2) and by this sector's employment of a small and decreasing proportion of the workforce (see Table 4.1; refer also to McKay, 1967, pp. 129–30) and further in relatively decreasing contributions to export income where it was previously dominant (see Table 3.1).

Government assistance has enabled many farmers to survive as the prices they received for their produce moved downwards while those they paid for materials and services moved up (McKay 1967). But although government help has prevented general collapses in any of the divisions of small farming, and the expressed intention is to advance the interests of this sector, it is the large landholders who emerge as the principal beneficiaries of government policies. As the 1974 report finds:

The family farm or business does not have the same access to the capital market as the company form of organisation. Where farm families have inadequate capital resource they may be unable to exploit size economies. In addition, where financial capital and reserves of credit (unused borrowing capacity) are inadequate, farmers may be unable to manage their properties efficiently because of the risk of insolvency. (par. 7.21)

It is true that, in general, family—as compared with corporate— enterprises are relatively disadvantaged in access to capital, but it is very much a sliding scale of disadvantage, with small farmers inevitably located at the unfavoured end. For as the report also notes: 'In the long run, market conditions are likely to force producers who have inadequate capital resources to sell their properties. It would appear however, that these producers are in most cases likely to be replaced by other farm families with greater access to resources' (par. 7.24). The report also acknowledges that family farms with adequate capital are at least as efficient as corporate enterprises, and it is unlikely that they will be displaced as the dominant form of organization in rural industries.

In town

There is no more clarity in the depiction of class boundaries in the township than in the surrounding district. The majority of the workforce is constituted of wage labour and most of these people hold jobs at the quarry at South. Without the quarry Marulan's population would fall dramatically and no doubt present a different face. There is no other stable form of employment which could absorb so many people. It is the principal single source of employment of full-time wage labour in the township. Over recent years it has drawn on average about twenty-five to thirty employees from Marulan out of the total quarry force of around 195 people—the rest come principally from Marulan South or Goulburn. Marulan itself is not, however, a company town, a description which more aptly attaches to Marulan South. There, from a total adult population of just over 100 people, slightly fewer than half are engaged by the company—Blue Circle Southern Cement. This includes nearly all South's adult townsmen. But the quarry's impact on employment in Marulan itself goes beyond the actual payroll. The limestone crusher in Marulan employs five people from the town and at least six truck owners in the township rely directly or indirectly on the quarry. Others pick up jobs from the quarry from time to time. Without it, more particularly without its generation of money movement, it is doubtful whether there would be a living for the three general stores' families. The effect on the service stations would be much less pronounced, as their revenue comes principally from passing traffic. The call for a doctor would certainly be reduced, and it is questionable whether his presence could be economically justified.

Although so many of the men in Marulan are employed at the quarry, they constitute a relatively small group, geographically and socially isolated from the wider Australian population of mine workers. For many it is a case of conscious distancing.

A past immigrant to Marulan, one of the more politically active quarrymen, astutely summed up his view in the following way: the workers at South are very solidary in their feelings towards workmates, but they are not militant over important issues like conditions. He claimed that they are not like their counterparts in other areas as they are rather passive and slow to respond to industrial issues. He attributed this to:

their conservatism which has its basis in a narrow and sheltered outlook. They are brought up in the district and they don't have any other experience. Either they have come in off the land or else they are following in father's footsteps—they left school early and went straight to the quarry. They would never initiate action—simply follow. When it was SPC (Southern Portland Cement) the management was much more paternalistic and there is some carryover of this today. This in itself inhibits militancy.

He also suggested that people in Sydney had higher expectations of working conditions and 'quality of life' than did Marulan workers.

Basically, his perception is in line with that of the company's management, although there are differences in interpretation and emphasis. Management expressed the view that the quarry is a union backwater. There are virtually no work issues, and disputes, when they occur, are more a consequence of personality clashes than concerned with union policy. Only if there is a perceived threat to local workers—people known to each other—does trouble erupt. A company representative said that even when there was a 'work to rule', the workers 'died of boredom' and broke it themselves after about three days. He said that until quite recently there were no solidary work groups in the unions, although that changes with the emergence of more charismatic leadership. Moreover, as unemployment in the area has increased, people draw lines of demarcation more strongly and there is a tendency towards the definition of one-man jobs (that is what they are), thereby making the job occupant less dispensable. While this suggests developing class consciousness, it has not crystallized in organized class action.

While broader union issues are not central concerns, personal relationships are very important. The local manager, living at South and in this instance acting as company spokesman, suggested this as another reason for what he termed 'the low level of industrial relations'. The cross-cutting nature of personal relationships weakens the development of workgroup consciousness. There are, for example, a number of sets of fathers and sons working at the quarry, and even though many of the younger generation leave the district quite early in their working life, many come back. There is a high level of dependence on local family networks, and family connections remain important in the work context. Women may be conduits in this system, but for male kin. Despite a generally peaceful workplace, I was told that a certain amount of inter-community rivalry exists between Marulan and Marulan South, together with an element of hostility. Firming particularly in the pub at Marulan, this rivalry takes the form of bickering and chiacking which carry over to work. Indeed, some demarcation issues have resulted from 'stirring' in the pub.

The management's view is that the men here are easily upset on a personal level. This was attributed to country people having very high principles and a low tolerance for insult. At the same time the spokesman suggested that the low level of impersonal disputes is because country people are used to long hours of hard work and do not rebel against work pressure.

The basic points I have discussed are contained in the information in Table 4.2 on the extent and nature of industrial action at the quarry over a two-year period, 1977 and 1978. The high tally of strike hours in 1977 is a consequence of profound disturbance in the cement industry generally. This originated at other sites although the quarry at Marulan South was drawn into the dispute. These data do weigh heavily in the table, but do not contradict the argument that the incidence of locally generated

Table 4.2 Strikes at quarry—Marulan South 1977-78

Date	Union	Local matter		Industry matter	
		Dispute	Duration (hours)	Dispute	Duration (hours)
1977 February	FEDFA TWU AMU AMWU	Suspension Duty refusal	13		
June	FEDFA AMWU ETU AWU TWU	Dismissal Duty refusal	20		
July	AMWU ETU FEDFA AMU			Wage claim	24
September	AMWU			Award payment	25
October	AMWU FEDFA ETU AWU TWU			Award payment	416.5
1978 January	TWU AWU	Worker driving self to doctor: minor injury	6.5		
June	FEDFA AMWU AMU ETU TWU	Suspension rolling over end loader	24		
	FEDFA AMWU ETU AWU TWU	Suspension reversing over petrol bowser	24		
July	FEDFA AMWU AMU ETU TWU	Suspension unsafe shunting	16		
			103.5 hours		465.5 hours
			569 total strike hours		

AMWU	Australian Metal Workers' Union
AWU	Australian Workers' Union
ETA	Electrical Trades' Association
FEDFA	Federated Engine Drivers' & Firemen's Association
FIA	Federated Ironworkers' Association
FCU	Federated Clerks' Union
SU	Shipwrights' Union
TWU	Transport Workers' Union

industrial disputes is low and tends to be personalized (compare the information in Table 4.2 with that in Table 4.3).

In conjunction with other factors it is apparent that the ties of community play a significant part in softening workgroup consciousness (see Pearson 1980, p. 173). Residual notions of ruralness prevail and insofar as they embody a politically and socially conservative outlook, and a sense of rural belonging, they are

Table 4.3 Strikes at Blue Circle Southern Cement Plant—Portland 1977–78

Date	Union	Local matter		Industry matter	
		Dispute	Duration (hours)	Dispute	Duration (hours)
1977 January	AMWU	Protest overtime allocation	24		
March	AMWU SU and FIA	Staff doing union work	24		
May	FEDFA	Refusal of claim	8		
June	AWU	Dismissal of employees for refusal to work	144		
July	all unions			Claim for over-award increase	48
September & October	all unions			Refusal of claim for over-award increase	552
November	AMWU SU	Retrench-ments at Charbon	24		
1978 February	all unions			Company's fail-ure to indicate position re appeal above	24
	AMWU SU and FIA	Staff member using tools	24		
May	AMWU & SU (boilermakers only)			National strike re award	24
June	AMWU SU and FIA	Staff working	24		
July	all unions			Apprentices rates of pay	96
August	FCU	Disability allowance	168		
October	AMU	Staff working	24		
December	FIA	Refusal of duty	48		
			512 hours		744 hours
				1256 total strike hours	

See Table 4.2 for abbreviations.

more likely to stand in opposition to urban industrial values in quarry work relations. By way of corroboration, in her work on a mining town in Queensland, C. Williams found that men from rural backgrounds were more likely to take a conservative position and express loyalty to the employing company than were their city counterparts (1981, p. 102).

The depressed level of commitment to proletarian ideals is also manifest in voting behaviour. Most Marulan townsmen are wage labourers, but at elections only 27 per cent say they support Labor, whereas 54 per cent see themselves as Liberal/National Party followers (see Table 4.4 and Aitken 1972, p. 110). There is little difference between women's and men's responses. It is rarely possible clearly to separate allegiances or preferences within the coalition, for while at the state level the candidate was for many years a National Party man, at the same time at the federal level representation was Liberal. Indications are that the National Party has a larger and more explicitly ideologically committed following. The voting pattern reflects the rural orientation of the community as a whole, compounded by the fact that the MLA for this electorate (National Party) at the time of this study lived and farmed in the Marulan district. This illustrates well Aitken's argument that if the political candidate for a small rural community is Liberal or National Party 'the Labor Party will find itself reduced to the ideological faithful' (1972, p. 98). Indeed the point is sharpened by reference to the handful of voters who at heart are traditional Labor supporters, but who are persuaded to back their local National Party candidate at state elections. Even apart from the fact that National Party support has been strengthened by the presence of a farming MP who was the party's electoral representative, I believe there to be a strong petty bourgeois orientation on the part of a great many of the town's men and women, wage labourers supporting the values of capital, which no doubt reduces the Labor vote. Their subjective orientation contributes to the circumstances which control their class position.

The three families of general storekeepers and the ten truck owner-drivers are petty bourgeois, and many Australians find the image of a small business proprietor generally attractive. 'In a very real sense the petty bourgeoisie is detached from the concerns of the working and middle-classes' (Bechhofer *et al.* 1974, p. 123) and their interests are not served by association with either group. In this context class boundaries may be clearly

Table 4.4   Voting patterns in Marulan

| | Town | | Country | | | |
	Women	Men	Women	Men	n	%
Liberal/National Party (state and federal)	35	26	13	14	88	61%
Labor (state and federal)	17	13	4	4	38	26%
National Party (state) Labor (federal)	4	2	1	—	7	5%
Other	—	1	—	—	1	1%
Not on roll	2	2	—	—	4	3%
Declined to answer	2	4	—	—	6	4%
Total	60	48	18	18	144	

Source: Random sample survey.

drawn but wage labourers are also attracted by the ideals of autonomy and ownership of productive property. Many will never realize these aims, but other Marulan workers have stakes, albeit small, in productive property—land, equipment or stock. This certainly detracts from any crisp silhouette of class relations. While wage labourers may entertain petty bourgeois ideals, many petty bourgeois have a proletarian past with which there are strong links in the form of experiences and through family and friends.

I do not suggest that in analysis and in practice there are not important differences between people having values about property and autonomy and actually owning property and therefore possibly enjoying autonomy. These differences are likely to be crucial in both discussions and relationships of class. But in this instance the convergence of values, coupled with the passage of people from wage labour to ownership (and more rarely from ownership to wage labour) and the incidence of people with a foot in both camps, robs the differences of potency.

The case of the truck owner-drivers is illustrative of some of the complications intruding into the everyday existence of petty bourgeois members and which also complicate analysis. In principle owner-drivers have the autonomy of the self-employed and on paper they do own their own means of production. But the cost of a truck unit is very high. A new articulated vehicle of the size and strength commonly used in Marulan in 1977 cost around $72 000–$85 000 (in 1989 the range is more like $150 000–$240 000). A prime mover itself was about $60 000 (today $100 000–$180 000). Even second-hand units, a much more likely proposition, are very expensive, and one in reasonable condition could at that time cost $30 000–$40 000 (now more like $90 000–$140 000). The company financing the truck purchase thus effectively owns the truck, and it might be said indirectly controls the labour of the driver, for some time at least. Trucks are usually seen as good for about four or five years, and accordingly this is the usual period stipulated for paying off a vehicle. But the burden of repayment is onerous, and the owner-drivers may be pressed into working for wages, which is very little different from the circumstances of many of their wage-labouring mates. This appears in principle to be comparable to the pressure of mortgages on land or debts on equipment of small farmers. However there are some important differences, for there is no bulwark of rural policies, and unlike their farming counterparts the truckies cannot, in their poverty, retreat into a subsistence or holding position—that is living off the land while deferring debts. For although small farmers are susceptible to market pressures they have the capacity to endure them, short term at least (Nalson 1977, p. 307). Most truckies do not even have that.

Several truckies have professed that they feel the same as any other men in town who work for South; their class position does not set them apart. Yet there is a difference, and that focuses on their productive property—their trucks—in which there is a high investment in financial and ideal terms. There may also be considerable emotional investment which is essentially masculine in character. According to one of the men, 'some of the blokes just live for their trucks, they say "bugger Mum" and have a real fantasy about their truck—spend all their spare time working on it—living in it'; perhaps more aptly, living through it.

The ambivalence of the truckies' class position is revealed in a series of Australia-wide truck blockades which occurred in the first couple of weeks in April 1979. It was class action with a proletarian cast but bourgeois aims. Originally, lacking support from the Transport Workers' Union in their requests of the New South Wales state government, a few truckies stopped to meet on Razorback Mountain between Sydney and Marulan, and announced that they would stay there pending negotiations and co-operation from the government. Then, in the course of their work, and without initial co-ordination, other drivers 'just rumbled into the revolution' (*Sun-Herald*, 9 April 1979) which spread in a rash of other blockades. Only one Marulan driver took his truck to a Marulan blockade, although another was 'caught' on Razorback and, ironically, another who intended to keep working was stopped at Marulan on his way to get a load. A couple of others offered to take their trucks to a blockade if required. Of ten owner-drivers in Marulan, one continued to work throughout the troubles—fearful he might lose his contract if he stopped. About five of the men supported the dispute, although this was largely by inaction; most others would have worked had they been able to.

The local community was itself ambivalent in response to the events. Some residents were supportive, others condemnatory. The publican was initially behind the truckies, but was less enthusiastic when his supplies were threatened. The sequel to this episode and answer to the dilemma was provided by trucks moving from Goulburn to the Marulan blockade, bringing beer up on their trailers. This was in response to the publican's request. The manager of the local limestone crushing plant—totally reliant on this form of transport—took meat down to the men at the blockade, as indeed did the Marulan butcher. Another non-owning driver, privately employed, would not work. About twenty drivers at South announced their support, although as members of another union they did not go out on strike themselves. A busload of shift workers from the quarry when passing the blockade were not so well disposed and, freely borrowing a well-worn phrase, shouted 'Run over the bastards'.

This dispute appeared to open a crack in communal relationships, but it could not clearly be traced along class lines, and it turned out to be no more than a hairline fracture which was soon closed. I have already noted that people are usually careful to avoid deep rifts which could become institutionalized and split the community, and this was apparent in the case of the truck drivers' dispute. There were certainly differences of opinion, but on the whole these were contained within a framework of amicable relations. Insofar as there were differences, they indicated the very smudged nature of class outlines and the ambiguous position of the petty bourgeoisie.

The people from the thin professional layer in the township are not seen, nor do they see themselves, as having any more autonomy in their work life than other townspeople. On the basis of their occupations (one medical practitioner, three schoolteachers, one clergyman), they are likely to command more respect than others, and because of the nature of the services they provide they can be seen to occupy a special place in the local social system.

CONCLUSION

The overriding impression gained of class relationships in Marulan is one in which oppositions and hostility, necessary components in focusing and sharpening class consciousness, play an insignificant part. In the country, class differences can be collapsed by rural–metropolitan oppositions. These are contained, expressed and vitalized in rural ideology. To be a country person and to value country living in Australia is largely to endorse the same sorts of attitudes and values held by most other rural residents, and one of the most important values is land ownership. Generally people do not concern themselves much with the extent to which ownership of property facilitates access to power, and thereby brush aside the implications for class and gender. What appears to be important locally is owning and working the land. This combination is highly valued. Landless labourers, small farmers, large landholders and townspeople all hold it in esteem. That is, people generally subscribe to the values which legitimate inequality. The crucial role of property in the determination of rural social stratification has been described by Stinchcombe (1961–62, p. 164), and McMichael stresses the significance of land as the first form of property in Australia (1979, p. 45). In the development of Australian capitalism other forms of ownership have become important, but the value accorded land ownership has not diminished and, quintessentially represented in pastoral property, it continues to confer both social and economic power.

In addition to farming land, Marulan people think ownership of any productive property is commendable and desirable. Ownership of, say, industrial property, may not be of the same order as land ownership, but it does represent an aspect of the same property-holding ethic. Class consciousness among waged labourers is, and it seems always has been, at a very low ebb in Marulan. In short, a bourgeois ideology is powerfully pervasive, and in its flowering as rural capitalism it has considerable impact, evoking heartfelt commitment from both owners and workers alike, whether from town or out of town.

While rural orientations are in themselves peculiarly potent, they are intensified in Marulan by the community setting, for it is at this level of historical and social force that rural identification occurs, when the local is stressed over the general. In the givens of rural community—the networks of interaction and dependency—there are elements for the dilution of class consciousness. What is given is what has come to be perceived and experienced as given (Gusfield 1975, p. 30); and on this basis people constantly stress the homogeneity of the district and the township, saying 'Oh! we're just all workers here' or at other times 'We're just all country people'. There is no doubt that people in Marulan principally cast themselves as participants in, or at least members of, an identifiable and definable community which appears to fly in the face of Metcalfe's comments (1988, p. 7) on the danger of methodologically isolating a community. This identification, apparent to me in the early 1970s, was no less at the close of the 1980s. Indeed, for a variety of reasons which have mobilized local effort—various historical commemorations, the bypass, landscaping the town—the notion of community has been strengthened. And it is in this setting that the composite significance of elements of the stratification system has particular potential for the exercise of power, despite all the protestation of sameness.

Thus, while there is an understanding of difference, the issue of class oppositions is both consciously and unconsciously kept to a low key by employers, the self-employed and by all but a minority of workers. The workers in this district do not constitute a class remnant, but because of the constellation of circumstances I have described, they have scarcely been incorporated in processes of class formation.

CHAPTER FIVE

IMAGERY IN ACTION

SYMBOLS AND GROUPS

Style of life provides the reference point from which individuals assess each other on a scale of social prestige and privilege. Assessment of lifestyle invokes intangibles such as attitudes and values and relies on objective attributes and symbols such as education, occupation, leisure patterns, association membership, type of house and dress. Thus status categories are created notionally on the basis of shared qualities but their culturally defined relationships take on a reality for their members in opening or limiting social opportunities. This includes monopolizing certain benefits; and the corollary of denial of them. It is significant that the value accorded to the constituent elements of lifestyle, all of which are dependent on past or present class relationships, is based on the viewpoint of socially dominant groups.

Many status attributes hinge ultimately on economic circumstances, but money alone does not secure status improvement. From the viewpoint of those who influence judgements of social styles and who have the power to include or exclude others from social combinations, lavish expenditure directed towards upward mobility may brand people as 'nouveau riche' if it is not tempered by what are established as the canons of 'good taste'. The catch-22 here is that it is the privileged who are best able to define 'good taste'; they effectively decree it and use it as an artefact of closure.

Status identification is often and clearly articulated at the local level, for status awareness generally is heightened not only in interaction within any one group, but by interaction—or non-interaction—between groups. It thus has special impact in the context of community. According to Schmalenbach, community does not belong to the realm of feelings or emotional experiences but 'implies the recognition of something taken for granted and the assertion of the self-evident' (1965, p. 334) in the existence of given relationships. It rests heavily on the network of interaction, ties and dependencies which are accepted as givens. Sentiment may arise, although not inevitably, from the recognition of participation and association, but feelings do not constitute community. They are instead products of it and therefore subsequent to it (see Schmalenbach 1965, p. 335). It is in this sense that communities are socially constructed (see Gusfield 1975, p. 31) and become what, through experience, they are perceived to be. Thus Marulan, in its self-consciousness, is a community. In it, people's awareness of social difference is pronounced in experience, for in daily life they evaluate each other's behaviour and act upon these evaluations. They reflect their understanding of their own and each other's status positions in face-to-face interactions, which at the same time cue the respondent's behaviour. There may be inconsistencies between individuals' evaluations but, overall, district residents share a broad understanding of the local system of social class.

It is neither useful nor possible to propose a tidy linear model of a status system in Marulan. Strata do not overlie each other in horizontal layers. The principal reason is that, like many other Australian country districts, the system in Marulan is riven vertically by the division between town (that is the people from Marulan township—the villagers) and country (see also Oeser & Emery 1954, and Oxley 1974). The fissure does not carry through to the extremes of the status scale, the highest and lowest ranking, but affects those in the middle ranges. The uppermost levels are always and only graziers, and the tail end is constituted only of townspeople. An added complication is that farmers and their families at all times have an extra prestige loading by virtue of the fact that they are 'on the land'.

The permeability of social-class distinctions in Marulan is principally an outcome of the numerically small population. Further, the scale of the local social scene reduces social options at the district level. One effect is that more people are attracted to greater participation in extra-local events, but locals adopt this alternative only to a limited degree—with the exception of high-status people for whom it is part of their way of life anyhow. Increasing withdrawal into the family is another response. Thirdly, and most commonly, when there is participation in local affairs common purpose generates a sense of closeness, and this tends to break down the less sustainable status barriers. Two factors mitigate the retention of such barriers:

1 From the point of view of many people participating in a social event there are probably few others of like status with whom to identify in that social interaction.
2 Differences between people may not be so developed that they can endure as group markers in the face of close and ongoing interaction.

Under these circumstances any rewards a group secured by closure would be offset by the extreme restrictions this would impose on its membership. Differences are recognized but strategies of inclusion and exclusion are not regularly invoked to emphasize sub-groups or sets.

Two lines of cleavage are, however, quite clear and remain unaltered by scale—the basic town–country distinction and the separation of the landed élite from all others. There is no question of the status barrier between the upper-status farming sector and 'the rest' (as they sometimes refer to themselves) being permeable or subject to dissolution, and although there is social interaction between country and townspeople, the division conferring greater prestige on farming as a way of life stands firm.

Esteem is said to attach to how parts are played; prestige on the other hand is claimed to attach to what part is played—that is, to the social position (Davis 1950, pp. 93–4, and following him Oxley 1974, p. 30). A warning is timely here: it is not easy to make a separation between the qualities of persons and of positions, and rigid dissociation can become a real threat to understanding. There are times when structural and personal attributes coincide, and even when they do not it is still frequently possible to trace the connections. Despite the dangers, however, the distinction is fundamental in questions of status evaluation. Participation in social affairs at the local level is not a determinant of status, but it does invest the actor with greater merit and thus differentiates between people ranked in the same status group. In this way, although esteem is a different form of social honour from prestige and awarded on a different basis, it can generate confusion in status evaluations. In Marulan esteem is associated with some activities which constitute an incipient form of patronage or, as it is so often, matronage—an attribute of lifestyle which is certainly status-conferring.

UPPER-STATUS FARMERS

At the top of the social scale and overarching town and country is the very small group of larger landholders.

All the families share a background of privilege. Even so, not everyone ranks equally in this group and for different reasons, only some of which revolve around the material symbols of lifestyle. Family and family connections count, particularly so in the district context. Some families have been in the district for over a century, others just over a decade. There is advantage in having a history of residence, but it is not only the historical connection which confers social honour. It is also crucial to have welded links with the district, both present and past, by interest and participation in local affairs. Most members of this group, women and men, are committed to social life and business ventures extending beyond the district and absorbing considerable time. But in attending local functions and thereby mixing with other residents, and in taking an interest in and supporting district affairs, some from this upper group earn considerable esteem.

The impersonal use of farm labour enhances a person's standing. It signifies social-class position. Precisely how this is achieved is not spelt out. Necessarily it relates to the scale and productivity of the operation but insofar as this is acknowledged, it is carefully stated not in economic but in social terms. Most people do not assert that the aim is to reduce the grazier's physical workload, although it is understood that as office and managerial commitments increase there is less opportunity to work outside on the property. Rather the social nature of the economic enterprise is stressed as being of consequence in this context. Farming, and more particularly pastoralism, is seen as both a worthy and prestigious occupation, in which the manual/non-manual labour distinction has always been inappropriate as a guide to status position, except as it may absolve the controllers from irksome tasks.

The social distancing that occurs with increasing reliance on others' labour no doubt contributes to status maintenance, but in the case of these owners there is little or no conformity with Veblen's view that 'the pervading principle and abiding test of good breeding is the requirement of a substantial and patent waste of time' (1957 [1925], p. 51). Rather, the work ethic is quite stringent and the expectation is not to increase leisure but to maintain and improve the property. It is not just a matter of the numbers—the hectares owned or the stock—but also how the place is managed and the quality of the land and animals. While these factors apply generally to this sort of rural enterprise, and have an obvious economic basis, it is again a matter of esteem throwing prestige into higher relief.

It is interesting to note that few of the women of this status group are not employed full- or part-time for monetary return; information which flies in the face of the notion that men profit vicariously by the conspicuous consumption of leisure by women in the household (Veblen 1957 [1925], pp. 68–96). As far as I can assess, there are neither more nor less returns to the men whether the women are in paid employment or not. It appears that what is being eroded is not the significance of the symbols of the conspicuous consumption of leisure in household or social tasks, but the non-acceptance of upper-status women working outside the domestic sphere. All these women continue to perform the tasks associated with domestic leisure, and with varying levels of paid help they continue to concern themselves with 'household adornment and tidiness' and household chores generally, and with the garden, which is seen to be an extension of the domestic arena. Nor do they disappear from social life, but maintain voluntary association memberships and generally continue to participate as they had before. The symbols are therefore retained and continue to be applauded, and they remain woman's responsibility whatever her other work.

Education contributes to status location, but any expectation that the farming élite would have considerably more education than ordinary farmers and their families is not supported. The similarities between these farming divisions apply to attitudes to both sexes and are based on common beliefs about woman's role and on the skills understood to be required by men in farming, although there is little difference in the patterns of education of women and men. If the evidence on the length of formal education does not provide a key to distinguishing grazing from ordinary farming families, the type of schooling does. Members of the grazing sector educate their children at private schools, at least from a secondary level, and there are, as Encel claims (1970, p. 154), certain schools which are favoured. It is a manifestation of the 'immodest tendency' of private schools to draw high-status children (see Connell 1977, p. 158).

FARMING FAMILIES

I do not include absentee farmers, either Pitt Street farmers or hobby farmers, in this discussion of social class. As I have indicated, they do not form part of the community as it is perceived by locals. Nor do they form a group themselves, and although locals may generally refer to them as a category, there is no implication of any group association. Indeed, most commuter farmers are socially invisible to each other.

The rest of the farming division in effect represents some diversity in many aspects of lifestyle, but is bound together by occupation and more particularly by a common pool of values relating to rural existence. Their geographic distribution imposes certain limitations and offers certain freedoms. These are common, and create mental bonds between people as well as affording bases for practical co-operation and association. The fact that farming families seldom build on the commonality of interests does not detract from the knowledge of their existence. Nor does it prevent them from being emphasized and acted on when the occasion is clearly seen to demand it. I stress, however, that although most members of the rural population only infrequently come together socially or for work, the shared circumstances and the common values create a backdrop for interaction. There is a pragmatic understanding of what Schmalenbach describes as the traditional ties of community (1965, p. 334).

Paradoxically, farming at this smaller scale is an independent venture, but one in which there is recognition of the need for interdependence, particularly in crises such as drought, fire, flood or rural recession, but also in a number of the ordinary issues and chores of daily and seasonal existence. Families and individuals in other settings face many of the same challenges and difficulties, but the rural context tends to exacerbate them and indeed creates more problems. Activities requiring co-operation and mutuality might include working for a school bus, shearing, shopping and child minding. Yet the desire for, and the sense of, independence is paramount in the farming enterprise and there is little inter-reliance beyond that which is strictly necessary for protection and basic economic co-operation. A rare outburst of discontent from one woman reveals some feelings of withdrawal and separateness borne of the basic occupational independence in farming:

There is too much criticism in the country—too much time to think— about nothing, or not much anyhow. A lot of it [criticism] comes from envy. They [the farmers] don't like being questioned and they don't like being queried, which is why they don't get together much in groups.

Her sentiments accord with Oeser and Emery's view: 'Essentially the farmers occupy similar class positions which produce *like* interests but they do not have *common* interdependent interests: rather do their like interests entail certain elements of conflict' (1954, p. 20).

It is clear that technological developments have provided the means of markedly improving the material quality of life of these farming families. Refrigerators, freezers, television and a great variety of other machines reduce the drudgery of much domestic life, with particular meaning for those more geographically isolated. And, of course, in outside farm work developments such as chainsaws, electric hand-pieces for shearing, as well as innovation and design improvement in innumerable farming implements, contribute to making the work less back-breaking, less labour-intensive and generally more efficient. It is easy, however, to accept and assume the availability of time and labour-saving equipment and therefore to underestimate its impact. Large landholders have either always had reasonably ready access to it financially, or relied on the labour of others as a buffer against much of the stress and tedium, but it is not so easy for small farmers to accumulate or borrow money, and despite the some-time help of neighbours they ultimately have to fall back on their own and their family's labour.

Of all modern manufactured articles it is probably the motor car that has made the most significant difference to the life of small-farming families, and each family has had one for years. As opposed to the grazing élite, most farmers only have one vehicle, and it is a family saloon little different from those of the higher-status group. Some farmers also have utilities. The township of Marulan is now only about one hour's travelling time away from even the most remote farm. Shopping or social trips to Goulburn are part of routine existence. Even if options are not always taken up, social vistas have potentially widened quite remarkably. Important as the motor car is, it has not created any revolution in lifestyle. Men attend more meetings and the family as a whole may go out more often, yet many farming wives lead very restricted social lives. The telephone provides the most usual instrument for social interaction. Nearer neighbours see each other, but there is a low level of participation in events beyond the immediate area. The most likely reasons are that:

- some of the women do not drive cars
- when there is only one car the man often has first claim to it
- a farmer's wife may be committed in farm work to a level where she has neither the time nor the inclination to engage in social activities which are construed as exclusively hers
- child-care arrangements are particularly difficult in the country and child minding is defined as principally women's work.

Inability to drive a car and not having regular access to it, as well as commitment to farm work, militate against the conspicuous consumption of whatever leisure there is. In principle, the problems of distance also arise for higher-status women, but when there are two cars, some kind of home help, and no demands made by farm work, those problems largely dissolve. Perhaps such problems never really had substance, given higher-status expectations of social extroversion. By contrast, the small-farming families have more restricted social horizons, and their orientations are more towards near kin and neighbours in the locality.

Many of the attributes used as criteria in status evaluation are simply inaccessible or without impact for this group. Not only is extra-familial social life restricted for practical reasons and from choice, but house and garden are remote and may not even be visible from the road. Unlike the oasis setting of most larger houses, the farmers' houses do not stand out in the landscape and only a few have a generally known history. The diversity that exists among farming families is not then generally appreciated by people outside the farming sector, for the setting in which the farmers act, as well as much of their social behaviour, lies outside the general ken. Their social position is evaluated principally on the knowledge that they are farmers and more or less of the same ilk.

TOWNSPEOPLE

One upper-status woman likened the population of the township of Marulan to 'a large family in the country'. All the people there were doing the same thing, she said, and the reason for this was the existence of the quarry—presumably because of its call on specific types of labour. Her view does hold some truth, although not all townsmen work at South, but it is perhaps more revealing as a comment on her perception than an accurate description of the social face of the township; the feminine construction of her simile is worthy of note. Interestingly, her view is held by many others, including farming families and townspeople, but it is not held by people in the 'rough' working-class group.

The employment picture in Marulan is complicated by an inconstant ingression of those living outside the district but prepared and able to travel to the town for work, and by job availability in Goulburn siphoning off local labour. In Marulan it is principally the service stations and their cafés, followed by the railway and the hotel, which employ the greatest number of people. Apart from the thin professional/semi-professional division of people who live in Marulan, working there or in Goulburn, the occupational range is narrow in terms of claims to prestige and it is weighted towards the lesser-skilled end of the range.

Despite the occupational differences between town dwellers, the variation in people's class position, and the potential for social differentiation which can exist in such diversity, most townspeople consider themselves to belong to one status group. The awareness of a common lifestyle is fortified by a locality consciousness, which from time to time is strengthened in the experience of communion. In town activities it is women who are particularly visible, whether or not they are in the labour force, and esteem attends their social participation.

For a few people the local social system is simply there—a kaleidoscope of interactions, ties and dependencies, incorporating all those eligible and wanting membership—but it is mainly peripheral to their existence. These few choose to remain apart in varying degrees, even to the point of almost complete social isolation. Such individuals or families recognize their residential affiliation but for most social action do not identify with the locality.

Newcomers inevitably feel a sense of separateness, of being outside. Some maintain the division and continue to interact with kin and friends outside the district, or even to cocoon themselves in isolation while in it. Others seek to break down any barriers they experience or suspect, either by active participation or by patient and passive waiting. Even though the host group of settled residents may not always be welcoming or encouraging, there is a general pattern of acceptance for those who seek it—particularly those newcomers who are willing to become members of and participate in voluntary associations.

Although no one tendered information on this matter, I suspect that some people have become alienated in the course of waiting for acceptance and incorporation. Their endeavours to resolve their liminality resulted in directing interests away from district affairs. The development or retention of outside interests and family privatization are responses of this order.

Newcomers can be outsiders for quite some time. One woman, exaggerating for effect, claimed: 'After the first ten years it's a friendly place, but you have to be here that long. Then they accept you. After thirty years you become like them.' According to others it takes about five years for a newcomer to be accepted, and it is newcomers from earlier times who make more recent ones feel at home. Because of the enveloping potential of the family, and their role in it, looking inwards, women who are not in paid employment are likely to feel a sense of separateness more keenly.

If some local residents remain aloof or are excluded, others, who do not share a similar status situation, participate with varying degrees of engagement in social life. The occupations (medical practitioner, teachers and clergy) and family biographies of people in this cluster, as well as their attitudes and values, would normally operate as a source of social separation from others, who largely perceive themselves as working class. It is no doubt easier for the former to penetrate the local social system than it is for working-class newcomers, and their concern with local events and relationships must, in part at least, be considered in the light of the limitations of their social and physical surroundings. Quite simply, there is a dearth of people in the district with whom members of this cluster might freely choose to associate, and who would choose to associate with them. They have only slight interaction with the large landholding group, and other socially like-minded people are further away. As the numbers in this cluster are so few, in the setting of community, status closure is neither desirable nor feasible from their point of view.

Most pursue extra-local social interests, but they also commit themselves, often vigorously, to the Marulan social scene. Other townspeople would not seek to exclude them because their skills, participation and social standing are seen as definite contributions to social life.

People generally describe themselves as working class, although some individuals or families do not fall clearly within this range.

As with the farming section, in recent times the widespread private ownership of motor cars has transformed the life of many country-town dwellers—a claim made also on behalf of television. There are, however, a number of people—older widows particularly—who do not own cars. In their youth, for most townspeople motor cars were much more of a luxury. And if a household could afford one, driving was a male prerogative, rephrased as a responsibility. Thus even if these women could afford cars now they could not drive them, and so they remain dependent on the goodwill of relatives and friends to take them into Goulburn, or elsewhere, for any reason beyond the basic food shopping, which they do locally. There is no bus service (school buses excepted) between Marulan and Goulburn; nor are there trains which could provide transport to and fro on the same day.

As we have seen, at one extreme the division 'townspeople' incorporates those who, under other circumstances, would be classified differently, including professionals and some other residents who might be seen as belonging more appropriately to a 'middle class' category. At the other extreme of the town population there is a social category described as 'rough'. For despite frequent claims that all people from the town belong to one group only—the working class—there are sufficient numbers of individuals who draw attention to differences to encourage separate consideration of a subgroup. Differences in sets of some objective attributes reinforce such analytical disengagement, although given a change in circumstances, a larger population and/or less local insularity, I would expect the subgroup to be fully differentiable. Neither conversion is likely.

'ROUGH' TOWNSPEOPLE

A few members of this numerically small subgroup (ten to twelve households) spend considerably more time at the hotel bar than other town residents; they are principally men and it registers as

one of their few social outlets. The widespread inferences that
most are heavy drinkers are ill-founded. Both town sections
provide a number of fairly hard drinking regulars, but in neither
case could the whole be characterized by the behaviour of a
minority of members. The label of heavy drinkers, no matter how
inaccurate, is often accorded this subgroup by some other townspeople, no doubt as a typification of worthlessness. One family
bitterly voiced their helpless resentment at the stereotypes foisted
upon them.

Nearly all the men in this group are employed and most work at
the quarry. Occupationally there is little difference between them
and other townspeople, except that the weighting is clearly towards less formal skills and labour qualifications. Neither is there
one area of settlement with which they can be identified—no
'wrong side of the tracks'. Rather, these households are distributed through the streets of the township. It is true that whereas
orderliness is a characteristic of most townspeople, 'rough' people
are relatively little concerned with it. Yet with regard to occupation, education, house size and dress, there is no real difference
between this subgroup and other residents. They live in the same
parts of the town; the men work at the same place as many
townsmen and some of the women have the same kind of employment as other townswomen, or else, in the same pattern, are
full-time housewives. Differences surface principally in attitudes
to lifestyle, for it is here, even given basically similar building
blocks, that dissimilarities become apparent. Quite simply, the
'rough' people do not care about the same things. This is what
other townspeople imply and this is what they say themselves.
They are locked in their own and others' evaluation of their social
location.

Contradictions and elusiveness extend into areas of social interaction and separation. 'Rough' people and other townspeople
may have a common workplace, drink together, gossip together
in shops and send their children to the same school, but there is
minimal or no contact beyond this. Subtly, on both sides, there is
an understanding of difference.

MARULAN AND BEYOND

The pattern of status in the Marulan district is neither isolated
from nor independent of broader patterns of status relations in
Australia. For certain reasons, most particularly scale and locality

consciousness, the system in Marulan does not replicate the national system. None the less there is a fit, apparent first at the wider regional level and then at the national. The fit is mediated by status awareness, which as Wild suggests, defines with whom you are prepared to mix on the basis of values and interest (1978, p. 97).

The symbolic configuration is one in which people separate out into clusters on the basis of interests and values (Wild 1978, p. 98). It is ideologically determined and although not everyone concerned may interpret it in the same way, it prevails as a system of values, giving direction to social interaction and reinforcing institutional forms (see Austin 1981). The highest ranking group, the grazing families, is concerned with family—past and present—and with making the property work for them. The emphasis is on relations of dominance. Among the middle ranks, including small farmers (who might be said to be working for their property) and townspeople there is concern for respectability and deference to authority, and there is increasing recognition that qualifications are a means to individual achievement. Certainly, people from this sector stress relations of independence, and they are thought to be achieved by members of the petty bourgeoisie. Yet, in reality, many small farmers are dependent on graziers or other employers for part-time work and truck owners are dependent on those who give them contracts and/or control the financing of the business. Although the working-class emphasis on collective activity through trade unions is low, dependence is apparent in some measure in kin networks, and working-class people are perforce heavily dependent on their employers.

People evaluate each other's lifestyles and interact on the basis of these social evaluations. Status behaviour is visible, it is the stuff of daily interaction and it is systematic, but the evaluations are not in their origin piecemeal and undirected. The ranking by people of themselves and others in a status system reflects a dominant viewpoint. It is the values and beliefs of this powerful sector of society which prevail. The power of their voice is legitimated by their status honour and their role in the productive process. At times those lower in the status system may resent the particular social evaluations put on them, but they do not have the power to change the accepted view. Usually they accept the evaluations with consent.

People's awareness of status evaluations at the local and more encompassing levels does not prevent them denying in the first instance the existence of local status differences.

SOCIAL VIEWS AND SOCIAL ACTION

Inevitably the experience of social relationships informs images of social class, but it is important to stress that the actors' interpretations of those relationships also accommodate dominant ideas of what they ought to be (compare with Chamberlain 1983). Whatever the confusions, the views people hold of the social structure are crucial in social process (Ossowski 1963, p. 6); what they say and think about social relationships contributes to the reproduction of the social system.

The ideological dimension of status is anchored in material conditions and, no less significantly, has material effects. Since women in Marulan, whether they are in the workforce or not, are the principal bearers of status messages, they are important agents in reproducing bourgeois hegemony and, interactively and no less importantly, male domination. The translation of images of social positions and relations into social action is not necessarily direct; there is no question that such imagery can be seen as simply determinant. Yet there is a strong connection between perceptions of institutions and interactions and the management of relationships, for people behave very much according to their understanding of systems of relationships, and their particular place in them. Thus while perceptions may encompass systems at their broadest level, they are more detailed when focusing on local systems of relationships. Social interactions have systematic qualities, but this does not preclude specific behavioural differences on the part of persons occupying analogous structural positions which may be attributed to differences in their evaluations of the relationships. Hence within the range of a general notion there may be a multiplicity of images, differently developed and impressionistic views, and even inconsistencies. This is hardly surprising because each composition is drawn from a variety of experiences in an individual's life, spread over considerable time (see Davies 1967, p. 3). Moreover, separate episodes can in themselves be quite complex, so that a composite abstracted orientation may appear as confused in any external appraisal (see Newby 1977, pp. 387, 402). On the basis of the kinds of variation in experience which can and do occur in basically the same structural context, there is absolutely no reason why people should have, as summations of experience, resolved and tidy models of how the society works (Pearson 1980, p. 143). In short, a general notion is different from, although it is built upon, particular images, and there is no encouragement to look for coherent models from individuals, much less from collectives of people, even though in objective terms they may share similar social-class relationships.

Townspeople and ordinary farming families are quite aware of the sorts of upper-status activities from which they are excluded—not on a personal or individualistic basis, but because of their lifestyle, which, whatever their aspirations, is circumscribed by their social position. Generally they are not inclined to participate in those upper-status events which are nominally open to them. Most locals accept that there is little point, after all, in setting one's sights on things unachievable or achievable only in the most qualified sense. However some people do feel rebuffed in their exclusion. For them it is not simply a given of social life, something to which they accommodate behaviour and attitudes: rather they cast social obloquy on the exclusives. The Goulburn Polo and Picnic Race Club is essentially a higher-status association, and the fact that its members come from this section of society generates exclusivity. There are no formalized rules which debar anyone, but nomination is required for membership and, combined with the annual subscription, which is something of a luxury expenditure for most workers, this keeps the club fairly exclusive. Non-members can attend functions but their separation is visible. Members and guests always have the best parking and at the races, for example, move between the privately organized marquees directly in front of the course, where food and drinks abound. Non-members picnic between the cars in their section of the car park.

Most Marulan residents, townspeople and ordinary farming people, are not in the least concerned about the picnic races or, for that matter, polo. They recognize their exclusion and accept it uncritically. One man, however, with an interest in horses, would obviously like to attend the picnic races. Yet the experience of physical separation would offend him, so he does not go. For him the whole event (and by implication the people) is pushy and his rancour is evidenced in the satisfaction with which he said, 'Once you had to be invited to go, now they've got themselves into financial trouble'. In this instance his view is embittered and sharpened by his frustrations. This sets him apart from many of his fellow townspeople.

The exclusion of upper-status people from lower-status activities and events is likely to be much more voluntaristic, that is they, not others, make the choice of whether to participate or not. The point here is that the separate nature of some social business underlines divisions in the social structure and people are aware of the divisions although their responses differ.

Against this clear separation of events associated with particular lifestyles, no doubt promoting the same feelings of togetherness on the part of the included but divergences in response from the excluded, there are also occasions which draw together people from different social positions. At most informal community functions—a church or local school social event—it is usual for members of the grazing élite, ordinary farming families and townspeople to be present. Everybody does mix with nearly everybody else, and some are more adept at crossing status lines than others, but within limits. Graziers and townspeople converse, exchange pleasantries and maybe dance together, but there is a tendency for people to be drawn back to their own immediate circle of social familiarity and security.

Thus while many people circulate and spread themselves socially at such gatherings, high-status people spend more time with other high-status people and so on. The difference is less clearly drawn between town and ordinary farming families, but even here it is more likely that people seek the company of others with whom they feel they have more in common. Social distinctions are both dissolved and reaffirmed on such occasions. The participants' responses and the images formed on the basis of this shared but separate reality reflect and then become part of it. The structural foundations of difference are, however, never shaken.

There is, then, a series of social events and circumstances and a range of relationships possible within them. Small wonder that social perspectives can be kaleidoscopic. The observer's desire for order may well be part of analytical expediency, but as Bottomore points out, even here 'indefiniteness may be inescapable, and may reflect the confused social conditions of the present time. There is no great virtue, after all, in having a precise and definite theoretical scheme which is quite disconnected from reality' (1975, p. 12).

While idiosyncratic images and models in themselves are not constitutive of a social situation, they may colour it. More importantly, as they collectively affirm tendencies in more widely held views, that is general notions, they do indeed form an element in the situation.

DIFFERENCES DENIED

There is an apparent and widely spread contradiction in the attitude of people on the question of social differences in the district. I have no doubt it is patently obvious to all residents that there are marked differences in style of living and life-chances—consequent on social-class positions and relationships—and consistently to deny them on the basis of real or ideal egalitarianism is ludicrous. Yet the immediate response on the part of most people is, in the first instance, to deny the existence of social difference. Three explanations bear on this tendency. First, the point made by Oxley is pertinent: 'Most egalitarian groups do not object to some members being better off so long as they do not claim to be better. Minor differences in economic class are acceptable but claims to special status are not' (1974, p. 53).

It is against an understanding of the essential common worth of people that a good deal of Marulan residents' recognition of their social relationships occurs. This is not to say that everyone in the district believes all people to be equal. Such a suggestion is, as I have already said, so far wide of the mark as to be absurd. Yet no matter what actual understandings people entertain as to either the intrinsic worth of others, or the distance in relative positions, they want to be seen as mindful of the doctrine of equal intrinsic worth and for the most part their responses acknowledge the pervasiveness of this ethic. After a very short time, however, in the same conversation or later, people generally qualify their statements in words or actions, or both, to allow for a more workable appraisal of difference. People espouse an ideal of egalitarianism—and it is a powerful ideology—while at the same time recognizing the reality of social inequalities. It is in this way that women and men can build into their purview quite extreme social differences while, at least in the first instance, acclaiming the social sameness of most district residents.

Certainly different lifestyles, carrying with them greater economic and social comfort, prestige and advantages, are claims to high social position, but this in itself does not appear to offend most Marulan residents. This is just the kind of given difference which can be manipulated and legitimated within a framework which can be made to display the impress of egalitarianism, particularly when relationships are personalized and when there are apparently common experiences and interests (see for example Newby 1977, pp. 300–11, 368–70; 1979, pp. 130–1).

As an ideal, egalitarianism draws most subscribers from relatively less privileged sectors of society. It also (like the beliefs and values underpinning status evaluations) operates as an ideology which secures upper-class interests. Members of this group are accorded the freedom to mix with whoever they choose at all levels of society. In doing so they demonstrate their worth and that of those with whom they mix. Yet the ideology does not give this social flexibility to lower-status people. If they have higher social aspirations and act them out, they are likely to earn the dislike and scorn of their peer group and those above. The ideology of egalitarianism, with all its contradictions, is an element of hegemony, and performs an integrative function, reducing the cleavages which affect the smooth workings of unequal class relationships. This is particularly apparent when an employer works alongside an employee.

It is worth drawing attention to a tendency evident in egalitarianism. While not exclusively so, it has a heavy masculine projection. Its application is principally to men in the society or to institutions dominated by men. Thus families may be incorporated but less often individual women, and women are seldom included on a collective basis, say as housewives. Women may see its relevance to men and women, men see it only to men. But social difference as a simple and known statement of relative advantage and disadvantage does not necessarily cause the disadvantaged to take exception. Some of the most privileged members of the community are neither socially exiled nor discriminated against because of their advantages. Derision and contempt are, however, directed towards those who 'think themselves better'; those who seldom participate in community affairs and who, when they are present, socially distance themselves as much as possible from all but high-status people. Then they are seen as 'snobby' and excluded in perceptions of the district resident group. Scornful comments such as 'Oh, her! She doesn't mix. She'd just about fall over you rather than speak to you' or 'No, there are no differences here which are important. The only ones who think they are better are the ones who don't mix. They come to the odd function but keep themselves to themselves', are heaped on their behaviour, and with little variation are expressed often enough. In such cases there is detraction of the individuals who are the objects of this type of criticism, but their behaviour does not impair the reputation of others in similar social positions. Their rejection is a consequence of their standoffishness: it is not the cause. Should aloof individuals or families of high status decide to mix more generally, they are more likely to gain social acceptance than lower-status newcomers to the district.

The second explanation as to why it is so common for people initially to avow that social differences do not exist attests their view of functional interdependence. It follows directly from the discussion presented above and hinges on the notion of community. A preparedness too readily to point up social distinctions suggests a willingness at least to acknowledge lines of division, of tensions, opposition and even conflict. While people do, of course, recognize that there is a range of social options and relationships, to invest social difference with discord is a denial of the understanding of what they perceive community to be.

Commonality does not presume equality, although there may be a high coincidence of shared factors, but it does de-emphasize difference. As Marulan residents take care to preserve the image of community—which means incidentally that their understanding of it is self-fulfilling—their inclination is to stress commonality. The complexity of the message is part of the apparent contradictions which are contained in the following type of response: 'There might be some differences between people here but there are no distinct groups. Anyway, when people here get together the differences disappear'. This same person a little later delineated three different social groups—the graziers, the smaller farmers and the people from town.

The third explanation of an apparently incongruent attitude to social relationships relates to differences and inconsistencies which people experience in the course of their everyday life. This is exactly the case of discrepant images, framed by various social contexts, which I have already discussed. Here the personal, aberrant aspect of social relations intrudes into stereotypical notions. Sentiment, born for instance of respect, affection, allegiance or gratitude, becomes a key in understanding this perspective. In Marulan there are several instances where women engaged in domestic work have, in the context of their work, developed quite close personal relationships with their high-status female employers. At this level there may be an exchange of personal information and services. Other people who mix independently with the same high-status women will form different images according to the context and nature of their interaction, or even lack of it. While in one sense this third level of interpretation is prior to the others, it also succeeds them. It is not of the order of the first two explanations in that it does not immediately demonstrate why inequality should be downplayed and sameness stressed—at least initially. What this view does is to take account of egalitarian predispositions and community orientations. It makes sense of everyday encounters as well as special district events which tend to minimize any stressing or acting out of difference.

I also draw attention to non-encounters, those social events whose existence is common knowledge but which are socially apart and whose boundaries are maintained. They emphasize difference and inequality. (The annual polo fixture is just such a case.) Yet as most of these behavioural modes and milieux are quite separate, they do not form a part of a common pool of experiences for district residents generally and therefore are beyond not only the pale of experience, but also of sentiment. They can be plotted into and constitute part of a universally accepted hierarchy of difference, but only impersonally. Their impact therefore is much reduced for most people.

The way people talk about social differences is more than an evaluation of the position of others (see Bott 1957, p. 163). As evaluative comment it is relative and therefore says something about the way in which the speakers seek to present themselves in enhancing or denigrating their social position.

AWARENESS IN CONTEXT

Social awareness is biased in its direction, depth and scope according to the social context and the position of the individual in it. Thus it is common enough for people to separate out two spheres, the town and the country, in their assessment of social relationships, and for them to be more outspoken in respect of their own social sphere. This does not imply any reversals of significance attributed to the prestige accorded to different groups, simply that familiarity stimulates a more detailed awareness and direct focus.

The attitudes of townspeople are well represented in the following responses which highlight the way in which ideology not only conceals but contributes to contradictions: 'There are ordinary workers, mostly from the quarry, then there are others, really just ordinary workers but they think they have more than they have'. This woman acknowledged the existence of the out-of-town population but was little concerned with them except to include, rather self-consciously, some élite grazing families in her social world, saying 'they always talk to you wherever they are'.

Another young Marulan woman said:

There are no real differences between people here, we're all really friendly people. We're just ordinary country people. Out of town might be different; some are higher up—like educated people. Yes, there are differences, like me and Mrs... She's friendly and you could talk to her anywhere but there's a difference—she's always so lovely, but me I'm always daggy.

Again:

This is a working-class town, there are no real social differences in it. Even when you take the properties into account there's not much difference. It's nothing like it is in England. It's what you want it to be here. Even if there are differences they don't count for much.

Some people recognize that social familiarity or separation affects awareness. One woman, at the outset of her conversation, said that because she had little to do with them she could not include people from outside the town in her evaluation, although when it came to scrutinizing the town there were no fixed groups which she could differentiate.

All these responses are from townspeople and sit centrally in the general range of their attitudes. Variously, they point up clearly both the initial rejection of difference and the sharpened town focus.

Interestingly, one woman who lived for many years on a farm and has subsequently come to town, showed an eye for detailed classification in both spheres. Her starting point was the rural division.

In the country the top includes the bigger property holders, like the...but they would always mix. Mrs...would enter into anything that was taking place. A bit like the Queen—there has to be a head, you have to have someone to hold in esteem. Big property owners employed people, and they lived differently—education and so on. That family always mixed. Then there are the medium-sized property holders. They are entirely supported by their property, they don't have to seek supplementary work. They are treated with more respect than the... [despised strugglers]. The lowest group in the country is the strugglers. They had smaller properties which couldn't support them and they would have to take up outside work. They did a lot of rabbiting. They were the people who would pick kerosine tins of blackberries and go and sell them by the side of the road.

Her discussion of status in town was more complicated. Marulan, she said, is an industrial area, and really all of Marulan's population is working class; but then she was swift to point to quite obvious exceptions to this blanket view such as herself, the doctor and his wife, the school's headmaster and his wife, and the category of exceptions grew as the discussion continued.

The townspeople's view usually takes account of the farming sphere, even though they are more aware of township relations; yet people from the countryside may overlook the town component of the district in their statements of social awareness. During one evening a farmer and his wife discussed district social differences at length without ever referring to townspeople. A resumé of their conversation is illuminating. The woman initially claimed there were three discernible groups in the country district; the man on the other hand started from an egalitarian premise and said he avoided thinking of status—it was too complicated and was not helpful. They both agreed, however, that in the past some families were 'a station above'. Education and money made them so, but ownership of a lot of land and background were also important. The conversation returned to the present and husband and wife agreed that big landholding families could be separated from other farming and rural people. He then made the point that apart from big old-family landholders, there was no social differentiation. His wife supported him and they also agreed that any social differences that might exist—and these would be relics from times past—have little effect on social relations in the district. As a series of statements on social awareness, this conversation indicates a country compass and it both disclaims and acknowledges social difference. It also subtly demonstrates consensus achieved by both husband and wife working through their attitudes, although in the final instance it was the woman who agreed with her husband. He in fact controlled the rest of that discussion.

Generally responses from farming people distinguished simply either two social orders in the country or, more frequently, two country and then one town division. Social awareness is projected in a number of forms and is manifest in what people have to say about their social world and in their social behaviour. It certainly takes shape in anecdotes and stories told of, often against, others. These embody values—condemnations, laudations or simple acceptance—not merely of the characters involved, but the style of life they typify. One townsman whose family previously had a farm recalled an incident involving a grazier who had wide popularity but who had been insulted by someone. 'He took off his coat, folded it so, and raised his fists—just like anyone else, even though he was a gentleman.' The description was offered as a creditable account in anybody's terms of an appropriate response to a slur by any right-thinking Australian man; the more so because of the subject's social elevation.

Some of the stories which circulated about small farmers in the past—the early selectors and their descendants—tend to be expressionistic in the Steele Rudd style, but deprecatory. On one farm, a claim goes, there was a blind sheep bumping around in the orchard. The farmer dismissed the matter saying, 'Oh! He was woolblind before anyhow'. Wool was precious to this farmer, as it was to small selectors, and when on another occasion a sheep looked as though it could become woolblind he clipped around one eye only—or so the story told to me with some malevolence has it. Other tales are bruited about a family who had one son who barked like a dog and was kept chained in the bath. Compounding the calumny, his brother and sister were said to have had an incestuous relationship. Their father demanded that they stay at home, claiming that in the corrupt and wayward outside world they could 'get into trouble'. These stories, and others like them, may well be apocryphal. Whether or not this is the case, they do exude malice and a detraction of, not only the individuals involved, but by extension a lifestyle. The stories are not known to townspeople. They came to me from higher ranks in the district. I do not know if they had currency among other members of the farming division. People tend to avoid such evaluations in saying 'We're all the same here'.

In the town itself what many townswomen, all socially prominent, saw as the social ineptitude of one 'rough' family was underscored by innuendos and more explicit stories about them concerning the organization of their daughter's wedding. She was to marry in the Anglican church in Marulan, the reception to be held in the local hall, catered for by the local members of the CWA, a common pattern for Marulan marriages. One CWA member sympathetically indicated that the family would need all the help possible in the arrangement and organization of details of the wedding as 'they simply wouldn't know'. Exasperated, as other women pressed various points, she said curtly: 'They will want it how we will want it!' Rather less charitably, another member summed up her perception of the family's base condition saying, 'They wouldn't even know how to behave in Church!'

THE CLARITY OF HINDSIGHT

It is plain that many perceptions of present-day social relationships either draw directly on past patterns or episodes or are at least partly graven by them. In Marulan, as in any local social system, the material conditions of history and oral history are constitutive (although obviously not exclusively) of both present actions and attitudes, and the past provides a bank of information from which present actors draw in understanding and acting out their social relationships. The past is also consciously invoked by way of comparison with present arrangements. Older residents have a richer store of memories and they are the people who tend to minimize today's social differences with references to past patterns of behaviour. One septuagenarian said that in town in the past, and in contrast to the country where there were more picnics and dances, 'If you were a worker there wasn't much social life before you got married. If you weren't the policeman, stationmaster, postmaster, schoolmaster or night officer, you weren't anybody'. Such fine ranking is largely irrelevant today, although he had obviously been sensitive to it and experienced its socially limiting effects. His wife said, 'It's less snobby now because the workers earn more money and it's more social'. In fact she went on to amplify how it was presently less social, and attributed this to the availability of motor cars, which take people out of the district and 'weaken its spirit'.

An octogenarian from outside town said:

When I was a boy, there was the aristocrat and the working people who were treated as inferior. If you were working on a property and if you ever had a cup of tea, it was in the kitchen. Nowadays people have lost their snobbishness and the working people are more educated and interesting to talk to. The old hard-core ones have died out. When I was a boy and my father used to take the butter into Marulan. . .on the run he left me at. . .[a large homestead], it was always with the servants he left me.

Age is a significant variable in the appreciation of social awareness. For a start older people have had a greater time-span of social participation. This has nothing to do with the breadth of social experience, which may include variety over time but can equally well be consequent on the richness of mix of relationships in an abbreviated time-frame. The time element is important in contributing to social awareness, however, because although basic structural patterns change little over a generation or two (outside revolution), structural relationships are still subject to adjustments and adaptations in features such as range, intensity or fastness. In Marulan the bonds of social maternalism and paternalism have slackened, distinctions are not as rigidly or as obviously maintained—people from various social walks do mix in district events and on certain issues join together in common action. The barriers are still firmly there, but in selected situations the gatekeepers less vigilant and the passage less inhibited, or so it is generally seen.

At the same time as having directly experienced or witnessed changes of this nature which have a personalism and immediacy which gives them impact, older people have a different hinterland of social background and information (insofar as it is deeper) which is indirectly available and which may be called on to highlight changes even further. There is a saga-like quality to their social experience.

TWO-FACED STATUS

People evaluate others on who they are, what their social position is; but they also make assessments on how they behave. Thus social awareness takes account of the attributional and interactional aspects of status.

Following Parkin (1972), Newby argues that much of the confusion surrounding the concept of status arises because there is insufficient separation of 'status as a reputational attribute of persons and status as a formal attribute of positions' (1977, p. 323). This is homologous with Davis (1950) and later Oxley's (1974) distinction between prestige and esteem. Littlejohn (1963, pp. 30–1) also refers to the reputational aspect of status as esteem.

Newby cogently details the connections and the differences between the two applications of status criteria and at the same time demonstrates their direct and indirect links with the class system. When individuals allocate status on the basis of a number of criteria observed from personal acquaintance, this is interactional status. By contrast, attributional status is located in the power structure of society and is associated with the positions people occupy.

Such attributional status, thus, emerges from the imposition of the social evaluations and moral judgements of those who occupy dominant positions in society. In view of this it is not surprising that the attributional status hierarchy tends to follow closely the class hierarchy in [British] society as a whole, for it legitimates economically based domination and converts it into authority. Thus the easily discernible criteria of prestige allocation are basically material—occupation, income, wealth and conspicuous consumption—and thus all attached to the economic order. This renders attributional status a universal system of prestige allocation which can be, and is, transferred from one local *milieu* to another. (1977, p. 324)

While the two aspects of status may empirically coincide, Newby holds that they should be seen as separate phenomena. As attributional status emerges at base from the class structure it is little, if at all, indebted to the reputational ranking of individuals. This independence cannot, however, be claimed for assessments founded on interactional status. Certainly judgements are particularistic and, as Newby writes: 'different social classes may even operate with differing criteria of *interactional* status under conditions in which their relative social separation ensures that these inconsistencies rarely become manifest' (1977, p. 325).

Judgements are none the less locked within the behavioural constraints imposed by position. Thrift among the rich is interpreted as meanness, generosity among the poor as profligacy. As another example, deference flows only one way, upwards, and the direction of dominance can only be down. It is not seen, either by peers or superiors, as behoving workers to issue directives or orders; yet the capacity to perform this function is seen as estimable in their employers. The origins of controls which emerge from the structure of society which affect behaviour, and evaluations of it, lie inevitably with the values and expectations of those higher in the social scale. The working class has but circumscribed liberty in writing its own behavioural brief—particularly in dealings with the more privileged and powerful. So while at one extreme interactional status can appear to be little more than differences in personal style, at the other it clearly acclaims the potential and limitations of structural attributes. At all times, even at a particularistic and personal level, interactional status is subject to approval and disapproval, to the checks which generally emerge from the power structure. It may or may not involve directly observable hegemonic relations. When it does not, when the interaction is between those from the same social group, it follows implicit but well enough known guidelines for behaviour in the social order. To stretch a maxim into a canon of behaviour: a cat may look at a queen, but it may not behave like one.

Despite personal variables, systems of interactional status are often constituent elements in hegemonic process as described by R. Williams (1977, p. 110). Clearly it is usual for the values of dominant groups to triumph, and although there may be rebels within the subordinate camp most individuals' actions comply with the attributional status order. It is within this order that behaviour may be esteemed or not.

According to their social performance, then, members of say the élite grazier group can be more finely ranked. This is exactly the same procedure that is adopted in hierarchical adjustments in the other social sections. After location in a broad social category—based on attributional status—individuals are more precisely evaluated on the basis of how they perform and how they are said to perform within this placement. In just this mould, for instance, a townsman said that education and home environment were recognized as social differentials which set the big landholders apart. He then made the point that the most exalted of this group were in effect 'down to earth' men, while others thought themselves to be 'up there'. Embedded in his comment is obviously the distaste which attends claims to social preferment and any signs of pretension.

CONCLUSION

In this section I have stressed the importance of views of social structure as elements in the recreation of it. Overall, the views of any particular social sector may appear unitary, although even at this broad level there may be variations in perceptions. At the levels of individuals, inconsistencies and even incoherence are more apparent because social awareness is after all based on and developed from experience, which differs between people and even for the same individual. A general notion, tied to particular social positions, is, however, constructed and developed and people see themselves and are seen to act within this framework.

Ironically, Marulan people usually deny status differences initially. The reasons for this reaction are located in an egalitarian orientation, and personal sentiment. The response is diluted and much qualified, however, by later comment and by behaviour. For this reason it is important to distinguish between what people say about social differences and their observed actions. Despite the denials which are sometimes expressed, people's behaviour in deference or social separation may just as forcefully affirm that difference.

Naturally enough people's awareness, manifest in what they say, is closely related to the social position of the particular subject. The understanding of townspeople, for example, will be much more finely detailed in respect of townspeople; the people from the farming sector will see that area in more detail. Awareness is embodied in what people say of various social groups in casual conversation and is crystallized in anecdotes and stories. In this way social boundaries are reaffirmed in the mind, which of course has consequences for action.

CHAPTER SIX

WOMEN IN MARULAN: INDEPENDENT AND TIED

Discussions on the position of women in society frequently assume a premise of dependence as a baseline for understanding. Despite some concessions made by sociologists to mutuality in personal relations (seen for example in writings as different as Veblen 1957 [1925] and Goode 1967), where it may be acknowledged that women as mothers and wives provide a support and service system for the advancement of their male relatives, it is usually perceived as one-sided dependence—of women on men. For all the inherent inadequacies of such an analytical stance and the ever-weakening fit of the model with experience, such thinking continues as strongly influential. First and foremost this dependence is located in the family, despite the fact that a whole series of difficulties and deformations of interpretation arise from the uncritical assumption that the family is *the* unit for reference in stratification studies (see Delphy 1984, pp. 28–39). Dependence is also recognized formally in law and administrative policies (Ryan & Rowse 1975, pp. 18–22; Larmour 1975, pp. 55–7; Bryson 1983) and informally in priorities and preferences in educational philosophy and practice, in the workplace, in business transactions and in general social relationships. It is explained and rationalized with, often quite strained, reference to biology and in insecure extensionist arguments with a naturalist foundation (see de Lepervanche 1984) and it is expressed in ideal and material forms which are reproduced in social practice.

Over the last couple of decades two persistent but contradictory views have surfaced in analyses seeking to offer explanations of women's position in society. On the one hand there is the view which takes the family as the unit of social stratification and which analyses women's social position from that perspective, thus seeing it as derived. On the other is the approach which argues the class commonality of women on the basis of their shared characteristics of oppression.

These views have been criticized and reworked many times and, although other sophisticated lines of questioning have been pursued, they tenaciously resurface in one form or another. In very different ways both take up the issue of dependence and both work from the family as a significant site of subordination.

In rural communities, for economic and social reasons, the family plays a central role in ideological and organizational forms and this work has, therefore, a strong family focus. This is not to imply that the family is *the* locus of women's oppression for, as Franzway, Court and Connell point out, given such emphasis, 'The family and the construction of sexuality tend to become isolated from production' (1989, p. 21). The same argument can be turned around to caution against interpreting the position of women in the economy as the principal determinant of gender inequalities. Franzway, Court and Connell also argue that the desire to identify origins and basic causes not only imposes static qualities on the analysis but must assume some kind of permanence of social forms and relationships, retrojected through time—a very dubious assumption. There is no doubt, for example, that patriarchy has existed, and continues to do so, outside capitalism. Yet given the social and economic value invested in the idea and practice of family in Marulan, it becomes fertile ground from which to examine the two approaches to women's social participation. The contradiction between them lies in the way one accords women social-class position by proxy only, that is through husband or father, and thereby underlines a state of dependence of women on men, while the other recognizes the force of the material and ideological dimensions of dependence but seeks to free women from the strictures of a dummy-like existence in analysis, and present them as having a separate class position.

The division of labour and the role of women in the family underpinning social relationships between men and women is undeniably critical for the assymetrical form of the relationships and their reproduction. It encompasses the unequal distribution of power between women and men, manifest in access to and control of economic resources—within the family and beyond it. It is, however, most important also to make the connections between the structure of labour in productive processes, and ideals of behaviour, especially as ideals may operate as ideologies. Widely held beliefs about the worth and structure of the family and about the family and male dominance in social and economic realms generally, are pertinent in this context. The value-charged beliefs about the family, and especially women's role in it, and those supporting the pre-eminence of men, at home and at work, are both part of the same ideological complex.

While the traditional family form, and women's role in it, predates capitalism, the sexual division of labour as a defining characteristic of capitalism (Game & Pringle 1983, pp. 14–24) serves, and in dynamic interaction is well served by, the ideology of family (Zaretsky 1976), with very material advantages to men in both realms. The ideology, which assumes the sexual division of labour, recreates the assumption of female dependency and perpetuates unequal relations between women and men. The ideal model of family presupposes, in fact requires, a male 'household head'—the breadwinner, the father. In this vignette other figures take their place more modestly around the family hearth.

FACELESS WOMEN AND WOMEN AS AN UNDERCLASS

By faceless women I refer to those women to whom sociological literature has denied an independent social-class presence. There is a danger that if the family, in the ideal form, is interpreted as the keystone of the stratification system (Goode 1967, p. 582; Parkin 1972, pp. 14–15) women will be doomed in analysis to live vicariously (Lenski 1966, pp. 402–3; Zaretsky 1976, p. 81). In such analyses the senior male holds the determinant position for all other resident family members, who are not on paper granted social independence until the family connections are terminated by death or legal separation, or dependents change residence. In the case of daughters marrying, their social-class position continues to be seen as derived, the reference being transferred from father to husband. Men achieve this pre-eminence because they are automatically and uncritically accepted as the sole, or in the case of working husbands and wives, principal, contributor(s) to the family income (West 1978, p. 225; Delphy 1984, pp. 28–39).

There are glaring factual inadequacies which emerge from assessment of assumptions which lock women, for all of their lives, into a secondary role in male-dominated families (see for example Acker 1973, pp. 175–8). Walby repeats the often enough raised questions: what of people who do not live in family units, or cases where the family is not classically constituted, where there is, for instance, no male head? And what of the instability of women's class position at marriage, at the death of a spouse or termination of his employment? The theoretical problems are many, but even accepting that women's social position is often anchored in the family, it is evident that women are not merely social shadows of men (see for example Oakley 1972; Frankenberg 1976; Middleton 1974; James 1979). Analysts who assume that women's position is a dependent one within the family tend to cast women in a shadowy role and deny them individual identities.

It is necessary to differentiate between an ideology of dependence—and even dependence in action—and an attribution of derived social identity which some sociologists (see Acker 1973) offer as an inevitable corollary of dependence. The ideology is formally expressed in the institutions of society, but even legal and economic dependence on male kin has not deprived women of independence in attitudes and behaviour in many social spheres. Within the Australian context reference to history is sufficient to demonstrate that this differentiation must be made, as women who have been economically, legally, and in other formally expressed ways dependent have, none the less, through their own efforts, established themselves as socially independent beings (Kingston 1975, 1977; Teale 1978). The published historical references are skewed in favour of the historically notable, but there is no reason to believe that other less remarkable women should have sunk their identity into their husbands' social image. Women are inevitably limited in social action by a host of structural constraints. So are men. The argument is that women are more constrained. This is true but it does not deny them an individual social presence and force. Generally women from working-class families may wield relatively less power than those from privileged families. However, even given the general principle that people who are in favoured class positions and who are ranked higher in status systems usually have greater individual social impact than others, it is not safe to predict that it will always be men who are prominent—representing themselves or their families. Despite the bias in the system which favours men in the power and prestige stakes, women's social presence may be greater than that of their husbands, and cannot be interpreted as derived. In Marulan, for example, although women may defer to their husbands in a good deal of decision-making within the family, they act and are perceived as acting as independent beings in respect of district affairs. In many cases women present the social face of the family. This is a clear reversal of what, in other contexts, has been advanced as accepted social form. In part for this reason and despite some apparent differentiation, I do not, in this study, seek to draw and sustain a rigid division between public and private spheres.

The dichotomy which has been theoretically delineated (for example Rosaldo 1974) may founder when tested empirically, but uncritical acceptance of it has contributed to interpretations of women's position in society as secondary and derived, and has therefore encouraged greater devaluation of it (see James' argument 1979, 1981). The dual conceptualization of two arenas of mutually exclusive social activity has been very pervasive, and it is especially the primacy and independence accorded the public sphere, as opposed to the secondary and dependent character-ization of private life (for all that it is accepted as a 'necessary and natural foundation' for public participation, see Pateman 1988), which is so devastating for women. Problems arise in the first place because private is made to elide with domestic (see Rosaldo 1974), and in the second because activity in the public sphere attracts more attention and is constructed and commonly accepted as more significant. Further, the concept of domestic is much bedevilled by imputations of triviality and inconsequence (see Oakley 1976), and because domestic labour is seen as an all-encompassing dependent state. The cross-cutting lines of female–male interdependence, notably in the domestic context and beyond in the interdependence of private and public life, are seldom etched in.

Rejecting the argument that women do not have a class position or a status presence of their own because of their dependent position in the family, a line of reasoning developed (see Mitchell 1971; Oakley 1976) which suggests that women's role in the family assures them of their own specific position in class society. Paradoxically, it is from the position adopted by writers like Mitchell that it became a seemingly easy step to view women as a class. Mitchell claimed that the very fact of being female and oppressed created the basis for bonding which lay outside the class system: feminism 'is, by definition, available to all women, whatever their class or previous political position: *it is about being a woman*' (1971, p. 96). These same common features, welded to a domestic frame, opened up the possibility of categorizing women as a class. The development of the argument is, however, difficult to sustain. Women do not necessarily or totally derive their social position from men to whom they are related, but at the same time they need not have class interests opposed to them (West 1978, p. 226), and the notion of conflict which inheres in class relationships may well be lacking (see Cass 1978, pp. 34–5). Further, although women have a shared awareness of their position as women in society, the development of consciousness has been generally checkered and uneven. Although the second wave of feminism vigorously stirred many women's consciousness, other social considerations (for example those of class and certainly of race) cross-cut and dampened it, possibly inhibiting its development in the first instance.

As Phillips argues, to suggest that women form a separate class 'is to take the argument further than many would follow, but as long as women are oppressed there is undoubtedly a common cause. Whatever pressures draw us apart, we have our shared concerns' (1987, p. 71).

Gardiner (1976) presents the case for women sharing a common state of relative disadvantage on the basis of their contribution in unpaid domestic labour, and from the fact that women work within the family for the good of the family—which has consequences for the broader economy. Certainly women's usual domestic labour relationships create conditions of commonality which draw them together, despite profound differences between their own or their families' class interests, for women's primary role is widely perceived as geared to the family, where they perform similar functions for family members, whether property owners or not. Women's commonality is embedded within the ideology of family. Through the ideology the reproduction of male labour-power is assumed. At the same time the ideology states that the family provides a refuge from the trammels and stress of the workplace in industrial society (Zaretsky 1976). It is a privatized haven said to restore men emotionally. The idea of haven alleged to exist within the family may be far from the reality (Cass 1974, p. 56), but it is an integral element of the ideology of the family. The idea of haven is, rather simple-mindedly, of a refuge created and maintained by women and enjoyed by men. The truth of it is that the family may be haven or hell for women and men as individuals, but this does not impair the ideology or a general critique of it.

Just as women's economic position affects their family location, so do women occupy specific places in the class structure, not simply because of their relationships to domestic labour, but also because of the way this influences their incorporation in economic institutions (Power 1975; Cass 1978; Giddens 1973, p. 288; Barron & Norris 1976; Delphy 1984, pp. 28–39; Curthoys 1988). It is true that women's domestic role cannot solely account for their specific position in the labour process. West, for example (1978, p. 249), holds that women are accorded a particular place in the structure of labour because of the sexual division of labour, the ultimate determinant of that placement being the forces of capitalist production (see also Barron & Norris 1976; Beechey 1978).

It is not a question of rejecting particular perspectives developed in the to-ing and fro-ing of the debate on causes of gender inequality. Not only have they contributed to our understanding, but they remain relevant. They simply do not provide total explanations. At this point recognition of the constitutive processes of class and gender is important.

The ideological and the material aspects of women's domestic roles are dynamically integrated with other elements in the structure of capitalism and thereby reconstitute the structures and the relationships. Inevitably, in capitalist Australia, the stress on the nuclear family with dependent wife developed as part of bourgeois ideology (Connell & Irving 1980, pp. 203–4). This image was held firmly before working-class women too, even though they were seldom in a position to choose whether or not they would enter the labour process.

MARULAN WOMEN

First and foremost it is quite clear that family position is important in determining the life chances of district residents— women and men. To be born to or marry into a grazing family provides very different economic and social expectations and advantages from those attendant on being a member of a town family. As there is a tendency in Marulan towards homogamy it is the natal family which is the more significant in defining the parameters of social expectations. Of course this applies as much to men as to women, possibly even more so given (so far as the farming sector is concerned) the operation of land inheritance. In terms of occupation, at least, men are no more and no less constrained or freed by parental occupations in their own occupational orientations than are women. This might be assumed to have considerable spill-over effect for other aspects of existence. It also suggests that most people, women and men, derive their status affiliations primarily, and in the majority of cases long-term, from their parental family. As people tend to choose spouses from similar social backgrounds, there is no real argument here to support the proposition that in marriage women derive their social identity from their husbands. Indeed, given that the family is a principal unit of consumption and it is on the basis of consumption patterns that status is evaluated, and given that this consumption is directed and managed by women, suggestions that women derive their status from their husbands are underdeveloped and misleading. This in no way denies the significance of class and the structural limitations on women, but certainly in the way in which they evoke social evaluations women are not, nor are they seen to be, reliant on the direction of men. Because of their input into domestic labour, women work to keep down the costs of maintenance and reproduction of labour power (Gardiner 1976, p. 117) and thus extend the value of their husbands' wages, a factor which is not only important in class terms but which underscores women's part in status systems. In short, women's social position cannot legitimately be presented as derived exclusively from their spouses', for although they may well be economically dependent on men, they have social autonomy—both as individuals and through their contribution to the overall social position of the family.

Beyond the productivity of domestic labour it is clear that women play an important role in maintaining or changing family status. In Marulan this is done, as Veblen (1957) posits, through household adornment and presentation, and through involvement in the district and extra-district associations and social functions. Considering the women from upper-status grazing families first, those who work full- or part-time in the labour force still have well-kept and well-furnished houses and attractive gardens; their own dress and image has not changed and they are as involved as they ever were in a broader social life. Men continue to benefit from the domestic assiduity of their wives, and although the women may also be engaged in the workforce this does not detract from the benefit men derive. It is not women's leisure which is critical in evaluations of family status these days, it is the effects which once were conspicuously achieved by and in a state of alleged indolence which provide the key. Thus, whatever women's other economic responsibilities and contributions, the domestic arena is still seen as a female province, and if a woman joins the labour force she may be expected to work much harder and on two fronts. Alternatively she may contribute money to pay for the labour of others to produce the same effects, although this does not absolve her from the responsibility for the household, or completely from domestic labour.

The bourgeois ideal of conspicuous consumption in domestic life is shared by other sectors of the population and constitutes an element of bourgeois hegemony. It is particularly evident in townswomen's participation in local voluntary associations. Most townswomen have come from working-class families and have married men with similar backgrounds and futures. From this baseline many women have improved their family's relative social standing in the district by their engagement in the interactional status system (see also Oxley 1974, p. 79). The women who are obviously engaged in district affairs are also concerned with the niceties of family consumption, and exercise care and attention in matters of food, dress and household detail. Twenty (39 per cent) of the fifty-one townswomen who are socially active outside the family also work in the labour force full- or part-time. As with the women from grazing families, it is not their actual leisure but the symbols of leisure which count as important in status evaluation.

On the issue of status, I refer to some figures for job training or education beyond school. Of the fifty-four women in the random sample survey who gave their occupation as home duties, twenty-one (39 per cent) had undertaken further education at a tertiary level. This compares with 38 per cent for all men in the survey (n = 48) who were educated beyond secondary school. One of the women had a university degree, seven had trained as nurses (two of whom had also done business courses), a further nine had been trained in secretarial/clerical work, and four in dressmaking— one of whom had also acquired certificates in wool-classing and music. It is not proper, nor really possible, to discard this infor- mation in interpreting women's status as derived. Even though these women were not and did not classify themselves as in the workforce, their skills enhanced their status position and would have allowed them to pursue their own specialist occupations. They had widely-known accomplishments, in many cases carrying more prestige than the skills their husbands brought to the workplace. All other status inputs aside, these women were accorded prestige on their own account by other local residents (both men and women) for this reason.

By their wage labour women also make direct financial contributions to the family, which in some (although indeed few) cases are equal to those of their husbands, and in other cases supplement it, making it possible for all family members to enjoy an improved lifestyle. In the definition of their own occupation as housewives, women appear to accept their ideal place in the family, and acknowledge their secondary role in the class system which diminishes their individual economic presence. Some women in part-time employment still style their occupation as home duties, and those who are employed casually but move in and out of the workforce according to pregnancies and the responsibilities of child care, also give their occupation as home duties. This is so not only when they are between jobs, but frequently when they are working for wages.

For others outside wage labour, their acknowledged position in the family as mother and wife hides their economic contribution. This is particularly evident among people on small farms and in other petty bourgeois enterprises. It is interesting that of the 173 women in the district whose names were entered on the electoral roll, only nineteen registered as having an occupation other than housewife, and of these, two were students. In terms of the pervasive model of women as housebound, these figures stretch further the tendencies manifest in the random sample survey. Of the seventy-eight women interviewed, twenty-four named an occupation in the labour force and, as previously stated, fifty-four said they were housewives. Eight of the housewives are over seventy years of age, and a further nine are over sixty years old and so would be unlikely to be in the workforce anyhow. Moreover, five of the housewives work part-time on their own account and six work in what is seen as their husbands' businesses; in the case of three of these women they work very nearly full-time. This expresses quite clearly Finch's argument that women are incorporated into the productive processes through their husbands' work (1983).

The position of farming wives is especially significant. In the maintenance or improvement of family social class, farming wives may not play such an obvious social role as townswomen do, yet their economic contribution may be both more direct and hidden. Three farming wives are included in the above figures of women who nominated an occupation apart from housework. Two work full-time on the farm and one acknowledges her heavy work commitment to her husband's farming enterprise. Despite their reticence, however, many other farming women have an important labour input in the farming process. The general applicability of Finch's work takes on very specific meaning in the farming sector where it is incontestable that 'a wife's incorporation in her husband's work consists both in her incorporation into the structures around which that work is organised, and the incorporation of her labour into the work done' (1983, p. 3).

Some elements of farm production take place in or near the house. They are therefore considered to be women's work and often not included in broad views of the farming enterprise. Running hens, milking and caring for the house cow and growing vegetables fall into this category of overlooked farm work, but none the less constitute important economic activities (although the goods are for home consumption). If women do not undertake this work it will certainly fall to the farmer, or alternatively and at greater cost, the provisions must be purchased. Men raise 'killers'—beasts marked for domestic consumption, but although this is food provision for the family it is deemed a male activity because it takes place outside the immediate household area and is more readily associated with general farm tasks.

Farm women are not confined to what can be interpreted as domestic chores. It may be that their education better qualifies women to handle the paper work of farming; in all events farming women in Marulan—in keeping with the pattern in other parts of Australia (see Gasson 1978, pp. 11–12)—are often responsible for handling farm records and accounts. However their contribution to the business goes a lot further than this. They may not be actively engaged in the smaller day-to-day decisions involved in running the farm, but most of these women have an important voice when it comes to decisions of some weight, even though they may be careful never to appear to stand in opposition to their husbands' inclinations. This too is in line with other Australian data (Gasson 1978, pp. 11–12) and the relatively intensified level of interaction between farming husband and wife no doubt enhances this tendency.

Although farm women are primarily identified with the household, there is not for farmers the strong division between home and place of work that exists for the majority of urban workers. It is true that a farmer's work will sometimes be in distant paddocks, but some fencing and stock work takes place in home paddocks, and machinery requires ongoing attention—usually done in sheds near the house. Conversely, most farm wives also participate in non-domestic farm tasks. This work may range from a few hours a week working alongside her husband, to a full-time farm labour commitment. Under these circumstances interaction is inevitably high, but, most importantly, the woman's economic contribution is a necessary and required element in the enterprise even though the impact of her effort may be diminished by the farm being run in her husband's name and commonly acknowledged to be his as opposed to theirs. Farming in Marulan, for all women's input and capabilities, is essentially seen as a man's game, as it appears to be elsewhere. Bell and Pandey's analysis of the representation in advertising of women and men from the farming sector shows that traditional gender-role stereotyping in rural society is doggedly resistant to remodelling (1989).

To return to the economic contribution of townswomen, there is another money-earning activity in which women participate as housewives. A number of commercially manufactured goods are sold and distributed through demonstrations held in private houses. These are generally known as 'partytime' activities and the demonstration usually takes place as a social event, with morning or afternoon tea being served. One woman estimated that over that year about forty different 'parties' would have been held in Marulan, although this was fewer than in preceding years because, as she said, 'parties go in cycles'. Plastic kitchenware, picnic and tableware, cleaning agents, batik and Indian lace goods, and fresh or dried flower arranging kits are the type of goods which are sold in this manner. A demonstrator gets 33.3 per cent commission on some lines, 25 per cent on others. Out of this she pays for token gifts for the guests and one for the hostess in whose house the event is held. Often of course the demonstrator is also the hostess. There may also be other minor operating costs such as petrol and car running. Usually a demonstrator clears 18–19 per cent in commission. Sales easily soar into hundreds of dollars. About half a dozen Marulan women act as demonstrators, although many more make their houses available and provide refreshments for which they receive not only the 'hostess gift' but also 10 per cent on what is sold, or alternatively another gift of that value. The hostess also receives a dollar for each further booking which is made at her 'party'. Sometimes a function is held to raise money for one of the local voluntary associations. For some women these activities return no more than the odd gift; for others, however, who work quite hard as demonstrators, the money made benefits the whole family. Hire-purchase debts can be more readily discharged this way, and otherwise unattainable extras bought, such as stereo equipment or furniture. Although this informal and statistically invisible work of women is often enough trivialized, it amplifies household finances, gives a boost to patterns of consumption and affects status relationships.

The overall figure for women in the workforce in Australia in 1980 was 46 per cent. The present participation rate is 51 per cent (Australian Bureau of Statistics, August 1989) and against this figure the Marulan evidence is for a very low level of participation. I do not attribute this to district women's disinclination to join the workforce (there is usually a waiting list for part-time jobs at service station cafés), but to the limits of employment in a small country town and the difficulties of travelling to and from Goulburn for women in one-car families. Marulan women uphold the virtues and values of their roles as wives and mothers, but they also see it as important or necessary to contribute to the family income and enjoy having money of their own and the companionship they find in the circumstances of work. Service station cafés, for example, establish the opportunity for friendships and provide a social world for some women. Even though they may no longer work there, past employees drop in for a chat and support, particularly, as one said to me, when there are 'rough patches' in domestic relations.

In summary the emergent picture is one in which women, like men, have social expectations and opportunities which are principally established by the social and economic circumstances of their natal families. Through marriage there can be changes in fortune, although as homogamy is more likely it does no more than endorse the position of both spouses. Within the range of contingent possibilities, however, people act to effect changes in their social existence which may not only have immediate consequences—say an improved status image—but also cumulative effects for the descendants. Women are just as much actors in this scene as men. True, men must be acknowledged as the key figures in the class structure as it is they who, in assumption and reality, have the primary responsibility for the basic economic maintenance of their household members, but economic dependence does not rob women of their own social identity. Economic reliance of women on men provides the rationale for, but not the evidence to support, the over-deterministic approach which adduces women's social presence as derived. At base this approach is underpinned by the ideologies of family and male domination which, in the process of legitimating female subordination, shuffle dependence around as cause and as consequence.

The clear evidence in Marulan is that through their efforts within the household, and outside it but within the district, women are primarily responsible for maintaining and improving evaluations of their own and their husbands' social position. They are no longer simply status markers, because through their actions they also become status makers. Men, on the other hand, play a slight role in the interactional status system of district social life.

I shall now concentrate more closely on the proposition that on the whole women share a common disadvantage, whatever their class position. As far as consciousness goes, there is no suggestion that Marulan women might perceive themselves as a class, their class backgrounds and allegiances and experiences are too variable to allow them to contemplate a transcendent unity based on gender. For two reasons a townswoman would never class herself with a woman from a grazing family in respect of common gender oppression. First, for all that social differences are initially denied, there are cross-cutting ties of social class connecting male and female consanguines and affines. Secondly, there is but a negligible or weak perception of female subordination, which in no way undercuts an ideology of male domination. I shall return to discuss this ideology in the following chapter.

Marulan women subscribe heavily to the ideology of family, and inevitably the role of mother and wife in it. In this they share sentiments and experiences in common, and it is largely because of their position in the family and the work they perform in it, regardless of their social relationships in the broader society, which suggests that Marulan women also share a common disadvantage. There are two intersective elements to be considered here: the impact of inheritance on ownership, and the potential of individuals to engage in relations of production in a capitalist system.

Marulan women have, and recognize that they have, divergent class interests, even though they are mindfully underdeveloped. A few women have inherited productive land or shares in businesses in which they retain an active interest, thus stressing their position in ownership and management. Others have been made partners or directors in their husbands' enterprises, and while in a number of instances this is no more than tokenism for the sake of spreading a taxation burden, in other cases the women are effective, even dominant partners. Yet the existence of broad class differences and individual variations need not contradict the proposition that women share a common disadvantage. It is worth mentioning that in most cases of dual ownership, despite work input and even if there is recognition on paper of the woman's equal claims, the enterprise is seen as the man's. When popular opinion does accord a woman rights and responsibilities in the business it is usually as a junior partner.

LANDHOLDING

In rural areas land is productive property. It is therefore particularly instructive in an examination of the position of women to follow through patterns of inheritance and ownership of land. In this discussion I am principally interested in rural land. Nevertheless, in the accompanying tables information is included on the transfer of town lands because although only some of this property is productive (this is really limited to shops), the male domination in the transactions reflects a broader principle—the understanding that men should control property generally. As people in rural districts which have developed from a rural base are conservative in attitudes to male–female relationships it is not surprising that the bias is so pronounced in this context. There is nothing peculiarly Australian in this for, using French data, Delphy points out: 'Domestic circulation (the rules of inheritance and succession) here *flows directly* into patriarchal relations of production' (1984, p. 19).

I examined records held by the Shire Council from 1917 to midway through 1977. As the data for the pre-1938 period are incomplete, my focus is on the years from 1938 on.

Men obviously exercise control over land. In all instances, save that of town inheritance, which is a relatively small sample, the category of 'men only' is significantly fuller than any other. Women own land, but it is evident that their role in land transactions is and has been minor. Their reduced presence in rural deals (compared with town) relates to the ideal connection between a family and its farm, which is a heady efflorescence of the principle of male control of property (Gould 1989). Properties, once established, acquire an identity and name of their own, a fact which is evident in the form of country addresses. Mail boxes, and in some cases signs, bear the name of the property. Only newcomers are likely to violate the convention and put their own names on their mail boxes. Yet the responsibility for establishment and maintenance of a property lies with a family, and ideally the family name will be linked through time to this land (see Williams, W.M. 1969, p. 77). Men carry the family name, and it is principally men who inherit and hopefully increase the holding. In the few instances in which women have inherited the land, it has been from men. Women do not inherit rural land from women (with one exception, see Table 6.1). Discussing the distribution of the estate of her husband's grandfather, a woman said that the 'girls' could have inherited land but preferred to be left money. In rural society, where the pattern of residence is ideally, and in practice generally, patrivirilocal, the land would have been of little use to these women. Thus, apart from questions of ideals, male inheritance of land is self-generating for practical reasons. There may be barbed messages for women here, because the patrimonial imperative and lack of financial independence can become problematical in the case of domestic violence and breakdown of marriage relationships (see Coorey 1989, pp. 123–4).

Aside from the ideal connection of land and family with a male head, the nature and extent of women's participation in the workforce means that women are less able to make large-scale purchases on their own account and, despite their labour expenditure in the family commercial concern, country women seldom earn economic freedom. It is usual for profits to be returned to the farm, the enterprise to which they are committed but from which as individuals they are economically excluded. According to Teale, since the very early days women have followed pastoral pursuits and numbered among pioneers in the development of rural industry. She states that by the 1900s there was 'a good scattering' of women holding pastoral property in their own names (1978, p. 234). In this region a scattering is what it remained—no matter that many went out to pioneer with their husbands, it was not common for women to hold land. In the 1899 *Sands' Sydney and Suburban Directory*, the first edition to include a Pastoral Section for the Goulburn Stock District, only four women were included in the list, which had forty-five men as principal sheep and stock holders. The ratio has changed little over time.

Two categories which are very poorly represented in the pre-1938 span became significant in the later period. These are 'men and women', usually husband and wife acting together in land transactions, and 'companies'. In the rural division the earlier entries in the latter category are usually family groupings, which may also include women as wives, daughters or sisters. The change since 1938 may represent an acknowledgement of women's contribution to the business in both management and labour. This will not subvert the principle of male control, for incontestably sons will have preference over daughters when it comes to inheritance of the land, but a potent reason for women's inclusion is that it provides a means of tax relief and facilitates the movement of money on paper. Both categories, 'men and women' and 'companies', received a fillip in early 1970 (Table 6.2). This was a period of economic buoyancy and, as is seen in the peaking of land sales in 1973, Marulan enjoyed the land boom. The increased number of sales was in rural as opposed to town land. During the early 1970s a number of rural estates were sold directly, or sold, subdivided and resold, to commuter farmers.

The dramatically increased incidence of 'men and women' buyers during the 1970–76 period is due not so much to any real improvement in the position of women as landholders, as to the influx of Pitt Street farmers where, as with family farms, women may have been incorporated as a ploy to avoid or reduce death duties and to reduce the level of men's personal income tax. This latter explanation is unlikely to apply in the case of hobby farmers—those on 16-hectare blocks or less—where there can be little expectation of making money, although in these instances the city dwellers may bring with them something of the changing approach to female–male relationships and thus register their land in the names of both husband and wife. The argument on death duties appears to stand, however, but the hypothesis is difficult to test, for the issue of death duties in estates passing from one spouse to another is no longer a relevant factor and land sales have slowed right down. Forty-eight per cent of the total number of transactions involving 'men and women' sellers occurred during the boom period. More impressive is the fact that 58 per cent of 'men and women' buyers for the 1938–77 period fall within this seven-year span. The bias is clearly weighted by transactions occurring during the 1973–74 period. Thus although from Tables 6.1 and 6.2 it might appear that women played a more significant part in land transactions than I have allowed, analysis of two of the categories in which the women appear, or might be placed, suggest caution in interpretation (see Table 6.3).

Land is only one resource which can be inherited (or purchased) and women may receive other legacies, especially in money and personal property, which are balanced against the value of the land even though they are not necessarily equal to it. Needless to say, the worth of rural land lies not only in its market value. It also offers some assurance of an economic future and grants the autonomy of self-employment which is part of the bourgeois occupational ideal. (These are, however, lures not always to be believed, given market and environmental exigencies, for example the drought in eastern Australia in the early 1980s. Small farmers with no economic backstop are particularly vulnerable.) In the country land is the basis for the most privileged class relationships, which can only improve in character and potential with improved quality and quantity of the property. Moreover, land ownership has symbolic value: it attests a person's worth and standing in the community. Insofar as women feature only marginally as land owners, and principles of inheritance direct that rural land revert to male ownership, then from this perspective women hold a secondary position in the class system.

WOMEN IN THE WORKFORCE

I have argued that women's economic contributions to the family, both direct and indirect, cannot be overlooked and should not be soft-pedalled. None the less, many women are economically dependent on their husbands, or at least 'families are often more materially dependent on men (who generally earn more) than on women' (West 1978, p. 226). It is, however, necessary to go beyond these two propositions, that is, that women work for wages and that they usually earn less than men.

There is a pointer to relative social positions in women's lower earnings. (Although the nature of the engagement in relations of

Table 6.1 Land transfers—Marulan and district 1.1.38–30.6.77

	Rural land				Town blocks			
	Inheritance or gift	Sales to same name	Sales to different name	Total	Inheritance or gift	Sales to same name	Sales to different name	Total
W → W	1		4	5	2		7	9
W → M	8	8	16	32	2	4	19	25
W → M + W	1	1	6	8	1	1	5	7
W → Company			7	7			10	10
M → M	33	56	165	254	6	9	90	105
M → W	12	1	11	24	8	1	16	25
M → M + W	11	4	48	63	2	5	36	43
M → Company		1	38	39	2		29	29
M + W → W			2	2	1		3	4
M + W → M		3	21	24		2	4	6
M + W → M + W		1	17	18		3	15	18
Company → W			4	4			6	6
Company → M			43	43			41	41
M + W → Company	2		16	18			10	10
Company → M + W			71	71			24	24
Company → Company	1		29	30			12	12
Total	69	75	498	642	22	25	327	374

M = man
W = woman

Table 6.2 Land sales—Marulan and district 1970–76

Year	Sellers				Buyers				Totals
	Men	Women	Men + women	Companies	Men	Women	Men + women	Companies	
1970	10		4	1	9		2	4	15
1971	10	1	6	3	6	1	9	4	20
1972	14	4	4	24	9	2	21	14	46
1973	20	6	12	70	23	5	51	29	108
1974	22	1	10	29	22	1	26	13	62
1975	9	2	7	15	6	2	17	8	33
1976	3	1	6	10	3	4	11	2	20

Table 6.3 Sex of single agents in land sales—Marulan and district

| | 1.1.38–30.6.77 | | | Pre-1938 | | |
	Rural	Town	Total	Rural	Town	Total
Women alone as buyers	22	33	55	18	22	40
Women alone as sellers	42	46	88	17	8	25
Men alone as buyers	312	169	481	146	86	232
Men alone as sellers	321	186	507	151	98	249

production is basic in class analysis, income as such is not a key to class relationships.) The question is, why do women earn less? Because of their position in the family, and because of male control of the workforce, women enter jobs which are characterized by attributes of 'dispensability, clearly visible social difference, little interest in acquiring training, low economism and lack of solidarity' (Barron & Norris 1976, p. 53). Barron and Norris state, and many others have subsequently taken up the point, that these are characteristics of the jobs, not of the individuals doing that work, although attribution of these features to individuals is often offered as a reason for the existence of a secondary labour market. Not only do women have a significant showing in jobs of this kind, but they are also strongly represented in casual and part-time employment.

Overall evaluation of the relative class disadvantages of men and women in Marulan is made more problematical by the numbers of men who are in occupations classified as semi-skilled and unskilled. Many of the jobs at the quarry display some combination of the attributes Barron and Norris describe. There is a floating work population which takes up residence in Marulan while engaged in such quarry work. For all that, there is relatively little job-changing in the male workforce. It is not loyalty to the company which promotes this stability but rather limited job opportunities in the district. People stick to the job they are in. It may not be their preference but it is what they have.

Reference to Table 6.4 indicates the low level of residential mobility, and not all the people in the category 'Less than 5 years' resident can be considered as transient. Some will stay for many years more. In the country, where work opportunities are restricted, job mobility is very strongly tied to residential mobility and there is little incentive, especially for those who were neither

Table 6.4   Years of residence in Marulan district

	Country		Town	
	Men	Women	Men	Women
Less than 5 years	4	5	7	11
5–9 years	2	3	7	6
10–20 years	2	3	8	10
More than 20 years	5	6	9	14
All of life	5	1	17	19
Total	18	18	48	60

Source: Random sample survey.

brought up in Marulan nor have kin there, to stay on after changing to a job in Goulburn.

In this respect there is a considerable difference between men and women workers. Very few women in wage labour stay at the same job for any length of time, although their employment possibilities are even more restricted than men's. The principal reasons are pregnancy and childbirth and then child care. As family claims are made on women, they move in and out of employment, and their unemployment is rendered invisible by their family position. This engagement in the labour force is not a feature of casual work but of high job mobility. For the same reasons, however, women have a high engagement in the part-time and casual workforce, which is not the case for male labour. From the point of view of the nature of Marulan women's participation in the labour process, most of them share a secondary, insofar as it is disadvantaged, position in class relationships. Inevitably, as with the data for inheritance and ownership of property, there are exceptions—some women have well-paid, secure jobs for which good qualifications are needed. They are not part of the secondary labour market, and tied to this and the qualifications which made them eligible for the jobs in the first place, their status position is comparatively high. This is not the general trend, however, which instead indicates a relatively disadvantaged position for women no matter what the class background of their natal family or their husbands' class position.

CONCLUSION

In working towards an understanding of Marulan women's social position, a curious irony has emerged. It stems from an evaluation of two conceptual approaches to women's relationships in these systems and local appraisals of women's social-class relationships. Both views are grounded in the family, a critical social form in rural society, and this invited review of them. But in essence the derived existence of women, written into one assessment, is not well supported by the evidence, while the latent opportunities to mobilize consciousness, identified in the second analytical approach, are eschewed. Despite the shortfalls, the perspectives cannot be discarded as irrelevant; both have a degree of explanatory value. Their inadequacy in Marulan relates to their failure to take account of male hegemony on the one hand and the role of consciousness on the other.

Women may act independently of male household members, improving the family status in presenting an image which is superior to one based on people's evaluations of the senior male's occupation alone. This is a long way from simply maintaining status. Yet, as I shall demonstrate in the following chapter, women are at all times keen to defer to the social presence and power of their spouses; and in presenting men as dominant in economic and social realms the women willingly fall into step three paces behind. They patently have the potential to be, and many are, status makers, and this is acknowledged by local women, for local women collectively. But when any individual woman speaks on her own behalf the portrait she paints of the family face is usually that of the male breadwinner referred and deferred to as the family head. I suggest that because of a developed sense of dependence which is the linchpin of ideologies of male dominance and family, women accept in principle a secondary presentation of social self, although in practice this behaviour frequently does not accord with certain patterns of social relationships which locals recognize.

Conversely, because of their actual position within the family, and the ideals of the female role, Marulan women, like other Australian women, share a specific position of disadvantage. That is, within any division in the class system their position, while it cannot be described as derived, is secondary. Women accept their casting in a secondary role but at the same time are blind to it as a basis for the development of consciousness. They do not seek to assert themselves as a separate social force. This attitude is well summed up in the contradictions apparent in what people say about gender relations, and how they behave, and even partly explained in the statement of one of the local women: 'Things are changing. A woman has as much chance as a man. All the women who go out to work here wouldn't if their husbands didn't believe in it. It's not a male-dominated society—was it ever? Women see themselves as having equal standing; they accept their place and seem to be quite happy with what's coming home.'

In the following chapter I shall take up more directly the matter of male hegemony, which has provided an underlying theme in this discussion, and look at power relations within the family as manifest in decision-making.

CHAPTER SEVEN

MALE AND FEMALE RELATIONSHIPS: POWERFUL BELIEFS

To recognize mutuality within the family in the maintenance, recreation or extension of class and status relationships is by no means to claim equality for men and women in their social roles; any such assertion would be manifestly wrong. An entrenched male hegemony is disclosed in accounts which trace Australian women's social position from the early days of settlement to the present (see for example Summers 1975; Dixson 1976).

In this chapter I turn to a closer examination of the ideology of male dominance in Australia, which, in association with the ideology of family and clear differentiation of sex roles, shackles women to a dependent position. As testimony to the persuasiveness and pervasiveness of both ideologies, many women have for years assented to this position and even been active agents in reproducing the circumstances for future dependence. Marulan, like most country districts, is conservative in attitudes to social relationships between men and women (see James 1981, p. 103). For the most part district women hold as irrelevant to their social existence the increasing consciousness of women's relatively disadvantaged position which is so widely acknowledged in metropolitan centres.

RADICAL FEMINISM IN THE COUNTRY

In an analysis of radical feminism Mitchell comments that 'Women's Liberation has not developed in rural areas, farming or peasant' (1971, p. 40). Her purpose does not lead her to develop this point particularly, although the very differentiation of country and city living implies a reason which is embedded in a backdrop of district lifestyles and experiences removing these country women from the social milieux which generate the preconditions for the emergence of a radical feminist consciousness. In the years since the publication of this statement I know of no changes which require its modification.

A report on the plight of rural women following rural recession, issued in the late 1970s (National Party Women's Section Central Executive Committee, n.d.) gives as number one in its list of findings: '65% surveyed, reported that they felt a definite loss of dignity, hopelessness, as "seven-days-a-week peasants", in fact like second class citizens, working long hours with little or no return' (p. 2). Later the report states that:

75% of wives are now involved in extra farm work, either while their husbands work away from the property or to eliminate the expense of casual labour. Duties include cutting thistles, wood, noxious weeds, hay carting, fencing, shed hand during shearing, milking alone, handling cattle, tractor work, midwifery with cows, irrigating, fencing and general farm work.

Many of these women are actually doing three jobs—working away from home, working on the farm and looking after a family and home, and this they claim is the most difficult task—to keep all this activity going. (p. 5)

This evidence would seem to provide grounds enough for the development of a consciousness of occupying a second-class and marginal position, as the backstop for the enterprise (compared with awareness, which is avowed). The self-image is, however, one of farmers' wives, and in this compound definition it is the farm which is stressed and which always takes precedence. The women are the wives of farmers whose enterprise, and thus living and lifestyle, is under threat, and so they accept the responsibility of undertaking extra farm work, or if possible paid employment.

Skilled or professional women generally do not appear to have much difficulty in obtaining work, whereas those who are unskilled find employment a real problem if not impossible and so their problems are compounded by a feeling of inadequacy in not being able to *help out* financially. [My emphasis]

All women are working long hours, with a number working from 14 to 16 hours per day. (National Party Women's Section Central Executive Committee, n.d., p. 6)

The report is a response to difficulties affecting women and which are seen to arise particularly in rural recessions. When times are tough the problems flow over to women from the upper echelons of the farming sector, who may normally be exempt, but these difficulties seem ever-present in some degree for women from the small-farming division, even when the going is relatively good. With a commitment to their husbands' concerns, and in effect a strong identification with them, it is easy to see why women on the land reject the claims of feminism which they feel might align them in opposition to their present interests. Even if they do not see such claims as leading to an estrangement of interests, for many women there is no question of active feminism conferring any advantages on them in their style of living. As one woman said:

Women's Lib gains no ground in the country because women have to come to the aid of the party. They have to help—or else. Men and women in the country share the same goals. I admire the women for having a go, but I never worry about not being liberated—it rocks the boat too much.

There is no doubt that in this case the farm could not have continued as a viable concern without the woman's input. Indeed she carried the undertaking; but at all times, in his presence and out of it, she deferred to her husband. One woman probed the matter further.

Women's Liberation in the country would get no back-up—country women are isolated from causes, meetings and the immediate pressures of the media. Possibly they might attend one meeting but then, with no intensity or frequency of interaction, they would just drift back to their life. Pitt Street farmers might change it all. Individual people in the country don't like change but country life isn't so great it shouldn't change.

The reason most often given for country women's lack of interest in feminist movements was that they are far too busy; city women on the other hand are believed to have time on their hands. One woman from a grazing family said only frustrated women were interested; it was a common charge.

In town, with the possible exception of some members of the petty bourgeoisie, work association in what is in practice a joint venture (for example general storekeeping), cannot be, and is not advanced as, a reason for lack of interest in the feminist movement. Moreover, with low levels of women's participation in the workforce the matter of time may be largely a red herring. Conservatism in this, as in other areas of social relations, is less tied to time than to inclination. The attitude of townswomen is firm: 'Marulan women are quite satisfied with their lot. There's no suggestion of thinking of Women's Lib'. In a discussion following exactly this sort of comment one woman attributed support for women's movements in the city to university students, a force which she pointed out was happily lacking in the country. Her rationale represents an apotheosis of conservatism, projecting outwards and onto an already suspect group her fears about the dangers of change.

It is not only women who claim contentment with traditional givens as the basis for their way of life. Although men are generally taciturn about the matter, they also believe in the adequacy of the rewards of sex-role behaviour; in effect that the satisfaction of being a wife and mother is sufficient in itself. It is after all an argument favouring men's social position and relationships in very material ways, although the men are diffident about expressing their views on this aspect of the topic. The following is an exception to this general reluctance:

People who choose to live in the country or who are brought up there are happy with their lot, whereas women following such movements in the city are fairly unhappy. Women from the country see what these organizations want and know they have it anyhow. They are secure in these things.

This view was expressed by one of the more educated townsmen, and the thrust of his comment is a common one—country women have all they want.

There is no evidence to suggest that the older women are more conservative in this respect than the younger ones, among whom I had at first thought there might have been the rumblings of disaffection with the constraints of being a woman in a small country town. The first two comments on the Women's Movement listed below are from girls in their late teens, the last two from women in their seventies. All four are from the town.

It has no appeal for me. In some cases they are right—for example men and women should receive equal wages if they are doing the same work.

I agree with that, but I don't support the whole movement, in fact I haven't taken much interest in it.

Men and women are equal—the men go to the pub and the women go to their parties, that's all they ever do. . .Country women are not worried by Women's Lib. They do what they are told but they are not worried. Some things are fair enough, for example wages, but they go to extremes.

I can't say why there's no support for them in the country. There is a time lag between city and country in fashions, hair and dress, perhaps it's also with Women's Lib. It's all right in moderation. Women should have a say, but not like Germaine Greer. . .I certainly don't believe they should be the underdog.

In my day the man was definitely the family head—the man of the house. Women's life was more confined. I wouldn't like to be a real liberated woman but it must be a little bit good. Nowadays there is more sharing—you aren't 'the one in the house'. It was my duty to do what I did. . .Feminism might be stronger in the city because women must feel they want to get out more when they're confined to their houses. I could always do as I wanted. I think there's more companionship in the country.

The message in these comments is the same—there may be room for some improvements in women's position, but certainly nothing radical. Women are after all basically satisfied, and this, it seems, despite an awareness of women's subordination or cynicism about the breadth of men's and women's social life in Marulan.

Townswomen here are just as untouched by feminist arguments as are women out on farms. Yet they are not actively part of a farming population and the pragmatic reasons given by and for farming women's lack of interest cannot apply. Despite differences in lifestyle certain elements in the pattern of social relations and social expectations are shared, for both sectors are distanced from the potential for intensity in interactions that city life offers. They are indeed removed from causes and meetings, and although the media may have just as direct and immediate an impact as in urban areas, this is much tempered by the small population and its closed-community nature. For some women this is compounded by near isolation in the nuclear family (see Williams C., 1981, p. 170). Many people are isolated for one reason or another, in metropolitan areas too, and in that context women (and men) may also be conservative in the matter of female–male relationships, although it is then even more difficult to disentangle cause and consequence. While isolation may have a bearing on conservatism it is but one factor among many and is far from a necessary condition. An overarching reason which helps generate traditional attitudes in Marulan is rural identification, and tradition decrees that the tried is not only the true, it is the best. A rural ideology leans heavily on acceptance of both the family in its conventional form and male domination and brooks no critical scrutiny of either. As I have argued, Marulan townspeople, for all that they are existentially like city people, who are labourers, shopkeepers, housewives and so on, know themselves as country people and subscribe strongly to the rural ideology.

MALE DOMINANCE—AN IDEOLOGY

In an examination of the relationships of husbands and wives within the family, Bell and Newby find that gender inequality persists not simply because men maintain traditional authority over women, but also because women continue in their belief and behaviour to endorse their own subordination. They write that many women believe that 'not only *do* their husbands possess greater power but that in the last analysis, they *ought* to do so' (1976, p. 154). In acting out subordination and domination, contribution and co-operation are required of both parties. In this way the ideal form can become the reality. Male hegemony is not, however, restricted to a familial form only; there is abundant evidence of its triumph in all social spheres encompassing female–male relations. Empirically men have the power in many ways, and this is obvious from information on land ownership and job security. Yet sometimes in both extra- and intra-familial forms the system goes awry, and men stand in jeopardy of losing the power. In no way is the strength of traditional authority destroyed, however, for as is often the case in Marulan and elsewhere, adjustments can be made to uphold the ideology. In those aberrant circumstances in which women come to the fore, the understanding that men ought to possess greater power is translated into the belief that they do.

Women on the land would seem to be in a strong position to change the image of farming as a male activity, particularly when they own land in their own right or even jointly with their husbands, but also by their participation in the business of farming. Instead they are satisfied by their efforts to return prestige to the whole family, but especially to men. This is evident from Pownall's thumbnail sketches of early pioneering women (1959) and is the essence of Grimshaw's argument (1980) that the material circumstances of pioneering promoted partnership in marriage.

Even so, women were mostly seen as junior partners, simply overshadowed by their husbands, though many subsequently took on sole responsibility for the running and management of the property. Despite the fact that husbands and wives were in practice partners, the widely held social view heaped laurels on pioneering men for their farming achievements. At the National Conference of Countrywomen in Australia in 1979 it was apparent that this continued to be the case, and although some claims for recognition of the importance of women's input and capabilities were advanced at this conference, most women were happy to have farming projected as a way of life for men. The claims made by women were generally tentative and for the most part the focus was on problems of family, women's employment, education and health. For many women these problems are acute, but this does not detract from, indeed it serves to reinforce, women's gender separation, and perpetuates the stereotype of 'the man on the land'. A salient point here, differentiating farming women from other women who have a heavy labour input into the family business, is that a farming woman's work is invisible to outsiders. Her husband knows and sees, but few others appreciate it. This is not the case with say shopkeepers or many another city-based small business.

With few exceptions farming women in the district make a considerable and necessary input to farm work but do not seek recognition for this, let alone equality with men. One woman said she felt that women and men were socially equal but 'perhaps women don't think they are as important. When it comes down to tin tacks, I like to see it is the man who makes the decisions'. Another woman, whose husband was in poor health and did virtually no physical work on the place, still felt that he should make all the decisions for the family and the farm. Quizzed further, she said that as they had always had so little money, if anything went wrong she did not want to be blamed for it. Her reasoning was sound, no doubt, but it obviously reflects the orthodoxy of male domination, for there was no question of her blaming her husband in the event of his decisions turning sour.

The following comment is unusual in that its author was much more forthright and condemnatory of men's behaviour than was usually the case. She none the less acceded to the ideology of male domination (that is, beyond the physical realm):

In the country men certainly have the upper hand, although women are the driving force. Men know the worth of women, but a lot of women are frightened of men—physically, and because of isolation. In town there are long periods of separation while the men are at work, the pub, or other activities, and this can offer a tension outlet. In the country relations are so close that the strain can be unsupportable. Women put up with it—what else could they do? Men need to see them subjugated because of their insecurity. They are not much good in a big pond so stay in a little pond—they only have themselves to argue with and they always win. There are always good men, but there are more of the other around here.

She went on to say that the thoughtlessness of men in being late for meals, or walking in with dirty boots, was an assertion of their right to dominate. Her acrimonious outburst was singular, and offsetting it is the evidence that the relative isolation and closeness of the life of farming couples can just as readily—more so if the information from Marulan is any guide—draw people together in experiences and in pursuit of common goals which in themselves diminish deep lines of opposition while they continue to give emphasis to male superiority.

Farming wives are commonly involved physically and in the business management of farming and it is true that farming men may undertake more household chores and child care responsibilities than do their counterparts from town. That is, there is some interleaving of sex roles. Yet it would be misleading to leave the subject at that. The reality is that men's involvement in the domestic sphere is still minimal. Because the separation between house and place of work is not rigid on farming properties, men do 'lend a hand' in a range of domestic activities, but not regularly and not if they are time-consuming. There is nothing to stop them cooking or dusting, for example, but these are seen to be female tasks and men do not undertake them; and no matter how well they are performed, they rank lower than male skills (that is those usually performed by males). Crutching sheep or marking (that is emasculating) calves may not be pleasant work but both carry the stamp of farming and therefore some prestige; by comparison housework is not prestigious. The point here is that while the women are quite active in what are traditionally seen as male domains, men venture relatively little into the realm of domestic responsibilities and work. They maintain a superiority by remaining fairly aloof from this field, as is witnessed in the fact that it is not that they cannot do this work, but that they do not care to. Any domestic task a man performs is to 'help out' his wife and this is a very different matter from undertaking the responsibilities on his own behalf.

The ideology of male domination is just as strongly adhered to in the town, despite women's influence on public life in the district, which appears greater than men's. This influence is strongly tied to women's high visibility in local voluntary associations in which men, on the other hand, play a much smaller role. I asked forty-two people—men and women from the town and out of town—whom they classed as influentials in the district. Five farming and grazing men scored twenty-three, against two nominated farming or grazing women who scored three. (Three of the men formally represented the district at state or local government levels.) These figures are consonant with the elevation of men in the farming division, although certainly formal positions of influence inflate the scores. In the town it is women's visible presence and influence, particularly in voluntary associations, which creates the greatest impact. On thirty-seven occasions twelve townswomen were cited as the influentials of the district, ten townsmen scored thirty times (see Table 7.1). The clustering of numbers around a few names underscores the influence of some people. One man from South was also named six times as being influential in the district. The reason he was proposed in three of these instances was specifically because he was said to have had a bad influence. For instance, he was said to be instrumental in having established in town the limestone crusher, which showers nearby residents with dust, and he is alleged to have been obstructionist over the Marulan town water supply, delaying it by years.

Shiftwork can have a profoundly disturbing effect on the rhythm of both private and public life, which no doubt affects the individual's potential for social impact (Williams, C. 1981, pp. 177–8; Department of Science & Technology Report 1980). Only three of the townsmen cited as influential work erratic hours. Both Ampol and Esso cafés, however, run a 24-hour service and women as well as men work shifts, waitressing and cooking. Moreover, women's lives are also thrown out of kilter when their husbands are on a shift roster (see also Metcalfe 1988, p. 33).

Table 7.1   Scores for people cited as influentials

Country				Town			
Men	Number of citations	Women	Number of citations	Men	Number of citations	Women	Number of citations
A	1	A	2	A	7	A	5
B	1	B	1	B	2	B	1
C	9			C	10	C	10
D	8			D	2	D	2
E	4			E	3	E	1
				F	2	F	2
				G	1	G	1
				H	1	H	1
				I	1	I	5
				J	1	J	6
						K	1
						L	2
(5)	23	(2)	3	(10)	30	(12)	37

(No relationship is implied by the use of the same letter.)

Most hold that they have adjusted to it and that they really do not mind any more; but even though they go to bed during the night shift when their husbands work, they still stay up to see them off at 11.00 p.m. or wait up for them if they are on the afternoon shift and prepare supper on their return. As most of the women also have children living at home, normal timetables revolving around school or work hours, meals and sleep, have to be adhered to, and preparation for the extra meal sittings resulting from shiftwork slotted in between. One summed it up thus:

You have to creep around the house while he's sleeping in the morning, cramming housework into other snatches of the day, sit up with him at night to get him off to the night shift, feed him at all hours as well as have the routine of the rest of the family to cope with.

Chambers' conclusion that '*Women are a central part of men's resources to overcome shift effects*' (1986, p. 321) is definitely relevant in Marulan.

Many men only work three shifts (that is they are never rostered on the late night shift) and one woman pointed out that from midnight to dawn was the only time she could rely on her husband being at home to babysit—so twice a week she works that shift at a service station café. She may manage a couple of hours sleep before she starts work at midnight, but that is all she gets for that twenty-four hours. She says she is used to it.

Six of the women proposed as influentials are married to men who work flexible hours and two of them work shifts themselves. Despite the fatigue which is caused by constantly changing living patterns and the social dislocation which is promoted, shiftwork alone cannot account for men's lower rating as influentials because it also has direct and overflow effects on women. Moreover, it is interesting that although Kandos is a shiftworking town, changing work hours do not seem to have had any profound effect on men's participation in social life outside the family (see Oxley 1974). Men are definitely socially active there. And while Metcalfe records the profound exhaustion and social dislocation experienced by shiftworkers at Kurri (1988, p. 34), there is no suggestion that it prevented them from participating in socially visible, and indeed significant, action.

What is important in this context is that women are acclaimed to have more influence than men. Men and women recognize and acknowledge this and even say that men and women in Marulan are equal, but they still cleave to an ideology of male dominance. Most sentiments expressed by women or men open with the comment that women and men are equal. It was only in the expansion of views, or in riders to them, that the ideology of male domination emerged.

According to one woman, for example, Marulan women believed male and female equality to be there:

partly because so many women in the town are working. The majority of men couldn't care less as long as things are getting done and they don't have to do them. But the majority of women prefer to have someone to lean on rather than shoulder all the responsibilities themselves.

As ever, in working through attitudes, people's responses involved a measure of confusion and incongruence. Despite the discord, immanent dispositions usually emerged. This was apparent in attitudes which either men or women often spontaneously introduced on an aspect of equality, such as whether women should be exclusively and unambiguously cast in a domestic role or whether this role could incorporate outside work and interests. For instance:

Men always have the edge over women. In Marulan though, women are not housebound, they play sport and so on and so are more or less equal. If men were really superior they would keep their wives in the house all day and she would have no separate activities or interests of her own— but they don't, so they can't be all that superior. Women here see themselves as more or less equal to men—but, well, the men have got to think they are superior.

Less complicatedly, another woman said, 'The men probably think "if the old girl has got to go out let her do something to keep her quiet" '. Some women respond critically to the mould of relationships between local men and women although they do not seek to change it, but rather to make adjustments, as the following observations demonstrate: 'Because Marulan is a labourers' town the men are fairly chauvinistic. The women work to get away from domination and to get a bit of money. Some men disapprove of their wives working because of their chauvinism.'

This last point is a sensitive one in this woman's family. She earns as much as her husband and he resents it. She said that like other men in the same position 'he finds it hard to take'. It is a threat to the superiority of his money-earning powers which has more generally diminishing social consequences for him. The traditional male right—restated as male responsibility—to work, although not denied by his wife, was obviously thought to be under challenge. Female dependence in economic spheres produces the subordination of women and simultaneously reinforces notions of the pre-eminence of men; and it was a commonly enough held view that married women ought not to join the workforce if others were thereby excluded from it (a condition which at times of unemployment virtually debars married women from entering the labour process). The CWA circulated a motion to this effect among its branches. At the meeting I attended, nobody dissented.

Rogers (1978, p. 155) proposes that where there is both ideological (notional) and behavioural differentiation between the sexes, that is men and women view themselves as fundamentally different from each other and act out different roles, there is the probability of interdependence and non-interchangeable roles. In Marulan men and women know there are such fundamental sex differences and it is obvious that there is differentiation in behaviour which is allied to differences in values and outlooks which are gender based. Everybody accepts and expects this differentiation; it is proper and it accords greater emphasis to male roles, although it is necessary to note that women do not consistently play out a subordinate status role and this too is generally recognized.

In their presentation supporting the statement of the widely held belief that men hold the power and ought to, Bell and Newby (1976) are only concerned with the husband in the control and management of the inequality of female–male relationships in marriage. This is a restricted view. Women may be subordinate but that need not imply passivity, and does not exclude women from contributing to and exercising control over the tensions inherent in the relationship.

In this study I have sought to demonstrate the potency of the traditional ideology of male dominance, even though the exigencies of daily existence may at times conflict with it. Men's position could be severely eroded by the disconformities of practice which improve and strengthen women's position. As a logical follow-on, it is women who regulate and relieve the strain inherent in the relationship by deferring to orthodoxy. Thus, by aligning their interests with those of their husbands, women defend male control and indeed replenish it. Despite the opportunities available to the women in certain social contexts, they do not seek to capitalize on the social advantages they enjoy, which would offer a challenge to this hegemonic relationship. In most contexts men have more power than women, and in those cases where this is not objectively so, women lend their support to ensure that what *ought* to be in fact *is*. The proposition that men ought to possess greater power is transformed into the belief that they do. This is a reversal of the elision proposed by Bell and Newby as legitimating male dominance. Not that they are mutually exclusive claims—to the contrary—for what is arrested for the sake of closer analysis is in fact part of the social process. The process is self-generating, as practices of everyday living carry with them meanings and values which are affirmed in experiences. It is something of a Gordian knot of belief and behaviour, although as process it is subject to adjustments and minor change over time, accommodated in order to preserve the essential nature of the relationship. And as R. Williams writes: 'while by definition it [hegemony] is always dominant, it is never either total or exclusive' (1977, p. 113). What is apparent is that the beliefs and behaviour of women and men in Marulan clearly manifest the dynamics of tradition which can be exploited so successfully in hegemony.

HAPPY FAMILIES

In the Australian domestic ideal, family is linked inextricably to home. Indeed, through women as catalysts there is a fusion of the two notions. Home is not just house, the bricks and mortar, weatherboard, slab construction or whatever, it is the dwelling transformed from being merely that by women in the family. Men are not homemakers; women mysteriously are said to have that capacity, and in bourgeois expectations should exercise it. Thus it might be equally appropriate to speak of home and of family as haven (although the same criticisms still apply). As the bourgeois domestic ideal coloured working-class views, and working-class people managed to exercise more control over the form their private life took, so the notions of home and haven became more pervasive. There is no indication, however, that in Australia's early history the oppressed working class, even though they had families and some sort of habitation (Connell & Irving 1980, pp. 126, 158–61), subscribed to the idea, let alone enjoyed the reality, of home as haven. Their oppression was not confined to working hours nor to life outside the domestic sphere.

With the end of transportation Australian society put on a more 'respectable' front, and as mercantile capitalism gained ascendancy so did the bourgeois family in its social and material setting (see Richards' comments on the strength of the Australian family and its resistance to change, 1978, p. 38). The family was invested with high value, and emphasis was given to the God's Police stereotype of women exercising a broad moral guardianship from within the family (Summers 1975). The Australian home became an inviolate institution invoked in economic, political and religious argument.

Marulan people put great store by family and the material setting of home, and thus the ideology of family is firmly set in a consumer frame. Those who cannot yet afford lounge suites, wall-to-wall carpets or central heating aim to acquire them as soon as possible. Meticulous care in housekeeping may not be a feature of 'rough' households, but they still have, for example, colour television, an assortment of domestic appliances and warmth, food and comfort. Home may be dowdy, makeshift, even chaotic, and this drops people on the social scale, but it provides the setting for family interaction. To marry is, properly speaking, to set up home.

The concept of family as haven may be a far cry from the

reality, but it is an ideal. Domestic privatization, as the withdrawal from social interaction, enhances the idea of home and family as providing a comforting retreat. Withdrawal is not always an option, however, and less so for some than for others. By way of example, one 'rough' family complained that they had no friends in town and that they were socially isolated. Even at school their children had a difficult time. This family had no car. Social insularity was forced upon them and in the foreclosure of choice their reaction was to acclaim the ideal. This instance is extreme, but there are many families who as newcomers experienced a feeling of separateness, and as a response emphasized the family focus which ultimately disinclined them to social activity. Then, prolonged separation made it difficult for them to participate. Even for those families in town who are involved in some way in district affairs, the emphasis is always on home and family. Primary responsibilities lie there, and people know them to be unfailing sources of greatest satisfaction. To abrogate these commitments is to invite censure and this rarely occurs. Needless to say, farming families are deeply committed to home and family life and this is bonded to the rural ideal.

One teenage girl from town claimed that people in Marulan got married very young because 'there was nothing else to do'. Her statement incorporates the ideal of marriage, family and home at the same time as recognizing other more pragmatic reasons which promote privatization. It is a pithy summary of the connectedness of ideal and practice. Domestic privatization feeds familism and is then embedded in its practice. It is true that young people in the district often complain of being bored. Very little is organized for them and they are not greatly encouraged to take matters into their own hands. Such organization (by selves or others) is not even very feasible as the numbers of any age group are so small. Further, transport is an ever-present problem for some of the youth and the lack of transport facilities emphasizes a family focus.

A minority make the break and leave home, going to live in either Goulburn or Sydney, with or without their parents' blessing. But when they leave most of these people are already in their late teens or early twenties. Many simply do not wait until they have the financial independence and the self-confidence to leave. They marry and stay. The pressures towards marriage are considerable. It is after all the ideal, and boredom and the promise of social independence as an adult make it an interesting alternative for young girls especially. On a general note, Cass observes that employment and education in rural parts are two factors promoting marriage at an early age for females:

Women in rural areas are much more likely to be married at younger ages than are women in urban and metropolitan regions. This is attributable to the scarcity of educational and employment opportunities for women in country areas. Those who marry at an early age are more likely to remain in the rural area, while girls seeking wider educational and occupational opportunities usually move to the bigger towns and to the coastal cities. This pattern highlights the small range of choice available to women in rural areas: induction into marriage at an early age is the most significant element in their set of life chances, while women in the cities are presented with a wider range of options, depending on their class. (1977, p. 148)

Poor employment prospects in Marulan, and in Goulburn, which has registered high unemployment over recent years, must certainly contribute to the high level of young women marrying in their teens, while the quarry opens the options for men a little more. The difficulties of employment may in fact encourage women to extend their education and training where possible, and Goulburn offers possibilities here. Further qualifications not only improve job eligibility, but the training period itself can bridge the gap between school and marriage, which is the primary and desired occupation in life for women, and which, if it offers, will interrupt and probably terminate the educational process.

Of the seventy-five women in the sample population, thirty-six (48 per cent) were married at twenty years of age, and another twenty-six (35 per cent) were married before they were twenty-six years old (see Table 7.2). In order to reduce the effects of any changes which may have occurred over time in attitudes to age at marriage, I extracted from the survey sample the figures relating only to younger women. Table 7.3 presents the ages at which people under thirty years and living in the district were wed. The numbers are small, but the same tendency towards early marriage, for women particularly, is apparent. Corroborative evidence, in which it is true there is some measure of data overlap, but which also covers people who were Marulanites but who have since moved out of the district, is provided by the Anglican Marriage Register. These figures are for 1970–77 and of course relate only to people who were members of the church flock or nominally Anglican (Table 7.4). Despite its larger attendance at

Table 7.2 Age at marriage

Age	Women	Men
20 years or younger	36	5
21–25 years	26	34
26–30 years	8	16
31 years and over	5	4
Total	75	59

Source: Random sample survey.

Table 7.3 Age at marriage—people thirty years and younger

Age	Women	Men
15	1	
16	1	
17	2	
18	1	
19	3	
20	2	2
21	1	4
22	1	1
23		1
24		
25		
26	1	
27		1
28		
29		
30		
Total	13	9

Source: Random sample survey.

fortnightly services, the Roman Catholic church in Marulan had no marriages celebrated in the same period. North Goulburn was chosen as the venue by four couples from the district who were wed. In three cases the bride was twenty, in the other fifty-one. The grooms' ages were twenty, twenty-one, twenty-nine and fifty-four. In all, this information supports the statement that women in the country marry young.

The store set by marriage emerges not only from the data on age at marriage but also from information on marital status (see Table 7.5). Of the sample population of 144 adults eight are not and never have been married. Five of this group are young men who are very likely to wed. The figures are low when considered in the

Table 7.4   Age at marriage—Anglican Church Register 1970–77

Age	Women	Men
16	2	
17	4	
18	4	
19	4	2
20	2	2
21	2	5
22	2	6
23	1	1
24		3
25		
26		1
27		
28	1	1
29		
30		
31		
32		1
33		
34		
35		1
36		
37	1	
38		
39		
40		1
41	1	
Total	24	24

light of information, drawn at around the same time, on the proportion of the Australian population which has never married although of marriageable age (Table 7.6). The same message is conveyed in the figures on divorce as the divorce rate is low. From the sample population, there were four unpartnered divorced persons living in Marulan. Not only is marriage in Marulan seen as an ideal state; in conformance with the ideal it is for life.

It is only through marriage that the ideal of home and family can be properly realized, creating fertile conditions for the subordination of women. Of course, marriage *per se* need not have this consequence, but when it is associated with an ideology of male domination and the economic and political consequences for women of a sexual division of labour as well as their role of child caring, it becomes a powerful vehicle for the transmission of

Table 7.5   Marital status

		Country		Town	
		Women	Men	Women	Men
Married:	a			1	
	b	4	2	9	7
	c	13	14	34	34
Single:	a				2
	b		2		1
	c			1	2
Divorced or	a				
separated:	b			1	1
	c			1	1
Widowed:	a				
	b				
	c	1		13	
Total		18	18	60	48

a = under 20 years; b = 21–30 years; c = 31 years and over
Source: Random sample survey.

inequality—the more so as the structure of its internal relationships is interpreted as a natural hierarchy.

Having undertaken an analysis of divergent views on the exercise of control by women and men within the family in 1975, Bryson wrote:

The outstanding finding is undoubtedly the key role of women in family decisions and activities. All the studies agree on this and it seems clear that the Australian wife/mother maintains a large measure of autonomy within the traditionally defined female realm. The husband/father apparently also maintains a large measure of autonomy in the household realm traditionally considered male, but the number of tasks he is involved in is relatively few. (p. 217)

The key words here are 'traditionally defined...realm'.

SPHERES OF ACTION

In the following discussion I examine responses in the random sample survey related to beliefs and action of both men and women, on female and male role behaviour in domestic contexts. One question concerned attitudes to married women joining the workforce, although it was not specified whether the work would

Table 7.6　Proportion of Australian population never married – 1977

Age	Men %	Women %
15–19	98.9	92.5
20–24	66.6	39.9
25–29	25.7	12.9
30–34	13.1	6.9
35–49	9.6	5
40–44	8.8	4.4
45–49	8.9	4.5
50–54	8.2	4.7
55–59	7.8	5.4
60–64	7.8	5.4
65–69	7.9	8
70–74	8.2	9.6
75+	8.1	11

Source: Australian Bureau of Statistics, *1976 Census: Population and Dwellings Cross-classified Tables*, Cat. no. 2426.0, ABS, Canberra.

be full- or part-time (Table 7.7). If the respondent felt that a woman's employment outside had an effect on her relationship with her husband, or with her children, she or he was asked to specify whether it strengthened the relationship or was detrimental to it. On the matter of wife–husband relations, there was some tendency from townspeople to disfavour women's employment but this was not very strong. Even so, beliefs that a woman's outside employment would have no effect assumed that it would not interfere with the execution of her household responsibilities. People on the land, however, believed quite keenly that a woman's place was in the home—or at least, as is the way with farmers' wives—around the home. It is useful here to recall Cockburn's findings that 'A man was no man if he could not keep a wife at home to minister to his comfort' (1983, p. 34). A positive effect of women's external employment perceived by a very small minority was the financial contribution women were then in a position to make to the family income, and a couple of working women also said that women could develop other interests, outside the home and family. Detrimental consequences ranged from those contained in totalizing statements such as 'The family is not a family unit' or 'They drift apart' or 'It puts a strain on the marriage', to quite specific problems such as 'You'd be too tired to bother with sex' and 'A woman loses her husband's respect and he exploits her'. The latter charge is also apparent in the state-

Table 7.7   Attitudes to women's working   (Does a woman's working affect her relationship with husband/children?)

	Country				Town			
	Women (n=18)		Men (n=18)		Women (n=60)		Men (n=48)	
	Yes	No	Yes	No	Yes	No	Yes	No
Relationship to husband(n)	15	2	15	3	36	24	28	20
Positive	2		2		5		5	
Negative	11		11		29		21	
Positive and negative	2		2		2		2	
Relationship to children(n)	16	2	17	1	44	15	38	9
Positive	1		2		3		1	
Negative	15		14		40		34	
Positive and negative			1		1		3	

(In three instances the answer was 'don't know'.)
Source: Random sample survey.

ment 'A woman is expected to do more than she should have to'. Predictably, neglect of household chores was a recurrent theme. As one woman said, 'You're supposed to stay in the house and do the work'.

Both town and country people generally deplore the effects on her children if a woman is working. One or two people suggested that the children might profit from an enlivened relationship as a consequence of the mother's expanded interests, but the common response was that a mother's working was bad for her children. They would be neglected. Latchkey children, unsupervised children, uncared-for children, are all the result of mothers working away from home. The assumptions embedded in this narrow range of reactions are that it is the woman's responsibility to care for the children (and there are no surprises there), but also that if the mother is absent the children will be neglected. The second assumption brooks no other possibilities than full-time maternal care of children.

The attitude that child care is a woman's responsibility is contained in the information on the ideal form of the division of domestic labour presented in Table 7.8, and in this case the data cover more than child care. In the random sample survey women and men were asked if they thought that there were certain tasks

Table 7.8   Attitudes to sex-specific domestic tasks   (Are
there certain jobs a woman ought to do? Are there certain jobs
a man ought to do?)

	Country		Town	
	Women	Men	Women	Men
There are	15	12	43	37
There are not	3	1	12	3
There are for women but not for men		5	3	7
There are for men but not for women			2	1
Total	18	18	60	48

Source: Random sample survey.

around the home which really ought to be undertaken specifically
by either wife or husband. The strong response was that domestic
responsibilities are sex specific. Very few people believed that
they were not, and it was women more than men who favoured
this view. When those who differentiated between female and
male jobs were asked to specify sex-appropriate duties, the lines
of division were easily drawn. Women's work was in the house—
cooking, cleaning, washing, ironing, mending and child care
were repeatedly cited. Men's work included house maintenance
and repairs, chopping wood, car maintenance, cleaning grease
traps and generally anything which was said to involve heavy
physical work. The division was often made along the lines of
either inside or outside, light or heavy, clean or dirty work. In
practice, of course, the tidy dichotomies break down as the
garden is more often than not woman's responsibility, carrying
shopping or moving furniture around for cleaning, and cleaning
itself can be heavy work, and changing soiled nappies must be
classed as dirty work. Of course many men do in some capacity
'pitch in' in respect of female tasks, but the differentiation of
female and male work is used and referred to as a demarcation for
action. An important point to note is that when men do 'lend a
hand' they are usually able to engage or disengage on their own
terms (see Cockburn 1983, p. 202).

Three of the townswomen who supported the idea of sex-
specific jobs said that this was not so for women but was the case
for men, and two reversed this, saying that there were no jobs
especially for men, but there were for women. Five of the country
men who believed in the differentiation said it did not apply to

women but did to men. In these cases the suggestion is that when a task is not sex specific the spouse is not only able to undertake it but can do so without eroding any gender image. For example, five men from the country category believe they have the ability and the social charter to do the same sort of domestic work as their wives. In reality it is more likely to mean *some* of the same sort of work. This may reflect their increased involvement in the domestic realm (a) because of some blurring between farm and farmstead and (b) as a counterweight to their wives' help on the farm. It certainly does not imply that they see women's domestic work *in toto* as appropriately performed by men. One townsman said that there were no jobs which a woman particularly should do and made it quite clear that by this he meant that there is nothing a man cannot do, not that it is properly a woman who performs some duties and a man others; this was unquestioned presupposition. He admitted that if for some reason he had to help, it was grudgingly.

Apart from attitudes relating to the ideals of sex-role responsibilities in the house, women were asked specifically if their husbands helped and in what ways, with housework, children and generally around the home. Their husbands were also asked if they contributed in these activities and if so how. Although there is broad agreement between men and women on the level of help given by men in housework, there is a slight tendency for women to allege that men give less help than the men say they do (see also Harper & Richards 1979, p. 187). Overall it seems that a little less than half the men in the sample help with housework. Further, the nature of the help varies noticeably between town and country populations. According to most townsmen and -women, over half the men's help was confined to 'the dishes'. A few more helped make the beds. Very few assisted in other areas. On the other hand, those men from the country category who lend a hand, do so over a wider variety of tasks. On several occasions help in three or more different tasks was cited (washing or drying up, making the bed, hanging out the clothes, shopping, etc.)

In this connection it is interesting to refer to Harper and Richards' work on the allocation of household jobs. They find that when women work outside the home, husbands tend to help more. This is not by taking on more household chores, but by doing 'a little more of the same kind of thing'.

More men help with children than are involved in any aspects of housework. Indeed most men are active to some degree in helping with the children and there is a high level of agreement between both men and women on this question. Both indicate that men's help is principally in bathing and dressing young children and driving older ones to sporting fixtures or other social activities. This type of help underscores the notion of family. For men particularly, it affirms familial bonds through contributions which are essentially pleasurable. Given the perceived structure of responsibilities, and the work routine of most people, men's role in child care need not and cannot be encompassing, and that it is in effect help or assistance should be stressed.

Very few men do not undertake the traditionally male jobs around the home—chopping wood, cutting grass and the like. Both men and women, in and out of town, attest their performance in this role.

The responses to these three questions are consonant with the expressed belief on the proper differentiation of male and female responsibilities in the domestic sphere. Around one-third of the married men in the sample do not help at all in jobs which smack of housework. The assistance given by others in helping out with a particular task or tasks is probably a gesture of goodwill, but seldom more than that—there is no thought of usurpation of responsibility. The incidence of men's help with children rises, but again it is the nature of their involvement which is significant, and it in no way detracts from the mother's primary role. Most men derive pleasure from such commitments and at the same time the paternal input enhances the ideal of family. Only one or two men cavil at performing what is in essence perceived as men's work around the home.

SEX ROLE BEHAVIOUR—THE REAL AND THE IDEAL

Pursuing the enquiry in the same vein, questions were asked separately of married couples about various aspects of family behaviour and decision-making. While in many cases the answers reflect what does, or did, occur, they are often subject to an interpretation of what behaviour ought to prevail. Generally there was agreement as to who made the decisions, but there was also a high level of disagreement which cannot be discounted.

The questions asked were:

- Who has responsibility for banking matters?
- Who has responsibility for seeing the lawyer?

- Who attends to other family business affairs?
- Who decided to buy the car?
- Who decided how to spend the last holidays?
- Who decided to buy the last household appliance?
- Who decided to buy the last furniture or furnishings?

Looking first of all at the instances of agreement between spouses as to who comes to the fore in such decision-making and in what particular connections, there is nothing surprising. Agreed joint participation on a number of matters which are major concerns of the family may to some extent run counter to the expectation of male exercise of authority in significant decisions concerning the family, particularly financial matters beyond day-to-day household budgeting. But overall there is little threat to the traditional order of decision-making in the family. Excepting decisions about purchases of household appliances, furniture and furnishings, which are patently women's domain, men were seen as exercising control. In the sample of country couples the differences were not so marked, but among town couples it was the voices of men which were identified as prevailing strongly.

The pattern of disagreement offers more food for thought. Disagreement can take one of six forms:

1 The husband claims that the responsibility for the action or decision lies with him; his wife says it is up to both.
2 The husband says it is up to both; his wife says that it is up to her.
3 The husband says it is up to him; his wife that it is up to her.
4 The husband says it is up to his wife; she says it is up to both.
5 The husband says it is up to both; his wife says it is up to him.
6 The husband says it is up to his wife; she says it is up to him.

There is a clearly discernible tendency on all but one matter (furniture and furnishings) for townspeople to devalue their spouse's contribution in action and decision-making, thereby improving their own; that is to answer according to one of the first three forms of disagreement set out above. Country people, on the other hand, do the exact opposite, that is accord their spouses more responsibility than they claim. They answer according to one of the last three forms of disagreement. Some explanation is required. I suggest that in town, while the ideology of male domination stands firm, women are often socially pre-eminent. The ideology is, therefore, being both challenged by the reputations and actions of some women and defended by the men. The challenge is neither overt nor direct, nor could it be, given the ideological commitment, but lies in the respected social presence of townswomen, and in their demonstrated (to self and others) capacity to organize and manage affairs on a business basis at home, at work and on a broader social horizon. While country women are vital to the farming enterprise, which indeed would not run so successfully without them, the image of the country men is much sounder, and there is no fear of women either throwing down or, more to the point, dropping a gauntlet.

CONCLUSION

Both men and women contribute to the reproduction of an ideology of male dominance, although there may sometimes be disjunctions between the ideology and aspects of practical reality. Marulan women escape from the dilemma that others so frequently find themselves in (that is the more they play a woman's role, the less individual freedom and responsibility they have) by upholding the ideal of male domination while seceding from it in many aspects of behaviour. But in their conservative endorsement of the ideology, by their experience of it and their presentation of it as the encompassing reality, even when they are wayward in its practice, they invest sex-role differentiation in the family and outside it with a self-sustaining force and the ideology of male dominance is legitimated in action.

The relationship between the ideology of male dominance and the ideology of family is complex; the values and behavioural expectations of each ideology are mutually reinforcing at many points. Marulan people's belief in the propriety of different and, at least in principle, clearly defined spheres of responsibility and action is apparent within the family, for although certain adjustments may be made towards an acceptance of joint undertakings in a number of realms, the traditional view of women's role, if not her capacities, is essentially unchallenged.

Janeway attributes conservatism in sex-role relationships to a fear that any alteration or change has revolutionary consequences. On the basis of what she calls a 'yes-or-no, either-or approach', any adjustment is perceived as destruction:

Negative roles, for example, which reverse the expectations and attributions of traditional roles, are much easier to assume and impute than are new groupings of traits and actions. Thus, a demand for change will often be seen as the threat to put down anything and everything old with a ruthless hand. (1977, p. 250)

At the level of major change this is persuasive reasoning, especially in the light of the very strong, even fierce defence of the interlaced ideologies of family and male dominance. But the very fear of change requires that adjustments be made, not to the principal tenets of the ideology but to some features of its practical application. And, of course, the utility of the form of particular relationships cannot be overlooked by an argument that conservatism is exclusively a self-sustaining force. Conservatism is also underwritten by the advantages conferred on certain individuals and groups who have power in any given system of relationships and who seek to retain their privileged position.

In the last two chapters I have been concerned with the power men have access to and exercise in gender relations. The social structure is, in many ways, biased towards male privilege and power, but these circumstances are defended and recreated by individuals—men and women. Women are aware of their own subordination and the power which men may and do exercise, but they assent to the principle of male domination. For some, and for a variety of very material reasons, there is no 'choice', but others, not subject to the same material pressures, also endorse the principle.

CHAPTER EIGHT

TRIAL BY FIRE

Over the years the Marulan district has been scathed by flood and fire. Both have claimed lives and in such crises the population is drawn together. Prolonged stress such as drought also has a bonding effect on the subject population although, lacking a commonly experienced and heightened peak, its social impact may be less focused and discernible.

My first experience of bushfire in the district alerted me to aspects of the social behaviour it generates. On that occasion our holding was strategically important. It became the field control point—the centre from which labour was directed and resources distributed. The figures in the landscape were men.

It was apparent that while the fire burned there was always work for men of all ages. It was not a place for women. Not only my husband but my 12- and 14-year-old sons were swiftly recruited. Yet when, with my daughter and a female friend, I offered my services in the field, they were declined. We worked instead where it was deemed appropriate for us—preparing food in our kitchen, which was already stacked high with mutton and corned-beef sandwiches, pikelets and lamingtons—'tucker' made by district women for the fire fighters.

Sociological interest in collective responses to disaster is usually concerned with disaster on a large scale. There are obvious reasons for this. Bigger disasters are more sensational and attract greater attention from the media and then from the public generally. They are also more likely to merit closer scrutiny on the part of government and other agencies, not only for the purpose of extending immediate relief to the victims, but in order to plan how to minimize the effects of future disasters, and in order to review organizations which can be mobilized with speed in future crises. To date it has been disaster of this magnitude which has attracted social analysis, for example the Netherlands Floods (Fritz 1961), the Arkansas tornadoes, and Hiroshima (Fritz 1961; Barton 1970), the Irish famine (Barton 1970), the Tasmanian bushfire (Wettenhall 1975) and Cyclone Tracy (Chamberlain *et al.* 1981). In discussing bushfire in the Marulan district I aim to draw on some of the findings from studies of disaster and to apply them in the context of collective stress on a much smaller scale.

Fritz's specification of disaster provides a base line for examining the Marulan instances, for although it focuses on large-scale social systems, local crises are also socially disruptive. He defines disaster as:

an event, concentrated in time and space, in which a society, or a relatively self-sufficient subdivision of a society, undergoes severe danger and incurs such losses to its members and physical appurtenances that the social structure is disrupted and the fulfilment of all or some of the essential functions of the society is prevented. (1961, p. 655)

Bushfires may be severely and extensively destructive in material and social effects. This was obviously so in the case of the Tasmanian bushfire (Wettenhall 1975) and in Victoria and South Australia in 1983.

In the instance of bushfire with which I am principally concerned, however, the period of most profound and general social dislocation was during the course of the fire, rather than subsequent to it. With smaller-scale disaster individuals may sustain heavy losses and their lives may consequently be profoundly disrupted, but vital social functions at the broader level are not impaired for long afterwards and the pattern of social interaction is quite quickly resumed.

It is useful to differentiate phases in circumstances of collective stress because differences in the nature of the impact at various moments in the crisis produce concomitant differences in social behaviour. Very broadly, there are three stages:

1   The warning stage, encompassing recognition of the imminent threat and then its onset.

2   The duration of acute stress, the period over which the disaster actually strikes.

3   The aftermath (see Fritz 1961, pp. 668–93; Barton 1970, p. 40).

This model distinguishes clearly who will respond, when and how.

Other variables obviously intersect. They include the scope or extent of the impact (including the size and type of area involved and the numbers of people and nature of property), the speed of onset, the length of time of the actual emergency and the social preparedness of those concerned (see Barton 1970, p. 41). There is also a basic difference between organizational responses and unco-ordinated help at the individual level which operates at all stages but for different reasons.

Disaster can prompt socially unacceptable behaviour, such as extreme self-centredness, panic, violence or looting, but its social effects are not necessarily negative. Considerable attention has been accorded to the unifying forces of disaster and even its socially therapeutic features (see for example Fritz 1961, pp. 683–92; Barton 1970, pp. 206–7), and it is in disaster that the notion of communion (Schmalenbach 1965) is particularly appropriate, for in the shared experience of crisis the ties and dependencies of community are thrown into high relief. Certain traditional relationships may be temporarily dislocated in the crisis period, for example status relationships may be suspended as a basis for authority. On the other hand, the differences between female and male roles are, if anything, emphasized.

Farmers in Marulan, as in so many other parts of non-tropical Australia, live in fear of summer fires. They are frequent enough occurrences in these parts of the Southern Tablelands, caused, it is often claimed, by the negligence of non-rural people. Shooters are prime suspects—they are seldom welcome anyhow and their unextinguished campfires are held responsible for starting bushfires. On one occasion two of the local volunteer fire brigade members were alerted to the presence of trespassers on their land. The locals crept up on a blazing but unattended campfire in a patch littered with beer cans. They heard shots and lay in ambush. Unfortunately the delinquent and drunken campers returned, firing indiscriminately at any object, moving or not. The locals were obliged to remain hidden and immobile for some time before they dared move to apprehend the culprits. One of the two locals concerned told me this story of a very recent event. It served to highlight and substantiate the distrust which is accorded outsiders. Apart from shooters, who are particularly blameworthy because they do other damage, there is considerable criticism levelled at the irresponsible behaviour of campers and ignorant visitors, although on the whole it is less embittered and takes the form of disdain.

EVENTS OF 1965

The unease experienced by district residents over summer months is not surprising given the frequency of fires and the damage wrought. They act as constant reminders of the most significant event in living memory affecting the district as a whole—the big bushfire of early 1965. It has become a historical marker. Present residents who lived in the district at that time form an élite in the experience of disaster. Their memory of the crisis remains clear and is recharged in the telling. Those who did not endure it or suffer its consequences in some way are, or up until the smaller fire of 1979 had been, uninitiated both in what the district has to offer, and in terms of personal involvement with large-scale fire. To fight fire attests district commitment and provides social recognition.

The fire of March 1965 took the lives of two men. It raged through virtually every part of the district and nearly through to the coast. The ash from it fell offshore for a week. The blaze is alleged to have been started from a fire made by telephone linesmen to boil a billy, despite a total fire ban. On 5 March, in high temperatures and fanned by strong winds, reaching 50 knot gale force at times, it broke out violently. At 2.00 p.m. on the 5th it was burning fiercely at Chatsbury: it had reached Greenwich Park by 6.30 p.m. on the same day. It had advanced to Marulan by 11.30 a.m. on 6 March, and then swept through the village of Tallong at 2.00 p.m. It raged for four days, and because it moved so swiftly much of the country was not completely burnt out; when the wind changed the fire licked back on itself and still found fuel. It was not until 9 March that it turned and took its toll in the Big Hill area of the district. So swiftly did it move, kilometres in minutes by some accounts, that first-hand descriptions of it are very geographically contained, and isolated individual experiences form a mosaic-like totality.

On farms individuals struggled to save what they could of their houses, stock, sheds and equipment. Everybody seems to have sustained losses of some order. Nearly all pasture was burnt out, fencing and stock losses were high, and many buildings—sheds and houses—were razed. It is not surprising that the abiding concern of the group captain of the volunteer bushfire brigade is bushfire. In 1965 he and his wife, recently married, lost everything on their farm—house, wedding presents, stock, fencing and feed. The *Goulburn Evening Post* of 9 March 1965 reported that 'Stock losses alone could easily exceed 100,000 but agricultural experts fear that many more deaths could occur through starvation on burnt-out properties'. This was for the whole fire-affected region. It was estimated that 30 000 sheep and 2000 head of cattle were burnt in the Marulan district and many hundreds of kilometres of fencing lost. The following day the *Post* published the information that 2300 bales of hay had been either received by the Department of Agriculture at Goulburn or promised for the fire-affected area, but the *Post* had already offered the salutory caution that because of the drought 'there was a limit to what could be offered' (9 March 1965).

The story of the postmistress at Brayton, a small hamlet, is illustrative of the cell-like experiences of the country residents. Brayton was a manual telephone exchange and provided the only means of communication with outlying parts of the district. The postmistress stayed at the exchange, endeavouring to keep all lines open. Linesmen had been sent to Brayton to keep the lines in repair: they clambered up and down telegraph poles which were burning at their bases and kept many phones working. The postmistress's husband, a farmer, had brought most of his sheep to a small cleared yard paddock adjacent to the house; a road nearby acted as a fire break between them and the blaze. Even so, with flying cinders and the radiant heat from the fire the fleece on some of the sheep's backs started to smoulder, and the linesmen interspersed their maintenance activities by helping to control this problem.

At one stage the township of Marulan was almost encircled by fire. People saw the threat as so severe that most men from surrounding settlements as well as many from Goulburn were desperately involved in the fight. Several people told me that because the men from Tallong and Wingello (two nearby small settlements) were at Marulan, these two places were underdefended and when the wind turned Wingello lost thirty-one buildings and Tallong twenty-eight. Marulan lost no houses in the town although the waiting shed at the railway station was burnt and townspeople saw their fences, garages and other out-buildings destroyed.

Some people evacuated Marulan. Many who stayed sought refuge in the hotel cellar. At this time the hotel had become an important centre, and the publican himself emerged as a 'natural' leader in organizing supplies of food and drink for the fire fighters. He proudly recalled that they never closed over the emergency period and that any man who came in with soot on his face was given a free drink and a ham roll.

This bushfire had long-term consequences and provided a catalyst in the lives of some locals. Most farming families had been experiencing lean times. Relentless drought and the rural recession created severe pressures. The fire decided the future of many people, who then moved off the land either to work for others or to take jobs in town. One woman said, 'It put the finishing touches to us. We just went backwards'. Other stayed; they took out further loans and set about re-establishing their farming enterprises. One couple told me that they had just finished paying off the loan which they needed to buy out the property from other members of the husband's family when they 'had to start all over again'. He took on shift work at the quarry, farming in his spare time. Others recounted that it was only recently that they had been able to pay off their overdrafts.

Everyone suffered in some measure, but small farmers felt the long-term consequences of the fire most severely, despite the comments of an upper-status person who said: 'A lot of people used it as an excuse to pass over existing failures. A lot of people made out of it. Really, the bigger you were, the harder you fell.' There is no doubt that many small-scale farmers were in a precarious position before this time, but simply to assess losses on the basis of scale ignores the recuperative benefits which attend occupation of certain class positions. Most small farmers were uninsured, unlike the owners of larger enterprises, and despite government emergency aid they could either not obtain the level of financial help which was necessary for rehabilitation or, if they could, many were fearful of indebting themselves to that degree. Past experience and realistic appraisals of future chances promp-ted extreme caution in money matters. These people were petty bourgeoisie, but in terms of capital accumulation they were really sustaining a way of life rather than running a business.

For many, of course, any style of life other than farming was inconceivable. They stayed on their farms and endeavoured to meet immediate expenses by taking on contract work—fencing, shearing and the life. While this provided some cash flow it reduced the time they could spend restoring their own farms, which were economically marginal at the best of times. This new turn of events, with a very heavy burden of replacement expenditure, ensured a continuing low level of productivity for this scale and type of enterprise. It was those already economically advantaged, with a range of options open to them because of their wealth, knowledge and network of connections, who could save or extricate themselves from this predicament. Moreover, in such cases it is likely that the disaster encouraged further rationalization (see Wettenhall 1975, p. 239).

In two instances at least, the economic pressures following the fire gave rise to circumstances which women later interpreted as a form of liberation from the domestic bondage of their farms. Both high- and low-status farming families were affected, and in these instances, after the initial rehabilitation period during which they helped re-establish the farms as operating concerns, the women went out to work to support the economic good of the family. Had the fire, in association with the drought and rural recession, not had such economic impact, the women said they would never have taken this step. Yet it opened up new areas of interest for them and allowed a feeling of independence. One of them said that the fire let part of her develop. Before that she had merely and mechanically done what was expected of her. In going out to work she discovered satisfaction and enjoyment in her own efforts.

The physical and social face of the district changed. Brayton, for example, was extinguished, it ceased to exist as a hamlet. Its losses in the fire included church, hall and school, none of which were rebuilt. Moreover the manual telephone exchange was incorporated into the automatic network and the post office was closed down. Much of the land sold by farmers who decided they could no longer make a go of it went, not to other existing farming enterprises, but to city people. Towards the end of the 1960s the general land boom had started and was a further encouragement to sell. Some farming families who had thought they could hang on were tempted by the high prices offered for land and decided to get out. They sold to developers and individual buyers. Subdivisions were passed by the council. More than 6000 hectares of relatively small holdings had been sold to commuter farmers by the end of 1969, and by the end of 1973, when the boom was in full swing, Pitt Street and hobby farmers had taken over more than 22 500 hectares.

The fire did not trigger totally new developments. It accelerated changes already in train. The farming population had been dwindling, with the ranks of small-scale farmers thinning out. There appeared little justification for rebuilding such a small community centre as Brayton. Motor cars had already made it relatively easy to go to Goulburn for shopping and entertainment. That part of the district wound down as a community with an independent social life.

FIRE: 1979

There have been many subsequent fires in the district. At the end of 1977 one burnt for three weeks in inaccessible country. None has approximated the disaster of 1965. In February 1979, however, there was an outbreak of threatening proportions which did considerable damage to local properties; altogether the fire swept through 96 000 hectares, including over 47 000 hectares in the Big Hill and Brayton areas of the Marulan district (Bushfire Council of New South Wales). Members of our family were directly involved in this crisis.

Whereas the 1965 fire unambiguously falls into the category of disaster, the 1979 event, because of its limited social scope, does not, and is more properly described as a social crisis. Yet the threat was there and hundreds of people were involved, although the disastrous impact was felt by only a very small group in the district. Even so, it incorporated on a small scale many of the social responses associated with large-scale disaster.

The crisis was the outcome of more than one fire. The first started on the Chatsbury side of the Cookbundoon Ranges, on Saturday 10 February, allegedly ignited by a spark from a drilling rig. The second, not far away, was reported to have resulted from a lighted cigarette thrown from a car around noon on Sunday. A wet spring had encouraged vigorous growth, and a very dry summer created optimum fire conditions. Initially the fire fighters tried to hold the fires in the rugged country of the Cookbundoon Ranges. Their efforts were largely successful with one of the fires but the odds were against them in the other, which moved from Chatsbury through heavily timbered ridge country. Men fought the blaze through Sunday and Monday and tried to backburn at night. Ironically this strategy failed because of heavy dews. On Tuesday morning a fierce wind of 40 knots blew up and the temperature soared. At one end the fire—the previous evening's backburn which had not backburnt—flared up, presenting a fierce front and spotting over many kilometres at a time. At the other end a dozer making a fire trail sent out sparks as it hit rock and another conflagration whipped away out of control. The front was many kilometres long and the sky ominously coloured. When the fires broke, jumping the fire fighters at one end, any real endeavours at co-ordinated and organized suppression of them collapsed. Some people returned to do what they could on their own places, others dispersed in scattered groups. Overnight, wind and weather changed, bringing relief, although the fires continued to burn along slightly altered courses and into other districts through Tuesday night and Wednesday. On Thursday they flared up again, although the worst was over by that time and the organization became more effective. An emergency situation (referred to as a 41 F, under the Bush Fires Act) had been declared by the Shire Fire Control Officer at 9.00 a.m. on Tuesday and was not lifted until 5.00 p.m. on Monday 19 February, when the fire was clearly suppressed or under control.

One man in the fire-fighting force was killed just outside the district. In the Marulan district itself three houses, several sheds, equipment and kilometres of fencing were lost. Stock losses were fortunately minimized because, as the fire had threatened for a couple of days before it broke, people were able to yard or bring most of their animals to home paddocks. The greatest effect felt by most people was the loss of pasture. Paddocks of feed, tall and dense because of the excellent spring growing conditions, literally went up in smoke.

FIRE FIGHTERS: FORMAL STRUCTURES AND INFORMAL PARTICIPATION

Wettenhall (1975, p. 44) records that the Australian volunteer bushfire brigade movement was established around 1900 as a response to the ever-present threat of bushfires. In New South Wales membership numbers around 69 000 fire fighters from nearly 2500 registered volunteer brigades. Overall authority is vested in the Bush Fire Council of New South Wales—a statutory body constituted under the Bush Fires Act 1949—which works in conjunction with local government councils. Apart from the administrative office bearers, there is a hierarchy of field officers. To locals they represent the real chain of command and constitute the fire élite. The senior bushfire officer in a council area is the Fire Control Officer (FCO), appointed by the local council. Group captains are responsible to him, and brigade captains to their respective group captains. Thus in Marulan the hierarchy is FCO, the group captain and his deputies and then the brigade captains and their deputies. Whereas the chain of command is rigidly observed from the level of group captain down— all of whom are locals—the FCO appears irrelevant in much of the fire fighting. He is not a local and therefore does not have the intimate district knowledge which is critical in overall planning and for organizing responses to specific and localized problems. He does not fight fire but is more a bureaucrat. In some shires the FCO works on a voluntary basis. Here, he is a paid employee of the shire council. His salary is taken out of the total fund allocated to council for bushfire fighting and thus reduces the amount left to maintain and buy equipment. This is advanced as a reason for local dissatisfaction. In all respects he is seen as an outsider, and although he is the most senior and responsible officer, everyone says that the real work is done in the field.

The Big Hill Brigade saw itself performing the key role in the 1979 fire and this was apparent in the earlier stages and again in the final days. The outbreak was in its area of responsibility, its members had knowledge of the country, and it was their property which was immediately at risk. All the office bearers and most of the members of this brigade are farmers—and nearly all are small-scale farmers. One or two members have houses and land in this section of the district but they work elsewhere and do not farm; the membership also includes a number of commuter farmers, of whom only some were present.

Big Hill Brigade was very soon joined by the Marulan Brigade. Its members are townsmen and farmers. Yet many non-member townsmen were quick to offer their services as they do when there is fire in the district. Men who are employed at the quarry are given time off to fight fire if it is in their part of the district, and their pay is not stopped so long as they can present a receipt signed by the brigade captain attesting their presence. Other employees with no vested property interests also fight fire in off-duty times and self-employed townsmen turn up. This latter category, which includes shopkeepers and truck owner-drivers, was not threatened immediately by the 1979 fire but many joined in the fire fighting even though, as their own income-earning activities were suspended, they stood to lose economically.

In crisis the community coheres and membership of it is countersigned in visible participation in events of the moment. In these circumstances behaviour acknowledging status differences is much diminished and the differences themselves are only as relevant as individuals like to maintain them—most do not choose to. Social divisions are not wiped out in crisis, for there is still some restraint in interaction, but they need not inhibit a reframed working relationship in which the hierarchy of status yields to other organizational forms with a different authority structure. Yet not all upper-status men participated. This is not a direct reflection of their status, immediately removing them from the hurly burly of action, but rather of their lack of commitment to others in the district, tempered by status considerations. That is, in the normal course of life some upper-status people have little or no association with lower-status groups here, and therefore their identification with the district community is minimal. For them it is an area of productive country rather than a social system in which they interact. Those upper-status men who did turn up identify strongly with the district and its people. Even so, there was a time lag before they came to help fight the fire—for some the delay lasted a couple of days after general mobilization. Directed by the fire captain in the area, the more sensitive fought alongside others where they were asked.

In many ways fire fighting has the nature of a social occasion attracting attendance. This is more obvious when the pressure is reduced. Presence is both prestigious and, if one's property is not at stake, in some measure enjoyable, particularly in hindsight as a fire provides a talking point long after its extinction. There is discomfort and fatigue, sometimes exhaustion and danger, but against and perhaps heightened by all this there is a feeling of excitement and togetherness. The glamour alleged (at least from a distance) to attach to the warfront exists in fire fighting. In fact the scene has been likened to one of battle on several occasions. There is of course the pall of smoke which hangs over everything and out of which men and equipment loom. There is also the behaviour which looks to an outsider like the confusion of battle, in the apparently random but purposeful movement of men. When the fire is burning fiercely there is also considerable noise—great explosions when a new stand of timber ignites.

As with any fire of threatening proportions, other formal organizations were involved. After the initial phase of fire fighting, units were called in from other parts of the shire and adjacent shires. Then, when conditions deteriorated further, units were also called in from Wollongong, other parts of the coast and from Sydney areas. The FCO also called for assistance from Goulburn and Berrima gaols and on Tuesday squads of volunteer minimum security prisoners joined the fighters. They were accompanied by prison officers, although at the fire they were allowed to separate and were put under the control of the chief fire officer who then deployed them as he saw appropriate.

Equipment is bought from monies allocated by the New South Wales Bush Fire Fighting Fund. The allocation is made up by a contribution of 25 per cent from government, 25 per cent from local council and 50 per cent from insurance companies. Marulan is not particularly favoured in this respect, for the total amount is determined by the council's contribution which is based on a maximum of 1/48 cent in the dollar on the unimproved capital value of rateable land in the council's area. This is not a big shire and it encompasses large tracts of scrub and rugged country. The low equipment vote is also in part attributable to the paid employment of the FCO. It is also true that in the past the local back-up organization has provided little in the way of extras.

In 1979 the two brigade tankers serving this district did not rate well against those from other districts. The events of that fire were cautionary and Marulan soon had a new tanker. Half the money was given by Blue Circle Southern Cement and half raised by the efforts of district residents, by donation and in fund-raising social activities. The Big Hill vehicle was (and remains) a temperamental old six-wheel drive with the potential of being a liability. Fortunately Big Hill now also boasts a new fire truck.

Apart from the few men who work a tanker, other brigade members fight fire with knapsack sprays, McLeod tools (a heavy rake/hoe) and, as the latter are in short supply, wet bags and at times branches. At the brigade level it is a fairly primitive operation, relying heavily on labour power which by itself and in the face of a large fire is but a token gesture. Fortunately some other equipment is also available. Some of the big local land-holders have their own tankers and others mount small tanks on the back of utilities and trailers and connect pumps to them. Bulldozers may be provided by the council and possibly by government departments such as Main Roads. Even so, the primary emphasis is on men, particularly when the fire fighting is in rough country.

Operating radio sets confers prestige upon the users, but this is perhaps the most contentious equipment. Each of the brigades has two Very High Frequency (VHF) sets which are used in the field. More than any other aspect of organization, the use of radio invokes ritualistic behaviour. It is perhaps the most important means of communication, although there are several factors mitigating its efficiency, and indeed some of the men state that it is a positive hazard. A fundamental problem lies in the military model for its usage. In the use of radio, language changes and becomes ritualized, which in itself sometimes obscures meaning, or at least clutters it up, but the problems extend beyond vocabulary. Radio users become very self-conscious, and in their efforts to comply with expectations of stereotypical behaviour and to express themselves clearly in the unfamiliar language, they can transmit precise but often unintended messages. Inevitably a lot of checking has to take place.

In the last couple of years some further bureaucratization in the use of radio has been instituted which finds no favour with field officers, who see this as a clerical decision. Now field units may not communicate directly with each other, but all messages must be directed through base. In terms of centralizing control the logic is apparent, but it does lead to some frustrating episodes. Unit A, for example, wants to get a message to unit C, but can only do it through Base. C, on the same channel, can of course overhear A transmitting to Base but must wait for Base to relay the information, and then in turn C's answer to A—which A has already overheard. It is not uncommon, with the extra input in the system, for messages to be passed incorrectly, although as both end parties can hear and are aware of the error it then becomes just a matter of time and tidying up for the official record. There is room for further vexation, for apart from units from neighbouring districts on the same radio band, visiting volunteer units are on different channels and cannot usually communicate with each other. Nor can the visiting helpers speak with other local units or even the control station in Goulburn; once out of sight at the fire they are also out of contact and rely on motorized despatches. This is obviously a limitation on the already strained communication system.

Being a woman, I was never present at the 'front' and hence relied on a number of interviews, gossip and snatches of conversation for my information. One of the more astute observers gave a stratified model of local participation at the 1979 fire, one cross-cutting the system normally in operation. He distinguished first of all the fire élite—those members of the local volunteer bushfire brigade who hold office and have access to superior equipment—particularly radio. In this instance the fire élite were the small farmers. It is this group which responds immediately to the sight and smell of smoke. The next division was 'the infantry', comprised principally of the rank and file of the local brigades. They used mainly knapsacks and McLeod tools, and did most of the hard physical work, deferring to the brigade captain or his deputy in this area. Then came 'the boys'. This category subdivides into two: first the parasites who drifted, according to my informant, from 'group to group, tea to tea, pikelet to pikelet'. Second, there was a highly conspicuous but independent group of mostly young men, some of whom had brought their own supply of alcohol. They were hard workers but did not usually seek or welcome direction. Above all, my informant said, they preferred to be doing their own backburn. He also drew attention to, and placed at the bottom of the scale, those people who were aware of what was happening but contributed nothing—the non-participators.

WOMEN'S ROLE IN CRISIS

Women do not go out to fight fires. Excepting the very old, no other category of adults is so completely without participant representation. There is no question of their going with the men or wielding any sort of fire-fighting equipment at 'the front'. As long as the fire is not immediately threatening their properties they move into their acknowledged sphere of action, which is preparing food for the fire fighters. They do this both individually and collectively. Women, supporting the men in one or two brigades in the adjacent districts, usually go to a rear base and distribute food, but this does not happen at Marulan, although the practice is to be reviewed. One woman from the town, in association with two Goulburn men, usually establishes herself as a first-aid centre somewhere near the action. This is not part of the formal structure of fire-fighting organization, however, and although men go to her for attention to minor injuries, her contribution receives only minimal acknowledgement.

Fire fighting is clearly not an arena in which women participate at a visible level. Everyone knows and accepts the reason: the task is challenging and strenuous, one requiring strength, stamina, grit and guts, qualities which are stereotypically male, and therefore antithetically exclusive of females. By the demonstration of these qualities in the crisis, indeed by just being in these circumstances, fire fighters achieve some kudos, which in turn reinforces the worth of the male image.

If the fire is not quickly suppressed and the crisis drags on, demanding a heavy and continuing labour input, then the burden, for farmers' wives particularly, also increases. The need for food supplies and refreshments remains, while some farming activities must be continued. In the absence of farmer and any other male labour, it usually falls to the women of the family to move temporarily into what are generally perceived as male roles, in order to do the jobs that cannot be postponed. Extra farm work is often a consequence of a fire threat, for stock scattered over various paddocks must be brought in to safer parts, and to areas from which they can be quickly mustered and yarded if the fire is close. As well, if in the fire path, the house and other buildings and equipment must be made as defensible as possible. Ironically, if it comes to the worst, this defence might be the responsibility of those female members of the family left at home. Thus women are excluded from participation in the forefront of the crisis in which social credit attends visibility, although their co-operation and participation is required at a less prestigious level. They contribute to what is generally viewed as the support system, both directly in catering and indirectly by keeping things running and by temporarily filling 'male' roles. Because it is only on a short-term basis that they undertake what are traditionally viewed as male tasks, they offer no challenge to the basically male character and management of these roles.

Direct participation in the formal arena of disaster is, however, a male preserve, and all able-bodied men are eligible. Except in the early stages of mass assault in response to other types of disaster which involve little warning time, I suspect this may be generally so. Women's services, as they offer what again is generally seen as specific sex-role competence, may be called on as part of the organizational response helping victims of disaster, but it is not usual for women actively to be engaged in any front-line organization, in the heat of the moment or after it. This view is in line with the argument presented by Chaney (1975, pp. 475–6), working in the broader arena of cross-cultural analysis of women— particularly in public affairs. She says that women tend to become active only in times of extreme challenge, and return to inaction when the crisis is past. There are calls on women's help in an emergency but this does not legitimate or institutionalize their permanent collaboration on an equal basis with men.

Analysis of the level of organization and participation of women during war offers an illuminating analogy on the exclusive nature of male activities in social crisis. (It is not an argument for the extension of women's responsibilities in war.) Even on the home-front there has been hostility to their involvement in war duties. Harrisson, writing of the blitz of London in the Second World War says:

Looking back from these Women's Lib seventies, the failure to use women in certain blitz situations seems astonishing. The feminine role in dealing with civilian and especially household problems emerges as grotesquely small. Matters of war were still planned by and for the male. (1976, p. 201)

Apart from drawing attention to the essential maleness of war, there are two points in this excerpt which require further comment. While the situation Harrisson describes seems ridiculous, it is indeed questionable just how far the exclusiveness of traditional roles in disaster broke down in the 1970s and even the 1980s. Moreover, the author himself seems to suggest that the female role should appropriately be a development of traditionally accepted and womanly activities.

Other writings concerned with war and women's role in it support the hypothesis that during times of crisis women are organized to perform auxiliary tasks. Ideally the duties are usually an extension of traditional womanly work, but women can and do move into what are commonly seen as male spheres of activity (Calder 1969, p. 194; Rupp 1978; Shute 1980, and even earlier during the First World War, Braybon 1981). This potentially volatile situation is, however, defused by recognition of its impermanent nature.

What becomes especially clear in the context of crisis is how the separation of male and female jobs is part of the ideology of male superiority which masks the real contributions women may and do make.

THREAT OF DISASTER, REALITY OF CRISIS: HUMAN RESPONSES

Like many other disasters, bushfires do not necessarily strike speedily, and this has an effect on the social behaviour associated with disaster which is related not only to the speed of onset of the fire but also to the scope and duration of impact. As it affected Marulan, the 1979 fire was relatively prolonged in its early phases but did not ever reach what would be termed socially disastrous proportions, and although some relief for fire victims was organized, a good deal took place on an independent and informal level as other unaffected members of the district, as individuals, spontaneously extended aid to those who had suffered.

With the memory of the 1965 fire ever present, people's awareness and fear of the potential for destruction of this sort of crisis was heightened, and the prevailing weather conditions magnified the threat. The scale of destruction which did occur constituted a relief to most people because it was considerably less than menaced. Yet the threat was prolonged. It was nearly three days before the district felt the fury of the fire; conditions remained critical for the following four to five days until it was clear that the blaze was well under control and unlikely to break out again—although it is true that nervous apprehension and stress were not as keen during this second period. The threat, however, persisted. The heat was great, smoke could be seen for many kilometres, and the smell of fire travelled over considerable distances, so that even those who were not at the fire itself, nor really likely to be imperilled by it, were infected by an anticipatory dread. During the waiting time, when the men were fighting the fire, contact between women intensified, particularly between those in the area thought to be endangered, but also among others who, by virtue of their district association, felt themselves involved. A high degree of mutual support became apparent in behaviour and in expressions of concern. Telephone calls (when the lines were working) increased, as did personal contact as women gathered to make or deliver food. The increased and intensified interaction was supportive but at the same time it sustained the level of suspense.

The prolonged period of onset in this case overlapped with the period of duration. From the beginning men fought the fire; as long as the fire was burning in the Cookbundoons, and it seemed that measures could be taken to contain it, it remained only in the onset stage. Yet this coincided with the early stages of the emergency. Because there is always a high level of preparedness in the district, attitudinally if not in material resources, the immediate response to the crisis from members of the local bushfire brigades was organizational but small-scale.

Even when the emergency became more acute it took some time for the organizational response to upgrade and cohere, and as the FCO alerted other agencies and called in the human and material resources at his disposal the approach became segmental. This was dictated by the terrain, and the scale and unpredictable nature of the fire. Individual responses to the crisis were slotted into this segmental organization which, after the early onset period, was loosely incorporated into a broader organized approach. The view of authorities such as the FCO is that the response was by formal organizations, yet in practice this frequently broke down to the independent actions of individuals and men in groups. Barton's comments on reasons for the breakdown of the organization of behaviour at various levels in an emergency social system are relevant here (1970, p. 127). Such breakdown may occur 'at the small-group or organizational level, because roles are not adequately co-ordinated for disaster conditions; or at the community level, because organizations are not adequately channelled'. In 1979 at the brigade level roles were co-ordinated both within and between brigades, the members of which are known to each other. The difficulties arose with the contributions of brigades from other areas, outside work units (for example prisoners) and individual volunteers. All are controlled ultimately by the FCO and in the field by the local fire officers from the relevant group or brigade, but they do not necessarily act in a co-ordinated fashion.

When the pressure was acute, unfamiliarity with the geographical area, with social networks and even uncertainty in individual relationships as well as the confounding effects of radio, all promoted a measure of fragmentation in response. When the direct threat was reduced, for instance when weather conditions became more favourable and the fury of the fire dissipated, co-operation was better controlled, and individual and group action adequately channelled. This was evident when big backburns were planned and executed at night later in the week. The heat had gone out of the moment and there was time to organize. Large numbers of men assembled as instructed and the operation was successfully carried out. It was not the case, however, when the fire was raging on Tuesday.

Organization at the small-group level collapsed on Tuesday with the fire breaking at both ends, jumping the fire fighters in one area. Clearly nothing could be done to contain it from the established field bases. The organized front disbanded at that point. The members of the Big Hill brigade also realized that their own properties were endangered and individually they returned to defend them as best they could. It took some hours for anything like co-ordinated effort to be re-established. As the fire swept on it was very much a series of separate stands made by small and independent groups of people. A party of prisoners saved one house, in other instances individuals battled to preserve their property. Along this section of the fire front no one knew what had happened to the organized groups of fire fighters or to any tanker.

The natural factors of adverse weather conditions at the time, the local geography and the unpredictability of the fire itself combined with the problems of co-ordinating individual and group roles to give rise to circumstances in which at one level the organization response disintegrated; it had been for most of the period of onset and duration only loosely articulated. Only after the height of the emergency passed was the organizational response sustained and effective, and even then it appeared to be of low order. The Big Hill brigade rallied to some degree to keep a watching brief on their already devastated area, although this was largely a matter of individual action. Many foreign units went home, others were sent to fight the fire which had moved out of the district, some continued patrolling. The organization was most obvious in the preventative measures of controlled back-burns in the aftermath of the main fire.

AFTERMATH ASSISTANCE

Relative to the tense and explosive conditions of the onset and duration stages the subsequent period was low key. Immediate assistance on an informal and independent basis was offered by members of the district community to people who suffered loss. Shelter, food, clothes and blankets were given to those in need; locals delivered hay for animals and were quick to offer agistment and other sorts of help. The needs of people and stock were thus swiftly met by district neighbours. Two service organizations from Goulburn were also quickly off the mark. Organizational response from bigger bureaucracies, which involved a collective contribution and invoked weightier administration, was inevitably more unwieldy and slower than the spontaneous and direct response of individuals and the service clubs, although the bigger bodies were able to offer help on a larger and more sustained scale. In this case the State Emergency Service and the Department of Agriculture organized a hay drive, but it was several days before the feed could be delivered and had it not been for local informal help, stock would certainly have suffered.

People may be moved to offer assistance either through sympathetic or moral obligation (see Barton 1970, pp. 238, 268–9). Sympathetic identification encompasses:

- primary group association—it was obvious how families rallied around
- secondary group association—in this case district residency
- emotional identification sympathy based on perceived similarity of victim and helper.

All three orientations motivated offers of help to fire victims. A moral obligation to help was most clearly evident in the reaction of some large-scale landowners. The obligation was, however, contingent on district or at least regional associations, and thus in some measure overlaps with secondary-group identification. One high-status grazier surveyed the damage a couple of days after the emergency, then took cattle on agistment (free of charge) and delivered hay to the impact area. Another large landowner avowed that it was the responsibility of his ilk to offer help in such circumstances. In the hay drive organized by the State Emergency Services and Department of Agriculture, the biggest grazier in the region donated 1500 bales out of a total of 2500 received. After the fire the state government provided relief to bushfire victims in the form of road and rail freight concessions of 50 per cent for transporting feed to fire-affected stock and for moving stock from a fire-affected property. The Rural (State) Bank also made available to victims of this (and other) bushfires, concessional interest rate loans, repayable over a long period.

CONVERGENCE

Possibly as a result of the limited scope of damage to people and property, and because of the extended time-span of the emergency, problems of convergence, so often beleaguering operations in an impact area, were virtually absent. It is true that in the duration period hundreds of volunteers arrived in the area, but this was so extensive that labour power was never in excess or numerically so great as to be embarrassing. The potential for independent action, particularly given a loose organizational framework, resulted in the ready absorption of volunteer efforts during and after the fire. There were relatively few sightseers and they were apparent after the crisis, but there was no great influx of material help, as there was no public appeal for anything but hay. Human material needs were coped with on an individual basis.

Apart from what might be termed disaster tourism, personnel convergence is usually associated with offers of help or some kind of contribution, either in the form of expertise, or in official visits by those whose presence may have symbolic meaning, for example in restoring morale, providing publicity and so on (see Wettenhall 1975, p. 219). Certainly the local MP and officials from concerned government agencies visited and/or flew over the area. There is obviously a social investment in doing this; sympathetic interest is attested to by a visit to key areas or even by some measure of participation in the action, and audience appreciation of visible involvement generally results in an improvement of social and political stocks. Such gain may not be recognized as the sole reason or even the underlying motivation for attending the crisis scene, yet it must be accepted as a consequence and it may be intended.

Another form of convergence behaviour was manifest, which reaped negative returns. Some district residents came to view the crisis on different occasions, not in order to help, but to assess threats to their own properties. They were then considered spectators and outsiders.

COMMUNION

The development of communion (see Schmalenbach 1965) among the affected and participating population is a predictable and significant social response to all sorts of disaster.

Fritz claims that conditions of stress generate feelings of belonging and unity which are not experienced under normal circumstances. He emphasizes the values which emerge in what he describes as socially therapeutic adjustments:

The widespread sharing of danger, loss and deprivation produces an intimate, primary group solidarity among the survivors, which overcomes social isolation and provides a channel for intimate communication and expression and a major source of physical and emotional support and reassurance. (1961, p. 689)

This heightened sense of interpersonal and district commitment was evident during and immediately following the fire of 1979. It constituted a central element in the spontaneous manifestation of the order of relationships referred to as communion.

Schmalenbach warns of the confusion which arises when an awareness of the connections and dependencies of the given and what he terms natural, bonds of custom and tradition, embracing blood and other relationships which coalesce in time and space to form the basis of community, are not analytically separated from the experience of feelings of belonging, that is of communion.

In recognizing their interdependence, community members acknowledge the pre-existence of the community. Mutual reliance is sometimes recognized as direct and strong—as against the continuing threat of natural disaster—and sometimes as diffuse and weak—such as the support for district, over outside events and interests. The acceptance of communal ties may contribute to hegemony, when the position of the powerful in the district is supported in ideal and material ways. In the range and types of bond, however, it goes well beyond what might be described as an element of hegemony—in this and other contexts. Traditional ties need not give rise to any particular feelings although some sentiments may be engendered by and directed towards the community. Whatever the case, such 'feelings are simply subsequent forms of experience at the level of consciousness. They are *products* of community' (Schmalenbach 1965, p. 335). Communion, on the other hand, emerges through emotion, although by its nature it is a transitory social phenomenon: it does not persist outside the events and acts which give rise to it. It may thus give way to a community order, not in direct metamorphosis, but by the recognition of pre-existing bonds.

In the common threat it presented, the fire drew people together in shared emotional experiences. Initially involvement was on a district communal basis; others were then drawn into the action. Feelings of communion developed among locals, and among outsiders and between both categories of people, in fact wherever the interaction of people was heightened by stress and excitement borne of common purpose. Those who remained outside, not only the area of activities, but aloof from participation at any conscious emotional level, had no part in the communion. Those women of the district, either directly or even more indirectly involved by the threat, who were emotionally drawn together over loaves of bread or the telephone, were members of the communion of fire even though they were personally absent from the centre of action. They became members by socially pooling their concern and commitment. After all, it is only when there is recognition of the shared experiences and emotions that communion can be said to exist. The unity and solidarity is produced by conscious association.

As Schmalenbach says, 'every experience of communion has the effect of establishing communal bonds' (1965, p. 337) and may heighten awareness of community. In this instance, after the intensity and excitement had passed, district residents who went to fight fire or shared in the communion in some way had, by their very participation, reaffirmed, in some cases redefined, their roles as members of the community. Outsider volunteers who experienced communion were none the less strangers to the district. They departed straight after the emergency and their presence left no social mark.

On the other hand, non-participant district members whose absence was either apparently unnoticed or taken as an indication of their indifference, were of course excluded from the feelings of communion, and this endorsed their communal invisibility and social marginality in district eyes. The limited scope of this crisis allowed most people to retain their privacy if they wished and thus made communion much more a matter of choice than in many disasters where the impact is extensive, making public and general people's experience of disaster. The communion of fire, while itself a passing order of quite intense social relationships, redefined district ties and made them more visible, and then gave way to the traditional interdependence of the district community.

CONCLUSION

Because of their impact, disasters become historical markers, reference points in time for other events (see Fritz 1961, p. 692). Their significance also stems from the social changes which so often attend diaster, wherein the style of community living, as well as the lives of individuals, are frequently altered. Social changes of this order followed the devastating 1965 fire. On the other hand, the fire of 1979, which because of the limited scope and nature of its impact I have termed a crisis rather than a disaster, does not look as if it will have long-term social consequences for the district as a whole. It was none the less an event which had general district significance at the time. For some period the threat was shared and recognized by most district members. The circumstances of crisis were experienced collectively. Most individuals were drawn into the drama, and the social scope of experience of the crisis was widespread. As such it falls into the range of those 'collective representations or symbols by which past, present, and future happenings become rated and dated' (Fritz 1961, p. 691).

While the crisis itself is intrinsically interesting and provides a frame for examining other dimensions of social relations, it is particularly significant in the context of this study for two reasons. First, it focuses attention on communion and through this stresses the importance of the general understanding of community which shapes perceptions of social interactions and indeed interactions themselves. Secondly, examination of behaviour during the emergency glaringly highlights the strength of gender and other divisions. The quiddity of the collective of fire-fighting men is never sullied by female participation and, although a temporary group, it is visible and memorable. In times of stress women also may shoulder different social responsibilities on a temporary basis, but these have no visible, nor it seems memorable, social impact. Their exclusion from the central and prestigious collective does not debar them from the communion but accords them a secondary position. Anthropological analyses have demonstrated the effectiveness of ritual in affirming and legitimizing what is understood as the proper form of social relations. The ritualization of gender divisions during the fire does just that: it underwrites male dominance.

In the social drama of the fire a new and unstable social order emerged in which there were no established barriers to some form of membership and certain traditional social cleavages were at least briefly reduced. Many were involuntarily drawn in simply by living in the directly threatened or impact area. Others committed themselves intentionally. The difference between intended and unintended association, in the circumstances giving rise to communion, is significant only inasmuch as some involuntary members, as fire victims, retained the spirit of communion beyond the period of actual emergency. As the conditions of crisis giving rise to the establishment of a communion of fire recur frequently, although in different parts of the district, so does the structure of intended and unintended subscription alter.

Individuals may purposefully commit themselves directly, that is, by volunteering their services in response to a particular event, or indirectly by their membership of organizations formally or informally established to provide assistance in such emergencies. In the 1979 fire another, albeit small, category emerged—those who despite their physical presence in the district intentionally remained outside the communion of fire—a communion which in its passing clarified the ties of interdependence in the district community.

CHAPTER NINE

CONCLUSION

When I began this project I had not conceived it as revolving so closely around the issue of power relationships. It is true that I was intrigued by the strong social presence of women in Marulan and how this might dovetail with the more general form of female–male relationships. I was also struck by the phenomenon of country-mindedness, and I had assumed that social-class differences would be significant. I had not at that time, however, thought to emphasize the common element in all these factors, which is the exercise of power; this focus became increasingly compelling with the passage of time. Nor had I given attention to the constitutive processes of different systems of power. As I became more familiar with local social processes it became apparent how the cast of power relations in one particular form is likely to reverberate, and interactively, in other social forms. Thus gender is critical in conferring and defending men's advantages in the class system in say the patrimonial inheritance of rural land or in controlling the circumstances of employment by constructing certain work as masculine and exclusively so. No less are the experiences of women in the home and in the workplace strongly grounded in their economic disadvantage. Moreover, although dominance in class position is not dependent on high status, nor is high status an inevitable outcome of ownership and control of the means of production (for example, neither management positions at South, nor management and ownership of a service station, a shop or the motel in itself confers high status or relies on it). It is clear that people dominant in the class system use the cultural language of status evaluations to defend and justify their class position. Also, social honour can provide opportunities for individuals and collectives to consolidate and improve their class position.

The rural ideology is significant because it is a way of looking at, talking about, and experiencing life in the country, including small country towns. It is also true that through it large landholders consolidate and advance their class position. The rural idyll is at the heart of the ideology and is therefore an important element in this hegemonic form. Both large and small farmers gain from other people's positive cultural evaluations of their lifestyles, although it is questionable to what degree small landholders are able to draw material benefits from these beliefs. Certainly the scope of the farming enterprise affects the ways and the degree to which the prestige endowment can be called up to return other benefits.

In the range of power relationships gender divisions are the most intransigent because they cross-cut and interact with all other social dimensions and it is incontrovertible that the general pattern in Marulan, as elsewhere in Australia, is that men are culturally dominant and women subordinate. Social-class advantages certainly expand women's opportunities in all manner of directions and ways, but they remain subordinate to men in the same social category. Strangely, rural ideology, in its practice so dependent on the very real and positive contributions of women, requires them to have no separate and autonomous position and to be represented as secondary (see Schaffer 1988).

It is common for both analysts and actors to see arenas of power either as those which are formally constituted and in which power is exercised as a known concomitant of responsibility—a property of the system—or as those outside formal institutions of authority where one party manifestly has the capability—the might—to assert its interests over those of another. This latter and informal exercise of power may also occur legitimately or illegitimately within formal institutions. The first instance embraces government at all levels, from the state to the controlling hierarchy in a church system to an individual school. An example of the second is economic pressure on political decisions (or non-decisions) brought to bear by sections of private industry (see Lukes 1974, pp. 42–4). As a system of power, patriarchy is legitimately exercised within formal institutions, for example through state structures and state policies (see Burton 1985). It is also exercised outside formal structures in everyday interactions in families, in workplaces and in leisure activities in ways which have general acceptance. It is also manifest in unacceptable forms inside and outside formally established structures. This is patently the case with domestic violence and instances of employment discrimination. The point it that male domination in one sphere supports, even secures, its exercise in others.

Lukes argues that the exercise of power influences people in *significant ways*. But the problem here is the identification of significance, which pivots on the notion of interests—in itself problematical. It is easy enough to see determinations of state as significant; impersonal political actions are readily invested with that weight. Such import is indeed written into the general understanding of polity. This is also the case with the visible or assumed workings of large-scale economic and other social forms, ranging from the Aboriginal Rights Movement to the Women's Electoral Lobby to the Rugby League. Even when the exercise of power is latent and/or connected with managing matters so that they are not in contention, that is so that they do not become issues, it may be identified at such formal or informal levels. It is harder to recognize power exercised in social relationships which are low key and ever present (see Allen & Barker 1976, p. 5); those ordinary, that is commonplace, interactions which for most people are part of everyday social existence but which constitute and recreate its form and which are therefore socially significant. There is nothing novel in such analytical awareness, for class analysis identifies the material bases of power relations arising from ownership and control of productive property which both give rise to what are seemingly the most ordinary social forms, and recreate them. Power relations are the reality underlying social process even at the most commonplace level, where the humdrum character of social relations does not invite such interpretation. Such is the case with gender relations, which are relations of power so pervasive and so seemingly ordinary that (at least until recent decades for many, and for others still) they were generally accepted and unchallenged.

Over the period of my research several matters intruded into the measured tenor of general social existence in the district. They were the protracted dispute in the cement industry, the involvement of truck owner-drivers in a national stoppage, and bushfire. The first two instances were characterized by overt exercises of power, and were initiated outside the district. Their provocation, the course they took and their resolution, revolved around economic and political issues. These disruptions to everyday life, with the potential for social conflict at the local level inherent in them, were controlled and minimized by people's acknowledgement of the ties of community. Nobody really wanted to rock the local boat. In both instances of industrial action the impetus for the action and that which sustained it lay outside the district. Most local actors were involved under circumstances over which they were seen to have no control. The fact that the majority did not wish to exercise such control is again evidence of a specific desire to retain the status quo. The bushfire was not the result of power play but social responses to it highlighted certain power claims and relationships. It underscored the assymetry of male and female power relations which, far from presenting a threat to the structure of relationships in the community, affirms community dispositions.

Marulan people's ideas about community relationships are functionalist and conservative. It follows that they make conscious endeavours to avoid or downplay circumstances in which rifts can occur and try to minimize the rifts themselves, whether they fall along class or any other lines. The recognition of the system of interdependence, which is the stamp of community, promotes a desire for social harmony, but in Marulan (and I suggest elsewhere) the notion of community is also conscripted in the services of hegemony, for it reinforces ideological pressures through forms of traditional domination. For example the ideology of land ownership, which legitimates the inequalities of social class and gender, does so even more effectively in the setting of community.

The ownership of land and the material capability to work it profitably is generally presented, and known to be, not merely in the interests of that landholder, but of the community generally. Those who work for landholders, as well as those who are less directly affected by their economic capacity, see their prosperity as contributing to that of the district, and thereby their own. They are aware of the economic dominance of landholders and, on the whole, endorse it in their attitudes and their behaviour. They recognize that their fortunes are hitched to this form of domination although they do not seek to renegotiate the relationship but rather assent to it and so recharge it, ideologically and in lived experience. Even if counter claims are advanced, and some people are critical of the social system and would seek to change it, these claims cannot be negotiated from a position of equal strength.

To recognize that ideology is part of lived experience does not mean that all aspects of existence are conformable with the ideology. Such complete concordance would imply that social behaviour is consistent in all its expressions—that any one person or group of persons will observe a coherent pattern of behaviour in any number of contexts. This patently is not the case. Moreover, there is the likelihood of some disconformity, given that specific interests—that is the interests of only certain sectors of society—form the base of ideology. Ideology, as developed understanding and consciousness, then, may have an internal consistency and be part of social process; there may also be disjunctions between an ideology and some aspects of social existence. However ideology also functions to gloss over and downplay the contradictions inherent in behaviour, including the nature of power relations and their material expressions, and the existence of dominant interests over others.

It is because of the persuasive qualities of its sustaining ideology that hegemony can be presented by the dominant as a legitimate form of cultural domination. And the general, and generally willing, contribution to its recreation—by the powerless and the powerful—further attests its legitimacy. Both dominant and subordinate groups may defend various forms of inequality along the lines that there have always been social differences and that they are somehow 'natural'—this is nowhere clearer than in patriarchal relations. In this context natural has two meanings. First, and manifest quite clearly in the Marulan evidence, it is traditional, even normal—which translates to right or proper—for some people to have social privileges and others not. Thus many people present the widespread distribution of a social form as an argument for its continued acceptance. Secondly, it implies that some people are born to social positions. This does not simply mean that an individual may be culturally advantaged or disadvantaged by the circumstances of her or his family, although somehow, by virtue of family background an individual may be seen by both privileged and non-privileged individuals in the society to be entitled to certain social deserts. Rather, there is the suggestion of genetically transmitted social difference. The notion of 'good breeding' affirms that, and the mysterious claim that farming can be 'in the blood'. Even when a tenet of equal opportunity is acclaimed—and it often is—it does not cut across recognition of basically different social starting points (see Oxley 1974, p. 45). Under these circumstances, when the already priv-ileged are further favoured, a belief in equal opportunity inevit-ably reproduces, and may even amplify, inequality.

There is a contradiction insofar as while people may willingly comply with the circumstances of their subordination they may also at times (particularly at the outset of a discussion), deny social difference. In such cases of denial people's uneasiness may be related to what they perceive as a devaluation of personal standing, not a rejection of structures of dominance. In the case of social class, for example, despite assertions of sameness, by etching out the ties of community and by virtue of their residence and position in the district, people can acknowledge the ob-vious—the social differences and inequalities—and with no threat to self (see Pearson 1980, p. 172).

In some measure acceptance of inferiority may be a pragmatic response in circumstances offering no real alternatives (see Aber-crombie *et al.* 1980). A paradox emerges, however, for while such reaction cannot be interpreted as voluntary compliance—it is a case of Hobson's choice—the subordinate may subsequently rationalize their inequality in conservative terms. It is a defence against criticisms of apathy, incapability and insensitivity which, it is anticipated, might be levelled at people individually or collectively.

In this sometimes strained consonance, criticism and hostility surface from time to time. Again, with no implementable options people usually seek to make the best of a situation which they cannot change. Acceptance based on these qualified premises cannot be construed as implying complete and coherent ideologi-cal integration—such unity may anyhow be an intellectual chimera. What is significant is that, despite tensions, Marulan residents generally accede to the conditions of their existence and the underpinning values, and they live them out day by day. Moreover, as Bottomore (Abercrombie *et al.* 1980, introduction) points out, the strength of the prevailing ideology inhibits counter developments.

Notions of hegemony depict the dominant as bearing responsi-bilities on behalf of the whole society. Thus high-status graziers should not merely have an interest in and concern for their workers, they ought to raise their voices in local matters and participate in district social affairs. In doing so they fulfil their social charge and in part demonstrate their right to power. Again, men have traditionally been presented as economically, legally, politically and indeed more widely socially responsible than women. The biological differences between the sexes have been rephrased as cultural differences in which men dominate. The ideology of male domination invokes physical differences which are incontestable, but which become translated to cultural capacities and incapacities and enshrined in social tradition. While the logic and propriety of this translation is increasingly under challenge, such is not the case in Marulan; here and elsewhere the relationship has long been legitimated on grounds of naturalism. Certainly in Marulan men exercise power and it is said that they ought to because traditionally they always have; that is, it has always been so and it is natural.

There are two points embedded in this discussion which on their own account are important in social process in Marulan. The first is that most local residents are disinclined to perceive power as exercised by individuals, and it is evident how this soft-pedalling of individual agency in power relationships is tied, as cause and consequence, to a conservative acceptance of given structural forms for their own sake. This again emphasizes the interlocking of tradition and legitimacy. Despite the locals' wishes to diminish its visible impact, individual agency cannot be discounted. It is a feature of social process. Both agency and structure are indissolubly tied and mutually dependent. Structures are created not simply out of their own past, but also by means of the agency of people as collectivities and as individuals and, of course, the form and potential of agency is precast by and in structure. The second point is that in hegemonic relations the dominated are aware of their position—yet consciousness, in the form of awareness carrying with it the motivation to action, does not characterize the subordinate response. Awareness of the assymetry in a hegemonic relationship is, however, necessary in order that people may not just be quiescent but may be encouraged to assent to it.

But a critical feature of hegemony is a sensitivity to danger signals, and therefore any challenge in the development of consciousness on the part of subordinate people is reworked in ideological terms by dominant groups. Hence Marulan women certainly have more freedom legally, economically and socially than they had, say, fifty or even fewer years ago, but they continue to support the ideology of male domination and to realize it. Over the years concessions have also been made in the management of social-class relationships in order to accommodate revisions in the attitudes and changes in the social circumstances of the subordinate. Such responses flow, albeit in an attenuated form, from the changes in the broader society. The transformations which have occurred at no stage remodel the essential nature of the local power relations, which are generally supported in both behaviour and beliefs by people at all social levels; hence the power potential and its actual exercise, which is the structural prerogative of the dominant, is scarcely diminished.

I do not believe that there is anything very special or distinctive about everyday life in Marulan. It fits into a pattern which prevails in other rural towns and districts, with or without an industrial component, and indeed the people are subject generally to the same structural constraints as Australian city dwellers. It is in this context of everyday life that power is less obviously exercised, but none the less with significant effect. It operates in objective structural terms and is manifest in subjectively motivated orientations. It prefigures the form and nature of social interactions although it may be neither apparently intrusive nor offensive. Some people resent specific instances of the exercise of power, but they generally accept the system of social relationships which gives rise to its exercise.

BIBLIOGRAPHY

Books and Articles

Abercrombie, Nicholas, Hill, Stephen & Turner, Bryan S. 1980, *The Dominant Ideology Thesis*, George Allen & Unwin, Sydney.

Acker, J. 1973, 'Women and Social Stratification: A Case of Intellectual Sexism', *American Journal of Sociology*, 78, pp. 936–45.

Aitken, D. 1972, *The Country Party in New South Wales*, ANU Press.

Allen, S. & Barker, D.L. 1976, *Sexual Divisions and Society: Process and Change*, Tavistock, London.

Austin, D. 1981, 'Ideology in Class Society: The Contribution of Max Weber', in *Class and Inequality in Australia*, ed. P. Hiller, Harcourt Brace Jovanovich, Sydney, pp. 28–39.

Australian Bureau of Statistics 1976, *1976 Census: Population and Dwellings Cross-classified Tables*, Cat. no. 2426.0, ABS, Canberra.

——1987/8, *Exports Australia*, Cat. no. 5424.0, ABS, Canberra.

——1989, *Australian National Accounts—Quarterly Estimates of National Income and Expenditure*, March Quarter, Cat. no. 5206.0, ABS, Canberra.

Bachrach, P. & Baratz, S. 1970, *Power and Poverty*, Oxford University Press, New York.

Baldock, C. & Cass, B. (eds) 1983, *Women, Social Welfare and the State in Australia*, George Allen & Unwin, Sydney.

Baldock, C.V. & Lally, J. 1974, *Sociology in Australia and New Zealand*, Greenwood Press, Connecticut.

Barron, R.D. & Norris, G.M. 1976, 'Sexual Divisions and the Dual Labour Market', in *Dependence and Exploitation in Work and Marriage*, ed. D.L. Barker & S. Allen, Longman, London, pp. 47–69.

Barton, A.H. 1970, *Communities in Disaster*, Doubleday, New York.

Bechhofer, F., Elliott, B., Rushforth, M. & Bland, R. 1974, 'The Petits Bourgeois in the Class Structure: The Case of the Small Shopkeepers', in *The Social Analysis of Class Structure*, ed. F. Parkin, Tavistock, London, pp. 103–28.

Beechey, V. 1978, 'Woman and Production: A Critical Analysis of Some Sociological Theories of Women's Work', in *Feminism and Materialism: Women and Modes of Production*, ed. A. Kuhn & A.M. Wolpe, Routledge & Kegan Paul, London, pp. 155–97.

Bell, C. & Newby, H. 1971, *Community Studies*, George Allen & Unwin, London.

——1976, 'Husbands and Wives: The Dynamics of the Deferential Dialect', in *Dependence and Exploitation in Work and Marriage*, ed. D.L. Barker & S. Allen, Longman, London, pp. 152–68.

Bell, J.H. & Pandey, U.S. 1989, 'Gender-role Stereotypes in Australian Farm Advertising', *Media Information Australia*, 51, February, pp. 45–9.

Bott, E. 1957, *Family and Social Network*, Tavistock, London.

Bottomore, T.B. 1964, *Elites and Society*, C.A. Watts, London.

——1975, *Sociology as Social Criticism*, George Allen & Unwin, London.

Bourdieu, P. 1979, 'Symbolic Power', *Critique of Anthropology*, 13 and 14, 4, pp. 77–85.

Braybon, G. 1981, *Women Workers in the First World War*, Barnes & Noble, New Jersey.

Bryson, L. 1975, 'Husband and Wife Interaction in the Australian Family: A Critical Review of the Literature', in *The Other Half*, ed. J. Mercer, Penguin, Ringwood, pp. 213–23.

——1983, 'Women as Welfare Recipients: Women, Poverty and the State', in *Women, Social Welfare and the State in Australia*, ed. B. Cass & C. Baldock, George Allen & Unwin, Sydney.

Buckley, K. 1975, 'Primary Accumulation: The Genesis of Australian Capitalism', in *Political Economy of Australian Capitalism*, ed. E.L. Wheelwright & K. Buckley, ANZ Book Company, Sydney, pp. 12–32.

Burton, C. 1985, *Subordination: Feminism and Social Theory*, George Allen & Unwin, Sydney.

Calder, A. 1969, *The People's War: Britain 1939–4*, Jonathan Cape, London.

Cammett, J.M. 1967, *Antonio Gramsci and the Origins of Italian Communism*, Stanford University Press, California.

Carne, J.E. & Jones, L.L. 1919, 'The Limestone Deposits of New South Wales', *Mineral Resources*, 25, pp. 137–43.

Cass, B. 1974, 'Images of the Family in Sociological Theory', in *Families: Australian Studies of Changing Relationships Within the Family and Between the Family and Society*, ed. M. Dawson, ANZAAS, pp. 51–7.

——1977, 'Family', in *Australian Society*, 3rd edn, ed. A. F. Davies, S. Encel & M. J. Berry, Longman Cheshire, Melbourne, pp. 138–75.

——1978, 'Women's Place in the Class Structure', in *Essays in the Political Economy of Australian Capitalism*, ed. E.L. Wheelwright & K. Buckley, vol. III, ANZ Book Company, Sydney.

Chamberlain, C. 1983, *Class Consciousness in Australia*, George Allen & Unwin, Sydney.

Chamberlain, E.R., Doube, L., Milne, G., Rolls, M. & Western, J.S. 1981, *The Experience of Cyclone Tracy*, Australian Government Publishing Service, Canberra.

Chambers, D.A. 1986, 'The Constraints of Work and Domestic Schedules on Women's Leisure', *Leisure Studies*, 5, pp. 309–25.

Chaney, E.M. 1975, 'The Mobilization of Women: Three Societies', in *Women Cross-Culturally: Challenge and Change*, ed. R. Rohrlich-Leavitt, Mouton, The Hague, pp. 471–89.

Clark, C.M.H. 1973, *A History of Australia*, vol. III, Melbourne University Press, Melbourne.

——1978, *A History of Australia*, vol. IV, Melbourne University Press, Melbourne.

Cockburn, Cynthia 1983, *Brothers: Male Dominance and Technological Change*, Pluto, London.

Coghlan, T.A. 1888, *The Wealth and Progress of New South Wales 1887–88*, 3rd issue, George Robertson & Co., Sydney.

——1969 [1918], *Labour and Industry in Australia*, 4 vols, Macmillan, Melbourne.

Connell, R.W. 1977, *Ruling Class, Ruling Culture*, Cambridge University Press, Cambridge.

——1980, How Should We Theorize Patriarchy, unpublished

paper delivered Macquarie University, Sydney.

——1987, *Gender and Power*, George Allen & Unwin, Sydney.

——& Irving, T.H. 1980, *Class Structure in Australian History*, Longman Cheshire, Melbourne.

Connelly, W.E. 1972, 'On "Interests" in Politics', *Politics and Society*, 2, 4, pp. 459–77.

Curthoys, Ann 1988, *For and Against Feminism: A Personal Journey into Feminist Theory and History*, George Allen & Unwin, Sydney.

Davidoff, L., L'Esperance, J. & Newby, H. 1976, 'Landscape with Figures: Home and Community in English Society', in *The Rights and Wrongs of Women*, ed. J. Mitchell & A. Oakley, Penguin, Harmondsworth, pp. 139–75.

Davies, A.F. 1967, *Images of Class*, Sydney University Press, Sydney.

Davis, K. 1950, *Human Society*, Macmillan, New York.

Delphy, C. 1984, *Close to Home*, Hutchinson in association with The Explorations in Feminism Collective, London.

Dixson, M. 1976, *The Real Matilda*, Penguin, Ringwood.

Eipper, C. 1981, The Bantry Bay Example: The Advance of Capitalism in County Cork, Ireland, unpublished PhD thesis, University of Sydney.

Eisenstein, H. 1984, *Contemporary Feminist Thought*, Unwin Paperbacks, London.

Encel, S. 1970, *Equality and Authority*, Cheshire, Melbourne.

——, MacKenzie, N. & Tebbut, M. 1974, *Women and Society: An Australian Study*, Cheshire, Melbourne.

Finch, J. 1983, *Married to the Job: Wives' Incorporation in Men's Work*, George Allen & Unwin, London.

Fitzgerald, R. & Hearn, M. 1988, *Bligh, Macarthur and the Rum Rebellion*, Kangaroo Press, Sydney.

Fitzpatrick, B. 1969 [1941], *The British Empire in Australia*, Macmillan, Melbourne.

Fletcher, B.H. 1976, *Landed Enterprise and Penal Society*, Sydney University Press, Sydney.

Frankenberg, R. 1976, 'In the Production of their Lives, Men (?)...Sex and Gender in British Community Studies', in *Sexual Divisions and Society: Process and Change*, ed. D.L. Barker & S. Allen, Tavistock, London.

Franzway, S., Court, D. & Connell, R.W. 1989, *Staking a Claim: Feminism, Bureaucracy and the State*, George Allen & Unwin, Sydney.

Fritz, C.E. 1961, 'Disaster', in *Contemporary Social Problems*, ed. R.K. Merton & R.A. Nisbet, Harcourt Brace & World, New York, pp. 651–94.

Game, A. & Pringle, R. 1983, *Gender at Work*, George Allen & Unwin, Sydney.

Gardiner, J. 1976, 'Political Economy of Domestic Labour in Capitalist Society', in *Dependence and Exploitation in Work and Marriage*, ed. D.L. Barker & S. Allen, Longman, London, pp. 109–20.

Gasson, R. 1978, The Role of Farmer's Wife in Australian Agriculture, unpublished paper prepared for the Australian Farm Management Society (South Australia) and the Agricultural Bureau in South Australia.

Gerth, H.H. & Mills, C.W. 1977 [1948], *From Max Weber*, Routledge & Kegan Paul, London.

Giddens, A. 1973, *The Class Structure of the Advanced Societies*, Hutchinson, London.

——1976, *New Rules of Sociological Method*, Hutchinson, London.

Goode, W.J. 1967, 'Family and Mobility', in *Class Status and Power*, ed. R. Bendix & S.M. Lipset, Routledge & Kegan Paul, London, pp. 582–601.

Gould, S. 1989, 'Family Problems of Farm Women', in *Women in Rural Australia*, ed. K. James, University of Queensland Press, St Lucia.

Gramsci, A. 1971, *Selections from the Prison Notebooks*, International Publishers, New York.

Grimshaw, P. 1980, 'Women and the Family in Australian History', in *Women, Class and History*, ed. E. Windschuttle, Fontana, Melbourne, pp. 37–52.

Gruen, F.H. 1970, 'Rural Australia', in *Australian Society*, ed. A.F. Davies & S. Encel, 2nd edn, Cheshire, Melbourne, pp. 340–61.

Gusfield, J.R. 1975, *Community: A Critical Response*, Basil Blackwell, Oxford.

Harper, J. & Richards, L. 1971, *Mothers and Working Mothers*, Penguin, Ringwood.

Harrisson, T. 1976, *Living Through the Blitz*, Collins, London.

Hindess, B. 1976, 'On Three Dimensional Power', *Political Studies*, XXIV, 3, pp. 329–33.

Hughes, R. 1987, *The Fatal Shore*, Collins Marvill, London.

James, J. (ed.) 1989, *Women in Rural Australia*, University of

Queensland Press, St Lucia.

James, K. 1979, 'The Home: A Private or Public Place? Class, Status and the Actions of Women', *Australian and New Zealand Journal of Sociology*, 15, 1, pp. 36–42.

——1981, 'Public or Private: Participation by Women in a Country Town', in *Beyond the City*, ed. M. Bowman, Longman Cheshire, Melbourne.

Janeway, E. 1977, *Man's World, Woman's Place*, Penguin, Harmondsworth.

Jeans, D.N. 1972, *An Historical Geography of New South Wales to 1901*, Reed, Australia.

Jervis, J. 1946, 'Settlement in the Marulan-Bungonia District', *Royal Australian Historical Society*, 32, pp. 107–42.

Kingston, B. 1975, *My Wife, My Daughter and Poor Mary Ann*, Nelson, Melbourne.

——1977, *The World Moves Slowly: A Documentary History of Australian Women*, Cassell, Sydney.

Larmour, C. 1975, 'Women's Wages and the Web', in *Women and Work*, ed. A. Curthoys, S. Eade & P. Spearritt, Australian Society for the Study of Labour History, Canberra.

Larrain, J. 1979, *The Concept of Ideology*, Hutchinson, London.

Lenski, G.E. 1966, *Power and Privilege*, McGraw-Hill, New York.

de Lepervanche, M. 1984, 'The "naturalness" of inequality', in *Ethnicity, Class and Gender in Australia*, ed. G. Bottomley & M. de Lepervanche, George Allen & Unwin, Sydney.

Littlejohn, J. 1963, *Westrigg: The Sociology of a Cheviot Parish*, Routledge & Kegan Paul, London.

Lukes, S. 1974, *Power: A Radical View*, Macmillan, London.

——1976, 'Critical Note: Reply to Bradshaw', *Sociology*, 10, pp. 129–32.

——1977, *Power and Structure*, Macmillan, London.

McKay, D.H. 1967, 'Agriculture in the Economy', in *Agriculture in the Australian Economy*, ed. D.B. Williams, Sydney University Press, Sydney, pp. 128–51.

McMichael, P. 1979, 'The Genesis of Settler Capitalism in Australia', *Intervention*, 13, pp. 39–78, 97–9.

McQueen, H. 1970, *A New Britannia*, Penguin, Ringwood.

Manheim, K. 1940, *Ideology and Utopia: An Introduction to the Sociology of Knowledge*, Routledge & Kegan Paul, London.

Martin, R. 1977, *The Sociology of Power*, Routledge & Kegan Paul, London.

Marx, K. & Engels, F. 1952 [1888], *Manifesto of the Communist Party*, Progress, Moscow.

——1965, *The German Ideology*, Lawrence & Wishart, London.

Metcalfe, D. 1988, *For Freedom and Dignity*, George Allen & Unwin, Sydney.

Middleton, C. 1974, 'Sexual Inequality and Stratification Theory', in *The Social Analysis of Class Structure*, ed. F. Parkin, Tavistock, London, pp. 179–203.

Mitchell, J. 1971, *Women's Estate*, Penguin, Harmondsworth.

Nalson, J.S. 1977, 'Rural Australia', in *Australian Society*, 3rd edn, ed. A.F. Davies, S. Encel & M.J. Berry, Longman Cheshire, Melbourne, pp. 304–30.

Neuwirth, G. 1969, 'The Weberian Theory of Community', *British Journal of Sociology*, 20, pp. 148–63.

Newby, H. 1977, *The Deferential Worker*, Allen Lane, London.

——1979, *Green and Pleasant Land? Social Change in Rural England*, Penguin, Harmondsworth.

——1980, 'Rural Sociology', *Current Sociology*, 28, 1, pp. 3–141.

Oakley, A. 1972, *Sex, Gender and Society*, Temple Smith, London.

——1976, *Housewife*, Penguin, Harmondsworth.

Oeser, O.A. & Emery, F.E. 1954, *Social Structure and Personality in a Rural Community*, Routledge & Kegan Paul, London.

Ossowski, S. 1963, *Class Structure in the Social Consciousness*, Routledge & Kegan Paul, London.

Oxley, H.G. 1974, *Mateship in Local Organisation*, Queensland University Press, St Lucia.

Pahl, R.E. 1968, 'The Rural–Urban Continuum', in *Readings in Urban Sociology*, Pergamon Press, Oxford, pp. 263–97.

——1984, *Divisions of Labour*, Basil Blackwell, Oxford.

Parkin, F. 1972, *Class, Inequality and Political Order*, Paladin, London.

——1974, 'Strategies of Social Closure in Class Formation', in *The Social Analysis of Class Structure*, ed. F. Parkin, Tavistock, London, pp. 1–18.

Pateman, C. 1988, *The Sexual Contract*, Polity Press & Basil Blackwell, Cambridge/Oxford.

Pearson, D. 1980, *Johnsonville: Continuity and Change in a New Zealand Township*, George Allen & Unwin, Sydney.

Phillips, A. 1987, *Divided Loyalties: Dilemmas of Sex and Class*, Virago, London.

Power, M. 1975, 'Woman's Work is Never Done—by Men:

A Socio-Economic Model of Sex Typing Occupations', *Journal of Industrial Relations*, 17, pp. 225–39.

Pownall, E. 1959, *Mary of Maranoa*, F. H. Johnston, Sydney.

Powys, J. 1981, 'Differences Between Old and New Settlers', in *Conflict of Values, Attitudes and Objectives: A Study of 'Locals' and 'Newcomers' in a New South Wales Farming Community*, ed. J.J. Powys, K.E. Hickey, M. Brown & J.S. Nalson, Sociology Research Monograph 4, University of New England, Armidale, pp. 42–53.

——Nalson, J.S. & Hickey, K. 1981, 'The Conflict Situation', in *Conflict of Values, Attitudes and Objectives: A Study of 'Locals' and 'Newcomers' in a New South Wales Farming Community*, ed. J.J. Powys, K.E. Hickey, M. Brown & J.S. Nalson, Sociology Research Monograph 4, University of New England, Armidale, pp. 54–74.

Richards, L. 1978, *Having Families: Marriage, Parenthood and Social Pressure in Australia*, Penguin, Ringwood.

Roberts, S.H. 1968 [1924], *History of Australian Land Settlement 1788–1920*, Macmillan, Melbourne.

Robinson, M.E. 1976, *The New South Wales Wheat Frontier 1851–1911*, Australian National University, Canberra.

Rogers, S.C. 1978, 'Woman's Place: A Critical Review of Anthropological Theory', *Comparative Studies in Society and History*, 20, 1, pp. 123–62.

Rosaldo, M.Z. 1974, 'Women, Culture and Society: A Theoretical Overview', in *Women, Culture and Society*, ed. M.Z. Rosaldo & L. Lamphere, Stanford University Press, Stanford, pp. 17–42.

Rose, D., Saunders, P., Newby, H. & Bell, C. 1976, 'Ideologies of Property: A Case Study', *Sociological Review*, pp. 699–730.

Rowbotham, S. 1973, *Woman's Consciousness, Man's World*, Penguin, Harmondsworth.

Rowse, T. 1978, *Australian Liberalism and National Character*, Kibble Books, Maldon, Vic.

Rupp, L.J. 1978, *Mobilizing Women for War*, Princeton University Press, Princeton.

Ryan, P. & Rowse, T. 1975, 'Women, Arbitration and the Family', in *Women at Work*, ed. A. Curthoys, S. Eade & P. Spearritt, Australian Society for the Study of Labour History, Canberra, pp. 15–30.

Sands' Sydney and Suburban Directory, 1899.

Saunders, P., Newby, H., Bell, C. & Rose, D. 1978, 'Rural

Community and Rural Community Power', in *International Perspectives in Rural Sociology*, ed. H. Newby, Wiley & Sons, UK, pp. 55–85.

Schaffer, K. 1988, *Women and the Bush: Forces of Desire in the Australian Cultural Tradition*, Cambridge University Press, Melbourne.

Schattschneider, E.E. 1960, *The Semisovereign People*, Holt, Rinehart & Winston, New York.

Schmalenbach, J. 1965, 'The Sociological Category of Communion', in *Theories of Society*, ed. T. Parsons, Free Press, New York, pp. 331–47.

Shute, C. 1980, 'From Balaclavas to Bayonets: Women's Voluntary War Work, 1939–41', *Hecate*, VI, 1, pp. 5–26.

Stinchcombe, A.L. 1961–62, 'Agricultural Enterprise and Rural Class Relations', *American Journal of Sociology*, 67, pp. 165–76.

Summers, A. 1975, *Damned Whores and God's Police*, Penguin, Ringwood.

Teale, R. 1978, *Colonial Eve: Sources on Women in Australia 1788–1914*, Oxford University Press, Melbourne.

Thompson, E.P. 1963, *The Making of the English Working Class*, Victor Gollancz, London.

Urry, J. 1981, *The Anatomy of Capitalist Societies: The Economy, Civil Society and the States*, Macmillan, London.

Veblen T. 1957 [1925], *The Theory of the Leisure Class*, George Allen & Unwin, London.

Walby, S. 1986, *Patriarchy at Work*, Polity Press, Cambridge.

Ward, J. & Smith G. 1978, *The Vanishing Village*, Quartet Books, Melbourne.

West, J. 1978, 'Women, Sex and Class', in *Feminism and Materialism: Women and Modes of Production*, ed. A. Kuhn & A.M. Wolpe, Routledge & Kegan Paul, London, pp. 220–53.

Westergaard, J. & Resler, H. 1976, *Class in a Capitalist Society*, Penguin, Harmondsworth.

Wettenhall, R.L. 1975, *Bushfire Disaster: An Australian Community in Crisis*, Angus & Robertson, Sydney.

White, D.M. 1972, 'The Problems of Power', *British Journal of Political Science*, 2, pp. 479–90.

Wild, R.A. 1974a, *Bradstow: A Study of Status, Class and Power in a Small Australian Town*, Angus & Robertson, Sydney.

——1974b, 'Localities, Social Relationships, and the Rural–Urban Continuum', *Australian and New Zealand Journal of*

Sociology, 10, 3, pp. 170–6.
——1978, *Social Stratification in Australia*, George Allen & Unwin, Sydney.
Williams, C. 1981, *Open Cut: The Working Class in an Australian Mining Town*, George Allen & Unwin, Sydney.
Williams, R. 1973, *The Country and the City*, Chatto & Windus, London.
——1977, *Marxism and Literature*, Oxford University Press, Oxford.
Williams, W.M. 1969, *The Sociology of an English Village: Gosforth*, Routledge & Kegan Paul, London.
Wolff, K.H. 1971, *From Karl Mannheim*, Oxford University Press, New York.
Wyatt, R.T. 1972 [1941], *The History of Goulburn, NSW*, 2nd edn, Lansdowne Press, Sydney.
Zaretsky, E. 1976, *Capitalism, the Family and Personal Life*, Pluto Press, London.

Reports

Department of Science and Technology 1980, *Shiftwork in Australia: A Study of Its Effects*, Australian Government Publishing Service, Canberra.
National Party Women's Section, Central Executive Committee (n.d.), *Report on the Plight of Country Women*.
Rural Policy in Australia, May 1974, report submitted to the prime minister by a working group.

Newspapers

Age, 11 May 1981.
Goulburn Evening Post, 9 March 1965.
Illustrated Sydney News, 31 March 1877. (Archives, Mitchell Library)
National Farmer, November 1977.
Sun–Herald, 9 April 1979.
Sydney Morning Herald, 14 September 1845, 11 January 1847. (Archives, Mitchell Library)

INDEX

action, in power relationships, 22–5, 28

activities, social *see* social. . .

age, feminism and, 134; social activities and, 145; social awareness and, 102–3

agriculture *see* farm; land; rural

bias, mobilization of, 24–5

biological basis, farmers, 44–5; graziers, 55–6; power relations, 187–8

bushfire, social behaviour in, 158–82, 186

business, women in, 121, 123; *see also* partytime selling; petty bourgeoisie

capitalism, family and, 108–9; gender inequality and, 53–4, 113; rural ideology and, 34–9, 64–8

cars and lifestyle, 85–6, 89

childcare, 86, 128; marriage and, 148; men and, 138, 140, 153–4; working women and, 151–2

city *see* rural cf. urban

class relationships, 53–78; women and, 54, 57, 60–1, 108, 111–12

closure, social, 57–9, 79

communion 178–80; *see also* community ties

community ties, bushfire and, 160, 178–80; class relationships and, 60, 70–1, 76–8, 80, 97; farming life and, 84–5

commuter farmers, 10–14, 40–1, 164–5, 186

conflict, in power relationships, 23–4

consciousness, power relationships and, 22–3, 27–8, 31–2; rural women's, 120–1, 132

conservatism, feminism and, 134–6; role reversal and, 156–7; rural ideology and, 49–50

consumption, family and, 114–5, 144

control *see* power

convergence behaviour, bushfire and, 177–8

country-mindedness *see* rural
ideology
Country Women's Association,
102, 142
crisis, social behaviour in,
158–61

death duties, 123
decision-making, family and, 117,
149, 154–7
disaster, social behaviour in,
158–82
division of labour, bushfire and,
171–3, 181; class and gender
and, 54; family and, 108–9,
151–4
divorce *see* marriage breakdown
domestic violence, 122, 185
domestic work, 83, 85, 112–15;
men and, 138–9, 152–4;
payment for, 62, 83; working
women and, 83, 151–2
domination *see* class; male;
power; status

educational opportunities, 83–4,
115–16, 146
egalitarianism, 95–8
emotional experience, 80, 177,
179–80; *see also* nostalgia;
sentiment
employment *see* division of
labour; work
environment, rural ideology and,
44, 124; *see also* bushfire;
nature

family ideology, 30, 32, 88, 107,
144–9; competing interests,
27; consumption, 114–15, 144;
decision-making, 117, 149,
154–7; farming life, 63–4,
84–5; industrial relations and,
70
farm men, domestic activities of,
138–9
farm women, bushfires and, 164,

172; rural recession and, 132;
social activities and, 86; upper
status, 83; work of, 62–3,
116–8, 137–8
farming and grazing industry,
7–8, 16–19; *see also*
commuter; land; rural
farming life, bushfires and,
163–4; education and, 83–4;
family ideology and, 38, 63–4,
84–5; labourers and, 16–7, 27,
56, 186–7; resident cf. non-
resident, 10–14; social life and,
16, 34–9, 55–8, 82–6
feminism, power relationships
and, 31; rural areas and, 131–6
firefighters, organization of,
166–71; *see also* bushfire
food preparation, as women's role
in firefighting, 158, 171–2

gender, inequality theories, 24,
53–4; research and, 4; roles,
131–57; *see also* male
groups, social, 79–90; crisis and,
177; formation of, 57–8; *see
also* social activities

hegemony, 4–5, 28–30, 186–90;
male, 129–30, 136–43
hobby farmers *see* commuter
home as haven, 112–13, 144–5
housework *see* domestic work

ideology, power relationships
and, 4–5, 30–2; *see also*
family; male; rural
independence, farming life and,
65–6, 84–5, 91; women and,
109–10, 129, 164, 189–90
inequality, consciousness and
conflict and, 23–4, 27–8;
denial of, 95–8; gender, 24,
53–4, 187–90; rural ideology
and, 77, 187–8
inheritance, patrimonial, 54, 64,
121–2

institutions, mediation of power and, 21–2, 25
interests, in power relationships, 23–8
invisibility of women, 17, 39, 54, 57, 60, 119, 137, 171–3
isolation, 46; of women, 131–2, 135–6, 138

labour *see* division; work
land ownership, bushfire and, 163; class relationships and, 34–5, 54, 77–8, 186; inheritance and, 54, 64; interest groups and, 26; rural ideology and, 61–8; women's position and, 121–7
lifestyle assessment, 79, 90–1; *see also* family; farming; rural

male domination ideology, 136–43, 189–90
male image, 39, 54, 136–7, 172
marriage, breakdown, 122, 148; early age and, 145–9; family ideology and, 109–10; upper status farming life and, 113–14; wedding patterns and, 101–2; women and, 138, 142
Marulan, 5–10; bushfires, 161–6; cement industry, 6, 18, 68–72; class relationships, 59–78; commuter farmers, 10–14; history, 3, 14–19, 38, 102–3; newcomers, 87–8, 145; quarrying industry, 6, 18, 58, 68–71; social groups, 87–90; trucking industry, 58, 74–6
moral guardianship, women and, 144
mothers *see* childcare; family

National Conference of Countrywomen in Australia (1979), 137
National Party, rural ideology and, 42–3, 48–9, 51; Women's Section Central Executive Committee, 132
nature, rural ideology and, 39–40, 45; *see also* biology; environment
nostalgia, rural ideology and, 41, 49–51

partytime selling, 118–19
patriarchy, 31, 53–4, 108, 184–5, 187
petty bourgeoisie, 60–5, 73–7, 91, 116, 144
pioneer women, 17, 122–3, 137
Pitt Street farmers *see* commuter farmers
politics *see* National Party; voting behaviour
power, theoretical concepts, 20–32, 57–9, 185
private life, 111, 144–5; *see also* domestic; family
professions, 76–7, 88–9, 100; women in, 132
property *see* land
public life, women's influence in, 57, 87, 111, 139–41, 156; *see also* social activities

research design, 2–5
role reversal, 156–7
'roughness' characteristics, 56, 89–90, 101–2, 144–5
rural economics, 34–7, 41–2, 67; *see also* farm; land
rural ideology, 30–52, 184
rural life cf. town life, feminism and, 135; status and, 14, 45–9, 80–1
rural life cf. urban life, feminism and, 133–5; ideals and, 36, 39–46, 190; young women and, 145–6; *see also* commuter
Rural Policy in Australia (1974), 66–7

rural recession, women and, 132–3
rural settlement, history of, 34–9
rural subsidies, 22, 51, 66–7

sentiment and social awarenes, 97–8
sex roles, 118, 121–57; *see also* division of labour; male image
sexual discrimination *see* inequality
sexual relations, working women and, 150
shiftwork, 139–41
skills, women's, 58, 60–1, 132
status, attributional *cf.* interactional, 103–5; awareness of, 98–103; crises and, 168; land ownership and, 55–7, 61–8; Marulan and, 79–82; rural ideology and, 46–7; women and, 92, 114–6
stress, collective, 158–82

structures, power relationships and, 21–2, 24–5

town *see* Marulan; rural
transport, 89, 145; *see also* cars; Marulan, trucking industry

voluntary associations, women and, 83, 139
voting behaviour, 73–4

war duties, women and, 173
women–women relationships, 97–8, 119, 174, 180
Women's Electoral Lobby, 185
work, women's, bushfire and, 164; class relationships and, 124, 127–8; farm women, 62–3, 116–18, 137–8; male domination ideology and, 141–2; marriage and, 146, 149–51; shiftwork, 139–41; town women and, 114–16, 118–19; *see also* domestic